# WE PIONEERED

## Arthur Shelford
### and
## Cyril Shelford

Orca Book Publishers

Second Printing, February 1989


**Canadian Cataloguing in Publication Data**

Shelford, Arthur, 1885 - 1979.
  We pioneered


  ISBN 0-920501-19-2

  1. Shelford, Arthur, 1885 - 1979. 2. Shelford, Cyril, 1921 -
3. Ootsa Lake Region (B.C.) — Biography. 4. Ootsa Lake Region
(B.C.) — History. 5. Pioneers — British Columbia — Ootsa Lake
Region — Biography. I. Shelford, Cyril, 1921 -     II. Title.
FC3845.067S53  1988        971.1'32        C88-091598-6
F1089.067S53  1988




Financially assisted by the Ministry of Municipal Affairs, Recreation and Culture through the British Columbia Heritage Trust and B.C. Lotteries.




Orca Book Publishers Ltd.
P.O. Box 5626, Stn.B
Victoria, B.C., V8R 6S4




Cover design by Susan Fergusson
Printed in Canada by Hignell Printing Ltd., Winnipeg, Manitoba.

*In memory of the Shelfords,*
*Jack and Safie, and Arthur and Millie,*
*and all of the pioneer families of the district.*

# Contents

# Foreword

This book is dedicated to the memory of my Uncle Arthur and my Aunt Millie Shelford, and, for the most part, it is their story as told by Uncle Arthur. My aunt and uncle played an important role in my early life in the north. Our two families were very close and we depended on each other for a number of things. My three brothers and I spent a great deal of time on their farm helping with the seeding in the spring and the harvest in the fall and doing other chores. It was like a second home to us. My Uncle Arthur loved good conversation. He would often set me down after the work was finished and we would talk about different aspects of national or international politics or whatever else was on his mind. I think that it is in part my uncle's influence that got me into politics later on in my life. At the very least, he certainly helped to develop my interest in that area.

During the dry years when the crops were poor, my uncle would come with us to the head of Ootsa Lake to do the haying. My brothers, John, Hugh and Myles, and I, enjoyed this more than anything else. And the best part was that we could sit around the campfire in the evening and listen to Dad and Uncle Arthur recall the stories of early settlers in the Ootsa Lake area. There were so many interesting people from all walks of life scattered throughout that sparsely populated country in those days. And our uncle was a great one for telling stories.

Uncle Arthur and Aunt Millie, like my mother and father, were true pioneers. They went into an area that was a wilderness and set about taming the land. They worked hard and earned their own way. Their independence was by choice and it was something that they took very seriously. Up until the start of the World War II in 1939, my uncle's yearly income was always less than $1,000. Their grocery bill averaged less than $30 a month. This bought them sugar (to preserve fruit, both wild and tame), rice, rolled oats and flour. Apart from a few clothes and the daily newspaper, they bought very little. Even after the War and up until the time they left the ranch, their income never rose above $2,500 a year until they got their pensions. Many times Uncle said, "I just don't know how people could spend all their pension to live comfortably."

Arthur Shelford was a keenly observant man and he had a wonderfully accurate memory. Like my father, he left England and came to Canada seeking adventure and opportunity and a life free from the constraints of British society. Like so many immigrants to this country he came because he saw the chance to live his life according to the way he saw fit. And that's exactly what he did. Uncle Arthur farmed in the Ootsa Lake region for fifty-six years. He was a very respected member of the community. But perhaps his greatest contribution to posterity is the record that he has left of his life and that of other pioneers with whom he shared the good times and the bad. And that is the real purposé of this book. I know that one of my father's greatest regrets was the fact that he never had the time to record the events of his earliest days in the North, especially the time that he spent hunting and fishing in the Alaskan wilderness when he first arrived on the west coast. I suspect that Uncle Arthur was at least partially motivated to write his memoirs by my father's regrets. And I in turn have been inspired to tell my story by the experiences and advice of both my father and my uncle.

When *From Snowshoes to Politics* was published last year a number of people reminded me of various interesting incidents and fascinating individuals that I failed to mention in that book. Several people suggested that I could easily fill another volume with other stories of life in the north. And, if time would permit, I suppose I could, for there there was certainly no shortage of interesting people living in the area around Ootsa Lake in the years when I grew up. But as it turns out I was already in possession of what I feel is an excellent record of the history of that area. Since his death in 1979 I have been in possession of my uncle's memoirs. I have always thought that they were worth publishing as a very accurate first-person account of pioneer life in the north. It would seem that now is an opportune time to do this. I offer some of my own memories of life on the ranch in the early days along with Uncle Arthur's story of his life in Canada.

This book then is dedicated first and foremost to Uncle Arthur and Aunt Millie. But it is also dedicated to all of the other pioneer families who shared that wonderful life that we lived around the shores of Ootsa, Francois, Whitesail, Tahtsa and Eutsuk Lakes and throughout the Bulkley and Nechako Valleys.

Cyril Shelford
Victoria, B.C.
September, 1988

# *Cyril Remembers*

# 1. Life on the Ranch

One thing my brothers and I enjoyed a great deal was going up to visit my uncle and aunt. In fact, we were always looking for an excuse to go as Aunt Millie would give us either rolled oat cookies (our favourite) or homemade hard candy, which would last in your mouth for over half an hour. Quite often we would take it in turns going, as four of us were too much for them to cope with — as I get older, I can well understand their problem.

In the early years the two families only had one churn, so we would have to walk up to their place, a mile away, every second day to deliver the cream so that Aunt Millie could churn it into butter and send butter back with us. The cheese was all made at our place, so the arrangement worked well for both. Most of the time two of us would go, as quite often we would see bears on the trip. If the bear was too close and scared us badly, the cream would be butter before we got to Aunt Millie's because we'd run so fast and shake it up.

Other times we would stop to catch fish in the creek that ran from Uncle's lake down past our ranch and on to Ootsa Lake. The fish came up the creek to spawn in the spring when the water was high; at that time of the year the creek would be about four feet deep and eight feet wide, so there was lots of water for us to get good and wet.

Our method of fishing was to take a sharp gaff-hook and climb out on a leaning tree or willow bush. If you were lucky enough to get the sun in the right position, you could see down into the clear water and spot the fish going by. If we could manage to hook one on the gaff-hook, we would then try to jump from the leaning tree to shore and pull the fish out before they got off. It took a lot of patience as often nothing would come by for half an hour or more. By that time, our interest would divert to squirrels or willow grouse drumming on a log nearby and, when the fish did appear, it would be past us before we could get our hook over it.

Willow grouse are interesting birds to watch during mating season in the spring. The cock will put on quite a show, strutting up and down a fallen tree to tell all other male grouse to stay away from their territory. Every five or ten minutes the grouse will sit down and flap their wings on the log, something which can be plainly heard over a hundred yards away. Very rarely, another male will come on the log and challenge the first grouse for its mate. In order to see a fight you have to stay motionless and out of sight — and you must also be willing to wait up to an hour before the grouse will perform.

My uncle often said the grouse act just like two young men strutting around to impress a girl they both like. The Franklin grouse/spruce hen — or fool hen as we called them — acted quite differently. They were so tame that a person could walk right up to them and they would only fly up in a tree eight to ten feet. In the spring the male is very colourful with its brilliant red comb. To put on a good show for his mate he will fly four to six feet off the ground, then stay in the same spot for up to a minute — he looks just like a helicopter waiting to hook onto a load. Only once have I seen two males doing the same thing, then landing on the ground and fighting just like two domestic roosters.

With all these things to divert our attention we occasionally set the cream jar down and forgot where it was. We all knew full well it was no use going back home and trying to explain how we'd lost it — we'd just be sent back to search and find it, even if it took until dark.

The most fun of all was to climb up in our Uncle's barn to find bird nests. He had three big log barns, each over sixty feet long, as well as a chicken house and a pig barn. There were lots of places where one could spend a whole afternoon looking and watching the birds coming and going as they fed their young. Again, if you sat absolutely still for twenty minutes to half an hour, the birds would go about their business without taking any notice of you.

Most of the birds nesting in the barns were robins, blackbirds (both the regular blackbird and the red-winged blackbird), and bluebirds. The latter were our favourites as they would get really tame if you stayed around them long enough. They would make their nest in a corner of the barn where the roof came down to the top log. Away

*Four young pioneers, 1922. Hugh, Cyril, Myles and John (l to r.)*

from human habitation they like to find an abandoned woodpecker's nest which is usually found in a dead tree or a live tree with a hollow centre where the woodpecker pecks a hole through the outside casing. The woodpecker then makes his nest down about eighteen inches to two feet on the inside, which gives them a lot of protection from the crows which are the very worst predator of birds' nests. The crow takes both the eggs and the young if he can reach them. However, a crow will not often go into a hay barn and the birds nesting there are fairly safe. As many as five or six pairs of bluebirds nested in both our barns and our Uncle's every year until D.D.T. and other chemicals came into use after World War II. The bluebirds decreased to one pair in less than five years. I've only seen one pair of bluebirds in the last twenty years — and haven't seen any for the last fifteen years.

Hugh and I would often feel sorry for the young birds' parents flying back and forth carrying feed back to their young, so we would go out and find a poplar tree or fireweed that was covered with green fly (aphids) and take a branch covered with them to the nests and watch the young birds peck them off the branch. It was surprising how fast they would catch on. However, it upset the parents and I'm sure they wished we would go away and leave them alone to freight bugs and worms to their young. There were several species of fly catchers that suffered the same fate as the bluebirds.

There are still many in society who try to hide the injurious effects of chemicals and try to find excuses for the loss of birds and say such things as logging has destroyed the old woodpecker nests, which is absolutely false. In the northern half of the province, for example, there are still hundreds of old woodpecker nests which haven't been used for years, and even if there weren't, it's surprising how adaptable nature is in trying to find other types of nesting places like they did in the barns in the early years of the settlers. The old log barns are still there, scattered all over the Interior and North. Unfortunately they haven't been used by bluebirds for years. The robin and blackbird have fared much better than the bluebird. Hopefully society will insist on the thorough testing of pesticides before they can be used. We all know the sad story of the loss of falcons over vast areas of the world due to the stupidity of so-called advanced societies in the careless use of chemicals.

In my opinion, the careless use of D.D.T. without proper research as to its effect on wildlife is the greatest crime ever committed by the human race. I must say that I have no confidence that many of the new chemicals used today are properly tested either. Unfortunately, it appears that a company producing these products can always find some professional who will assure the general public as to their safety. There can be no doubt that the use of these chemicals has tremendously increased the production of food for the world's population; nevertheless, this has been done at a terrific cost to the quality of life in rural areas.

Uncle Arthur and Aunt Millie always grew all the vegetables, fruit, eggs, and meat they could eat. Their garden never did see an ounce of chemical fertilizer or spray of any kind — only good old barnyard manure. It was amusing for us to watch Uncle and Aunt jump when people from outside the district came in and said how lucky they were to have such a good garden. My uncle would quickly say, "It isn't luck. It's work that makes a good garden." My aunt was a great believer in the premise that nature supplied all our needs in the way of nutritious products if only we had the will to do it.

In the spring of each year my aunt insisted on a natural tonic which was made from dandelion roots boiled as a tea drink. When I went up to plough their garden, potato and turnip patch I always had to have a cupful to get my system in order for the coming season. After that I could have a glass of home-made dandelion wine, which my uncle would pour with great care so that he didn't spill a single drop. We would then sit back and solve all the political and farm problems affecting the nation. Sometimes the conversation would get so interesting that Uncle would offer me another glass, which would bring my aunt to her feet. She'd then point her finger at my uncle and say, "Arthur, don't you dare give this young man another drink as he has to drive that big tractor down that narrow road to his home. I simply won't let you be responsible for an accident." And that was the end of my second glass of wine.

My uncle and aunt used the dandelion in many ways — everything from making wine, salads, tea to drying the leaves to be put in a moose stew during the winter months. My dad also spent hours trying to keep dandelions under control — always a losing battle. It seemed that for every one Dad cut down, five came up. He had a two-inch blade on a handle which would cut the root two inches under ground level. If you didn't cut the root that far down, it would come right back up again. Dad spent days cutting down dandelions each year.

My uncle made pretty good wine from dandelions, rhubarb and white and red currants. He even tried Saskatoons and huckleberries, which were fairly good; however, they were more often used for jam. In normal years, there were seldom many berries close to the ranch and we had to go near the mountains five miles away before we could get any number. We always looked forward to the trip once a year to get a winter's supply. Quite often we would take a blanket and stay the night so that we would get in two days' picking. Under good conditions we could pick three or four gallons a day.

The real work came when we had to pack the berries home. You couldn't pack them on a horse unless they were a little bit unripe; otherwise, they would turn into a mush. Huckleberry pie has been my favourite since I was very young. We would also go miles to pick both high-bush and low-bush cranberries. The high-bush cranberries grow on a bush about five feet tall and in clusters of twelve to sixteen berries in a clump. In good years you can get a whole handful at a time, which makes them very quick picking. A good picker can fill a three-gallon bucket in less than two hours. The low-bush cranberries are quite different and grow only in swamp areas on vines no larger than a piece of thread. Unless you look carefully, it seems as if the berries are just growing on the moss. They are very small and you have to be a very fast picker to get more than two gallons in a whole day. The low-bush cranberry is just like a Christmas cranberry, except far smaller.

My mother and aunt used low-bush cranberries for making pies, which are very good. The low-bush blueberry was also a favourite for pies, jam and preserves. These grow on a small bush, which is no more than two inches high. Fortunately, these were found close to the ranch on areas burned over by fires eight to ten years before. These were often picked by using a comb or, better still, by soldering two-inch nails onto an eight-ounce can. The picker would slide the nails or comb through the bush and the berries would fall into the can. Picking can be done very fast, especially if the fall frosts come late. The blueberry leaves drop off in late September or early October, leaving only the berries still on the vine. During the early years more of these were picked for winter use than any other berry. The wild raspberries came up quickly after a forest fire — normally in less than four years. These were easy picking. In early times small forest fires were set so there would be a plentiful supply not only of berries but also of good wild game feed, which improved hunting a great deal close to the settled areas. In those days timber other than for building houses and barns was considered quite a worthless weed that destroyed cattle and game range. Isn't it funny how our outlook changes.

Both my father's and my uncle's ranches were infested with rocks. My three brothers and I did everything possible to avoid picking them. Once rock picking was mentioned, Myles and I would tell Dad that we'd heard the cows bawling out on the range and suggest that we should go and see what was going on. Most times, of course, Dad didn't buy our story and told us we could go as soon as we had picked two wagon-loads. We often had to go and help our uncle pick rocks as well. On Uncle Arthur's property the rocks were so plentiful that he would take a wagon out in the field and just park it for us to fill up while he was clearing land with the team of horses. We could fill the whole load without ever moving the wagon. When we got the box full, he would take it away and dump it, then bring it back for us to fill up again. For some strange reason Dad loved picking rocks, so we'd let him do it whenever we could get away with it.

Land clearing was done mainly with a team of horses, an axe and a grub-hoe. The small stumps the horses could pull out with a logging chain. If the trees were too big, we had to first cut the big roots so the horses could pull them out. With the really big ones, it could take an hour to pull out one stump, so it was not surprising the small acreage that was cleared by most of the early settlers. The very large stumps were blown out with blasting powder. My Uncle Erland could set up a dozen stumps loaded with enough powder to blow them out of the ground, then light them all one after the other and still have time to get far enough away before the first went off. He would have a long fuse with twelve nicks in it so that as he got to each stump a flame would shoot out of the nick and light the fuse before going on to the next. It all had to be timed just right so that you reached the next stump just as the flame came out of the next nick in its fuse.

Every year in the spring and summer we were sent up to Uncle's to weed the potatoes and turnips. In return for our labour we would have a share of the crop. It was difficult for us to grow potatoes at home because our land was susceptible to late frosts. Around the first of July it would knock the potatoes down. My uncle's farm was only a mile away, but it was at least four hundred feet higher in elevation and didn't get frost from June till September. In some years the frost didn't come until as late as October on Uncle Arthur's land. The rows of turnips and potatoes were often two hundred yards long, and it took a long time down on your hands and knees to pull out the weeds that grew in the rows. The ground between the rows was cultivated with a horse, which helped a lot. The worst part of the whole business was the black flies and mosquitos which came in by the millions in late May and June. We would get so bitten that we'd look like we had measles when we got home in the evening.

In the fall we would all go up and help pick the potatoes and take some of them home to the root-house, where we kept them all winter and spring for use till the new ones came in August. We would grow about three tons of potatoes for our own use and sell a sack once in a while and still have enough left over for seed for the coming year. Most years we would grow five or six tons of turnips for our own use and for the cows.

For as long as I can remember, my uncle was a dominant figure in the Farmer's Institute of B.C. Not only was he Secretary of the Wistaria Farmer's Institute, but he was also Secretary of District B, an area which covered the whole of the Skeena and Bulkley Valleys and the Queen Charlotte Islands. Even though the farmers of such a wide area faced different problems, Uncle Arthur could always come up with resolutions for the convention that delegates from all areas could support. He always went to the convention armed with ten or twelve resolutions. The best resolutions brought before the convention were selected to be presented to the provincial cabinet when they had their annual meeting with the Farmer's Institute.

Resolutions presented to the membership covered a wide range of topics. There was always one on the need for electric power in rural areas (before the 1950's even the towns and villages in the north had no power and had to rely on gas lamps, washing machines, etc.) and the issue of improvements to road and rail transportation was never neglected. Sometimes there were also resolutions presented that showed the sense of humour that I feel was basic to the way of life of the pioneers of the north.

I can well remember a lengthy discussion on one resolution directed at the auto manufacturers for doing away with the crank to start cars. During the cold days in the fall many cars simply wouldn't start using the battery. They either had to be cranked or towed by a team of horses. I remember one day down at the Post Office when a group of us were standing around watching Cliff Harrison try to start his car. He cranked it a couple of times and then jumped back and walked away when the motor kicked back and nearly broke his wrist. Someone else came to give it a flip. At this point, Bob Nelson had just the right quip. "You don't have to do that," he said. "Cliff already wound it up."

Another resolution presented at the Farmer's Institute Convention that caused a good deal of talk was one dealing with the colouring of margarine. This will seem strange to people today, but at that time only a white margarine was sold. It came with a packet of colouring which the housewife had to stir in if she wanted it to look like butter. The Institute supported the dairy producers who opposed the colouring of margarine and approved a resolution by Jacob Lund for the government to disallow the colouring of margarine unless it was coloured green. Incidentally, Tilly Ralston achieved her political fame in championing the cause of coloured margarine. But I'm afraid she didn't do it by following our Institute's resolution to colour it green.

The resolutions that managed to get passed at the District B convention would be sent to Victoria, along with those from all other areas of B.C. They were then voted on by the provincial delegates, known as the Farmers Institute Advisory Board. The best eight or ten would be presented to Cabinet when the Board met with them once a year. Never a year went by without one or more of Uncle Arthur's resolutions getting to Cabinet. And he was there every year to speak in support of them.

There is no question that the Farmers Institute Advisory Board for many years had more credibility with government than most farm organizations. They not only had a good voice on rural policy matters, but also brought in supplies such as feed, seed, fertilizer, fuel and many other items at a reasonable price, because they could buy in quantity. Uncle Arthur's involvement with the Institute went beyond just going to meetings and conventions. He also wrote hundreds of letters, not only for the Institute, but also for individuals who had a problem and who didn't know how to write a good letter that would receive attention.

There are so many stories of how the free thinking and innovative mind of the early settlers carried them through the many difficult situations. Everyone had a remarkable story of their own about how they coped with the trials of living on their own in isolated area far from the centres of supply. One such story is contained in the following chapters, and I'm sure all those thousands of people still alive in Western Canada who can relate to that way of life will enjoy his account of all the hardships and joys of the early pioneer's life.

All of us Canadians who came later owe a great deal to the pioneers' foresight, energy and especially their deep-rooted sense of fair play and honesty and their commitment to caring for others, all of which should set a good example for society today.

# 2. Fishing and Hunting

One of the most enjoyable events of the winter in the early years was going ice fishing with my father and uncle. We would get up really early and get the cattle, sheep, pigs, chickens, foxes and mink fed, and the horses fed, watered and harnessed before daylight so that we could get an early start for the three-and-a-half mile trip to Morrison Lake to spend the day fishing. Once we reached the lake, my dad or uncle would go up to Jock Morrison's cabin to see if he had any fish eggs. Fish eggs were the very best bait.

Jock Morrison was a very friendly bachelor who lived in a small cabin fifty yards above the lake. He had a nice view of the little lake which was slightly less than a mile long. He never kept more than ten cattle and two horses; he cut all his hay by hand. He had a big, old scythe that had a three-foot curved blade with a four-foot handle coming up vertically from one end. This allowed the operator to cut a swath three feet wide in a circle around him. He would then step forward and do the same thing. A good man with a scythe could mow a half acre of hay a day. If the weather was good, he could then rake it up with a hand rake and put it into hay shocks the next day. If it happened to rain, he would have to let it half dry then turn it over to allow the hay underneath to dry before it could be put into a hay stack. Even after the horse and mowing machine came in to the country, my uncle scythed hay in among the trees where he couldn't go with a mower to get a little extra feed right up to the time he retired. If nothing else, this activity certainly kept him in good shape and he didn't have to take any other exercise.

When we went fishing at Morrison Lake, my brothers and I always wanted to go along to help get the fish eggs as we would sit back and chuckle as Jock would get his big sugar bowl down from his rough hand-made cupboard and dig the raw fish eggs out from down at the bottom of the sugar. He claimed this was the very best method he knew to keep them fresh. He maintained that "sugar-cured" eggs wouldn't fall apart when you put a small clump on your hook.

Our fishing lines consisted of about twenty feet of strong sewing thread wrapped around an old sewing reel. This made it easy to wind up when you caught a fish. In cold weather, though, the line would freeze as soon as it came out of the water and you couldn't wind it up. All you could do then was poke it back in the hole to melt when it got in the warmer water. We would always light a fire, either out on the ice or under a tree on the shore so that when you got cold you could run in and warm up by the fire. You would tie your line to a small willow so that if a fish got on while you were by the fire, you would see the willow branch jumping and run out to get the fish before it got off.

Jock was a good host and would call my dad and uncle in for a cup of tea. We always got a real kick watching them try to get a spoonful of sugar without getting any fish eggs. Like most others at the time, Jock kept a good garden and was able to live quite comfortably on $15 or $20 a month. This money came from a little trapping in the winter and selling three or four steers a year in the fall when the community cattle drive went out to the rail line once a year. Sometimes too he would be lucky enough to get a few days work on the road in the summer. Mainly this consisted of cutting some of the high stumps sticking up in the wagon road or replacing a bridge over a creek or culvert.

It's interesting to note how the early settlers were able to cope with problems without any training whatsoever. When there were jobs that had to be done, people simply got together and did them. Normally a foreman was chosen — without extra pay because in most cases there was no pay for anyone. The foreman directed workers on what to do, and everyone worked hard to get the job done. It was their road or bridge and they wanted it improved so there was lots of cooperation.

The bridge over the Nadina River at the head of Francois Lake was quite a feat of engineering in the early days. The bridge was more than 150 feet long. And the building of the new road, which had to cross over half a mile of swamp and muskeg, was claimed by many to be impossible with the limited equipment available. That equipment consisted of nothing more than horse-drawn wagons and scrapers which could move less than one square yard of earth or rocks at a trip.

Billy Kerr, an old-time settler in the area, had a lot to do with the original construction of that road and did a tremendous job. The first attempt to create a road bed with rocks and gravel failed altogether as the road fill just sank in the soft bog and muskeg. The next try also looked to be nothing more than a dream when the crew of thirty men set to work cutting the willows growing on the swamp. The willows were about two to four inches in diameter and twelve feet long. The men laid the willow pieces more than three feet deep, crossways, on the swamp and proceeded to dump the rocks and shale on top. To the surprise of most people, the weight of rocks matted the willow brush together and held the weight of traffic going over the swamp. In those days this was the most ambitious project ever attempted in the area. What is even more remarkable is the fact that the road, with slight improvements, is still used today by a large number of people. Even the big logging trucks of today use the road on their way to Burns Lake and Houston.

This type of project was carried out by many of the early settlers in all parts of the province. It shows what can be accomplished by people with a common goal and little or no formal training when there is nowhere to go for help. Today very few would consider doing such a thing and even if they did, they would run into so many government regulations that they would be held up for months or years. The early community halls, churches, ball diamonds, and hockey rinks were all built in the same fashion and were a great credit to the initiative and determination of the early settlers.

During the Depression of the 1930s nearly all the road improvements were done by the settlers who did road work to help pay their taxes. This system worked well for both the government and the settlers. The government had no money to build roads in remote areas and the people of the area had no money to pay taxes. Without this system many people would have lost their land for not paying their taxes. Above all, it was a way of making people feel good because they were contributing something to the development of the district. Even people on relief, who received $30 a month, were required to go out and work on the roads. This consisted mainly of shovelling gravel into the wagons, which were then hauled by horses to the worst section of the roads. The gravel was used to fill up a mud hole so that loaded wagons could get through without getting stuck.

One of the early duties of the Public Works Department was to make a run over the road system first thing in the morning to pull out unfortunate people who had got stuck during the night. Those people would have had to spend the night in their cars or make a fire under a big tree and camp out. Up until World War II nearly all the cars in the area were put up on blocks for the winter — that is, until the end of May when the snow melted and the ground dried up enough for the cars to move again.

I remember well when my uncle bought his first car and learned to drive. All four of us boys would sit on a log close by to watch Uncle start up. The clutch in those early cars was very touchy and would start up with a jump. This would make Uncle put his foot back on the clutch whereupon the car would stop. He kept doing this and we thought he was trying to copy a rabbit hopping down the road. Uncle Arthur never did master the motor on any piece of machinery, even though both my uncle and aunt took a lot of interest in what made them work. If the car quit working for some reason, they would phone for help from one of us.

One time Myles and I were asked to come and see what was wrong with the car. We checked first to see if it was getting gas, then the spark to see if the electric system was working. We soon found it wasn't. Myles said, "We will have to get a coil from town as this one is burned out." My aunt said, "Oh! That's interesting, but will that stop it from running?" Even with their lack of understanding about the workings of a car, they certainly did get a lot of enjoyment out of it. They were able to go visiting people in the area, as they both loved meeting and talking to people and going to dances.

In the early days when the car first came to the district, the roads were only wide enough for one vehicle, so one or other had to find a wide spot in the road in order to pass. This was sometimes quite difficult, and one would have to back up some distance to find a suitable passing place.

Another experience that I'll never forget was the first bear hunt that I went on with my dad, Uncle Arthur, their cousin, Herbert Plumb, and my three brothers. I was in my early teens at the time. It all started in the early spring before the snow went when John and Hugh found a bear den in a swamp while out squirrel hunting. The bear had dug a den under an old tree stump that had broken off in the wind. He was still in the den as it was too early for grass to be showing on the south slope of hills. The early grass comes up long before the snow goes in the timber areas. However, the boys saw the bear tracks where he had come out to take a look to see whether spring was really coming. Apparently, he didn't like the look of it — there was still three foot of snow around the den — and so, he went back to sleep for another week or so. We were short of fresh meat at that time of year as the moose and deer were too thin after the long winter. Therefore, it was decided to try and get the bear which, according to John and Hugh, was likely a two-year-old, judging by the size of his tracks.

Early next morning, after all the farm animals had been fed and watered, we all set out on snowshoes. Once the den was located, we were all directed to a position from which it would be impossible for the bear to get away without someone shooting him. The four of us boys were armed with .22 calibre single-shot rifles, while Dad had an old 30-40 rifle which he'd brought down from Alaska. Dad's gun had a worn-out barrel and didn't shoot very straight at more than fifty yards. Uncle Arthur and Cousin Herbert each had a good 30-30 rifle. It was decided that Arthur would come from behind the den and try and scare the animal out. Herbert was stationed out in front to shoot the bear when it appeared. Herbert was a short, heavy-set man with bow legs, who didn't moved very fast under normal circumstances. Uncle Arthur would also shoot the bear from behind if Herbert missed. If all this failed, the other five of us in the second line would get it for sure.

My uncle moved in very quietly, took off his snowshoes and proceeded to jump up and down on the ground above the den. At first nothing happened. Herbert, thinking the bear must have left before we got there, lowered his gun. Just at that moment the bear dashed out of the den. The poor animal was so frightened that it ran right between Herbert's bowed legs, went about twenty yards, turned and then dashed right back into the den. During all of this not a shot was fired! And it was probably just as well as someone besides the bear might have been killed. There were a lot of trees and brush around the den, so it was hard to get a clear shot with the bear moving so quickly.

That bear was fast, but not nearly as fast as Cousin Herbert after the bear had run between his legs. Herbert was long gone before the bear ran back to his den. What a sight it was! And it all happened so quickly! The rest of us couldn't stop laughing long enough to shoot. Eventually we managed to compose ourselves and our second assault was successful. Herbert and Uncle Arthur both shot the bear as he dashed out of the den. That bear turned out to be excellent eating — and well worth the effort of the hunt. But Cousin Herbert didn't think it was much fun chasing bears out of a den and never went with us again, except on rabbit hunts, which he considered safe.

Bear fat was a necessity as far as my mother and Aunt Millie were concerned. Every fall when the bears were good and fat, they would encourage us to go hunting so that there would be lots of fat that could be rendered down into oil. This oil was mixed with moose fat. The latter when rendered goes into a very hard block; however, when mixed with bear oil ( 75% bear oil and 25% moose fat), the conglomeration was very much like lard, which both women used for making pies. My mother liked it better than lard. The women also used it for making soap. However, for this purpose, the proportions of the mixture were reversed. All during the Depression, this was the only soap used for washing clothes and dirty hands.

Young black bears are very good to eat, especially when they've been eating berries. However, if they are living on dead salmon along the rivers and streams, they are terrible and taste just like a rotting fish. Ed Blackwell used a lot of bear meat — much of it was used to make cured hams, which was done basically the same way as for pork. Many other settlers smoked the bear hams along with moose meat. The meat was cut into strips about three-quarters of an inch thick and hung over a rock until it was smoked enough. It was then dried to take on the trap lines. This is what the Indians call 'jerky.' Many of the old-time trappers would stuff some of this in their pack-sacks and that was often the only food they took on a one-day stay away from their base camp. The Indians used a lot of this when game was plentiful; however, before the white men came in with rifles, game was hard to get unless the animals could be chased through a narrow gorge and then either speared or snared as they went through.

During the spawning season fish was far easier for the Indians to catch. Especially in the salmon runs in small streams, the Indians could use their hands to catch the fish. In the larger streams, the Indians used spears, gaff hooks and various types of fish traps. The latter devices were the most effective and are still used today in some areas. For the most part, fish traps are the most effective method of catching only the type of fish you want; one is then able to let the others go on their way to spawn. The incidental catch of steelhead by the gillnet fishermen and seiners on the coast has eliminated the steelhead population from many rivers and streams and has seriously depleted them from many others. This is a difficult area to regulate with our present fishing methods of harvesting salmon. No doubt, it will have to be changed in order to save not only the steelhead, but also the spring and coho salmon. This will not be easy with so many people making their living using the present harvesting methods.

# 3. Pioneers

Something that amazes many people today is the question why so many people left all the comforts of home and emigrated to the bush country of northern B.C. and other provinces. There were thousands who came from nearly every country in Europe to settle in a new land. Many trekked great distances over miles of uninhabited forests, lakes and rivers in order to reach an area they had never seen and knew nothing about. The one thing they did know was that there would be none of the comforts to which they were accustomed. At best, there might be a little log cabin.

Most of the cabins in the early days had only two rooms, a tiny bedroom and the kitchen which served as dining room, sitting room, etc. The beds were bunks made of boards or flattened poles with a straw mattress. The cabins were seldom more than five or six hundred square feet. When the first child arrived the family would build a lean-to onto the cabin which would be eight to ten feet square. The big log home we all hear so much about was quite rare and one that was a thousand square feet on one floor was nearly unheard of. However, quite a few had two floors that gave them a fair amount of room.

There was generally a barn for the cow, pig and chickens which all lived together for warmth in the winter. Of course, there was an outhouse at the back. You often had to tramp through two or three feet of snow in the winter with temperatures far below zero to reach it. Toilet paper was nearly unknown right up until after World War II. The old Eaton's catalogue was the normal paper, but only after the new one came in. It was considered a real luxury to have the paper from the

Japanese oranges and apples at Christmas. The service given by the T. Eaton Company to the rural dwellers was far superior to anything we see today. The average rural family obtained all their supplies, other than food, from Eaton's. Supplies consisted mainly of clothing, footwear, guns and shells, axes, and carpentry tools. One of the best features of company policy in those days was that if you ordered an item from the catalogue which they didn't have they always sent something of better quality. Therefore, when ordering, we always hoped they wouldn't have that particular item so that we'd get something better.

I remember when my brother Hugh ordered his first .22 rifle, it was listed at $4.95. He was so happy when Eaton's were out of stock of that particular rifle and instead sent him a far better one, listed in the catalogue at $10.25. This kind of thing happened quite often, so it made ordering quite exciting to see what you'd get. The company deserved a lot of credit for this policy as no one got stuck with not getting something they badly needed.

An example of how many people came into the area was Barbara's mother, Alice. The latter had married Arthur Eastment on May 13, 1919 in England. Arthur, who had come to the area in 1909 and who had later joined the army and served overseas in France during World War I, returned shortly after his marriage to make ready the house for his new bride. In order to get to the homestead, Alice came across Canada by train to Burns Lake and then by horse and buggy to Francois Lake. All her personal belongings came the same way, of course. Her destination was Colleymount, twenty-six miles up the lake. There was no road of any kind, so she and her husband had to load everything in a canoe and paddle up the lake to her new home. She and her husband lived at Colleymount and had one daughter, Doreen, who later married my brother, Hugh. Then Arthur Eastment died in 1923 at the age of 42 and Alice went back to England with Doreen. However, after her life in the west, she soon found she didn't like living there, so she returned to Canada. Later she married Del Cassidy, who had looked after her place at Colleymount while she was away in England. They were married in September 1924 and lived at Colleymount, where Alice ran the Post Office and Del had a small store and farmed for many years. They had three children — Marjory, Ken and Barbara.

It would be nice to know what some of the pioneer women thought after leaving a nice home with modern conveniences and landing in a remote area like this. There was no water except what you carried by bucket from lake or stream. In the winter you'd have to chop a hole through the ice each morning in order to get water to make coffee, cook and wash clothes. The bath tub was a round tub about three feet across and sixteen inches deep. The water would be heated in pans on the woodstove, then poured into the tub where several in the family would take turns having a bath. There was only room to sit in it, so no one could relax in a nice hot bath tub after a long, hard day's work.

One of the most interesting friends of the Cassidy family was Tom Allen, a bachelor, who lived nearby and who spent Christmas with the family every year. He was a good cook and often went out to cook in road, rail and mining camps in the summer. He could make the best pies and cakes you could find anywhere. He was a very interesting fellow with an excellent sense of humour.

One evening some of his old friends came to visit him and have a few drinks. As the evening progressed, they got to feeling good and decided to play a game of seeing who could shoot a pistol the best. Tom had a calendar hanging on the wall of the bedroom with a picture of cowboys and Indians on it, so everyone decided to see who was the best shot. The loser would buy the next bottle of rum the next time he went out to town. The target was either a cowboy or an Indian in the picture. They had lots of fun until the ammunition ran out and the bottle went dry.

A few days later old Tom came down for church and someone spotted holes darned in his one good pair of pants. When Tom was asked how he got the holes in his pants, he bluntly answered, "Don't ask such silly questions." But he couldn't keep the secret. People finally found out that Tom had had his pants hanging on a nail in the bedroom right behind the picture and the bullets had gone through the board wall and through the seat of his pants.

Another interesting story that my dad and uncle laughed about for days was the one about a trapper who had a cabin up the Whitesail River. Like all other cabins, it didn't have a lock on it. The main reason for this was that, first of all, there was no need as there was practically no theft in those days. People respected other people's property. Secondly, it was understood that a cabin should be left open in case of an emergency. Someone caught out in a storm knew they could come in for shelter and food if need be. Most people, therefore, left a coffee or lard can full of rice, rolled oats and flour. It was also understood that whatever was used would be replaced as soon as possible.

One evening in a storm a doctor and an engineer out on a hunting trip came ashore to spend the night and sit out the storm. After they made themselves comfortable and had had a bite to eat they sat around discussing why the trapper had his stove up on blocks nearly as high as his shoulder. The doctor immediately came to the conclusion that it was because he had a bad back and didn't want to bend over to stoke up the fire. The engineer disagreed and insisted that it was because the trapper wanted to keep his sourdough under the stove to keep it from freezing. Of course the two made a wager on this. Just then the trapper came in. He'd been cutting out his trap trails for the winter. The doctor and engineer immediately asked the trapper to settle their argument to see who was right. The trapper laughed and laughed. It was a couple of minutes before he could answer. The reason was simple, he said. He didn't have a stove pipe long enough to reach through the roof if he left the stove on the floor, so he raised it. This is just another example of one of the shortcomings of today's society — that of trying to find complicated answers to very simple problems.

I can still remember how shocked Aunt Millie was one evening when some strangers happened to get on the wrong road and ended up at my uncle's place, not long before dinner. Myles and I had been up helping to cultivate the potatoes and turnips. We'd been using an old cultivator and one horse, with one of us leading the horse, while the other used the cultivator. It would take us all day to do the potatoes and turnips. The black flies were bad at that time of the year, so we were always glad to finish before six o'clock, as the flies get worse in the evening.

We had just finished unharnessing the horse and putting it out to pasture for the night when two couples drove in and asked for directions on how to get to Burns Lake, sixty miles away. Like nearly everyone else who came in close to meal times, they were invited to stay to dinner. We sat around listening to the conversation, thinking it was quite dull, when just as dessert was being served, talk drifted to how best to reach a workable arrangement with your partner in marriage and how best to settle disputes. One of the ladies was fairly heavy, while her husband was small. She was telling our aunt that sometimes in marriage a woman has to exert herself or else she will get pushed around by a domineering man. She also went on to explain how she finally got fed up with her husband trying to dominate her. One day her husband got so miserable, the woman looked him in the eye and said, "You've gone too far this time." She went on to say that when she hit her husband he spun around like the knob on our out-house door; however, there was a far better understanding in their marriage from that day forward. Needless to say, her husband had little to say.

Myles and I laughed so hard that we were sent out of the room. Aunt Millie was so shocked that a wife would hit her husband that hard that she was pleased to see them go.

I suppose today one would think that most of the people that you would find in isolated settlements would be a rather uneducated lot. But that was certainly not the case when my father and my uncle settled on their farms. There were, in fact, people from nearly all walks of life carving homesteads out of the wilderness. The level of education varied from one extreme to the other. What all of these people seemed to share was a desire to live their lives independently. Very often too the early settlers were those dissatisfied with the quality of life in the large cities in the old country. I know that there were men who had been lawyers in Great Britain who had left that country and their profession simply because they could not bring themselves to defend criminals they knew were as guilty as sin.

Another characteristic that many of these people shared was a strong interest in reading. I suppose this is not a surprising fact given that this was an era long before the advent of radio and television. In terms of recreation, there was little else to do but read during the long winter evenings. During the rest of the year most people worked fourteen to sixteen hours a day, so they had little chance to read. People read for entertainment, but they also read with a sense of purpose, a sense of education. I'll always remember how much we looked forward to receiving months-old newspapers from England when I was growing up. It didn't seem to matter that the news was out-of-date; it was still news to us!

One day in the late fall when I was still a boy, a prospector stopped at the ranch on his way out of the district to record some claims. He had walked over from the coast, more than one hundred miles away, after spending the whole summer in the mountains looking for minerals. When he arrived at our place, he still had one hundred and sixty miles to walk before he got to the Recording Office in Fort Fraser. He told us what a leisurely summer he had spent and that he was confident that his claims would make him lots of money so that he could go to all the capitals of Europe that he had read so much about.

After visiting for a spell and sharing a cup of coffee, the old prospector went off to use the outhouse. It just so happened that not too long before this Dad had lined the seat of the biffy with sheep hide so that it wouldn't be such a shock to sit on during the cold winter days. When the prospector returned from answering nature's call, he said to Dad, "You city slickers sure do have a soft life with all the modern conveniences!" He went on to explain that he was referring to the fact that last year's Eaton's catalogue was hanging on the wall to be used as toilet paper, while all he had out in the bush was moss and leaves. I guess folks are right when they say it's all relative!

That prospector of course stayed for dinner and spent the night. And we all stayed up late into the evening listening to his tales of how he had outsmarted the grizzly bears, and had been able to find enough rabbits and grouse to carry him through the summer. All he carried with him for basic supplies were rice and rolled oats; all his other food came from what game he could hunt or trap. He apparently had come down the coast from Prince Rupert as far as Kemano with an Indian guide. He had made a base camp and then prospected the area close to where the Alcan power house at Kemano was built years later. Each time he had gone up the mountains to do some prospecting he had taken forty to fifty pounds of his summer's supplies on his back and had cached them close to the west end of Tatsa Lake. This would become his second base camp once he had prospected the first area. He had lived under these conditions before and had had the sad experience of a bear or wolverine destroying all his supplies. As a result he cached his goods up a big tree and put tin around the trunk in order to stop anything climbing. (A wolverine is worse than a bear if he gets into a camp. If he cannot eat everything, he will urinate on what is left to keep other animals away. There is such a stink left behind that nothing will touch it.)

After moving his camp many times, the prospector arrived at our ranch with enough supplies left to get to Fort Fraser provided he was lucky enough to find grouse, squirrels, ducks or fish. After spending eight months with only a spruce tree or balsam for shelter, he was ready to spend the winter with some farmer who needed help. He didn't want any pay — only board for the winter. Then, once the snow melted in the spring, he would be once again on his way to find his fortune.

There is no question that many of those early prospectors knew what they were doing as nearly all of today's mines were found and recorded soon after the turn of the century. Most of the claims were dropped and picked up again when technology had advanced enough to make it economical to mine these low grade properties. Granisle and Noranda Mines on Babine Lake were two of the many ore bodies found in the early days which were recorded in 1912 and then dropped due to the cost of assessment work required each year to hold the claim. However, later, they were picked up when prices were right and the extraction technology had improved.

My father and uncle both had many interesting stories to tell, yet there is no doubt there are fascinating stories to be told by nearly every pioneer family. To my mind, there is one thing that stands out more than anything else when it comes to tales of the early days and that is the sense of humour and hospitality that is always evident in these stories. No matter who came along or when they arrived, the kettle was put on within a few minutes of their coming into the house. In nearly all cases, it was considered an insult if anyone left before having a meal.

I remember one day when I was at the Wisteria Post Office. The post office was just a room adjoining the home of Mr. and Mrs. Bob Nelson. That room was not only a post office but was also a home away from home for all of us. We lived eight miles from the Nelson's and would come in either by wagon or sleigh. On cold days in particular, we were always offered a hot cup of tea, cocoa, and cookies or cake before leaving for home.

One cold day when I was there a stranger came in on horseback after a long ride. He was invited in for a cup of tea and decided to eat his lunch while in the warm. He had no sooner taken it out of his pack-sack than Bob Nelson put a stop to that.

"When you are in my house, you eat my grub," he said. And that was that. The visitor put his lunch away and was served a meal by Mrs. Nelson. This kind of thing happened more than once.

Mail day was looked forward to with a good deal of anticipation as the post office was a good place to hear all the news about what was going on in the country. Nearly everyone would collect an hour before the mail was expected to arrive and then visit together until the mail was sorted. During this wait many community projects were discussed and often the time for a meeting was set to plan how best the project could be carried out.

The Nelsons had a lovely big yard and each of us had a favourite tree that we tied our team of horses to. Like most others, we carried hay in our wagon or sleigh to give the horses a feed before we started the trek back home.

Many times two or three of us would make the trip for the mail: one to drive the team, and the other two to watch for rabbits and squirrels along the way. One would watch the right side of the road, the other watched the left. But for some strange reason it always seemed that the driver would see the most game. If it was a nice sunny day in the winter, the rabbits would come out of cover and sit on a high spot to get the most warmth from the sun. In order to feed all our foxes and mink that we were raising, we had to take every opportunity to get feed. On a good day we would get twenty or twenty-five rabbits before

*A view of the home ranch and part of the hunting/trapping area seen from my uncle's ranch. Mt. Wells in background.*

we got back home. If the weather was dull and cold, and few rabbits were visible from the road, we would tie up the team of horses near a willow swamp and hunt. A couple of us would walk into the swamp at one end and chase the rabbits to someone waiting at the other end. This manoeuver did two things: firstly, it got a few rabbits or squirrels; and secondly, the walking got you warmed up after the cold wagon ride.

In those days a wagon and sleigh were status symbols — in much the same way a nice car is today. Those with a nice comfortable sleigh stood a far better chance of getting the girls to ride with them. Before we got a car, we would often catch a ride to the community dance with Uncle Arthur and Aunt Millie. They had quite a fast team of horses; it would only take us an hour to get to the dance if the sleigh trail had been well broken. However, if a big snowfall came the day before the dance, it could take a lot longer. In order to break the trail so that we could get to the dance, we would take a team of horses, different from the one we were going to use at night, and break the trail four miles to the next neighbour's who we knew would be going and who would have the trail made to the hall so that the travel would be better. By doing this, we would have a fresh team to go at night. We could always make better time coming home as the horses were anxious to get back to the warm barn and good feed.

The first person who arrived at the Community Hall would light the fire, as it took some time to warm up the big building. As people arrived, everyone would crowd around the fire to get warm after the sleigh ride. One night when it was very cold one of the girls backed up too close to the big stove and caught her dress on fire. There was no water in the Hall, so, as quick as a flash, a big rancher picked up the girl, ran out the door, and from the edge of the porch dropped her into the deep snow. Once the fire was out, a coat was put around her and she was brought back into the Hall. Fortunately, one of the ladies found her something to wear.

There would be very little liquor at those early dances. On rare occasions there would be a bottle of home-brew. Very few people had money to buy liquor. This was true virtually right up to World War II when a few bottles might show up. Still I'm sure everyone had as good or better a time than they do today. Today, with all the liquor available, too many people sit and drink rather than getting out on the floor to dance.

The big wood heater in the Community Hall was hand-made out of a forty-five-gallon gas barrel. A square was cut out of one end and hinges bolted to hold the door. A catch was welded on to keep the door shut, with four legs welded onto the bottom to keep the barrel away from the floor. Gas barrels made an excellent stove, especially to warm up a large building that gets really cold when not in use for a week or so. The Community Hall was a frame building with no insulation in the walls, so it would get cold really quickly when not in use. It was built by community labour and the logs for the lumber were cut close by at the little sawmill owned by the Harrison brothers. The shakes for the roof were all cut by hand out of old growth pine, which made really good shakes — ones nearly as good as cedar shakes or shingles.

Their first taste of life in the north must have been quite an experience for many teachers. Most of course were women and many were very young, right out of Normal School. On top of that many came from the city where they were used to all the conveniences of modern life. Very often the small country school represented their first jobs as teachers. It must have been a little bit frightening and I'm sure it often took a good deal of strength of character to stick it out.

Elsie (Eccles) Parker, now living in Manhattan, Kansas, was kind enough to send me her recollection of her first experiences as a teacher. She came to the little school at Streatham on Ootsa lake in September of 1929. The following is her account:

When I entered the market for my first job as a 'school marm' an older lady in Victoria cautioned me, "Go anywhere in B.C., but stay away from Burns Lake. It's a terrible place." A young male relative had taught somewhere in the area, and apparently was not at all happy with it! I travelled north to Prince Rupert on the *S.S. Prince George* together with two friends from Normal School, Dorothy Howes and Vera Beechey. On the way we discovered that we'd be teaching at Wistaria, Ootsa, and Streatham respectively — and that we'd reach our schools via Burns Lake!

We clambered off the train at Burns Lake in the dark of night, spent the night at the Omineca Hotel and rented a car and driver the next day to take us to Ootsa Lake. I believe it was Andy Ruddy, a well-known local character, who drove for us.

At the Bennett's hotel at Ootsa Lake, Vera got out. She went inside, but before long came back to the car looking quite shaken. "They all put down their papers and stared at me!" she said. Later on, the Bennetts proved to be one of the nicest families in the area with which to board.

Next stop was for me at Streatham. Down the sloping road to the lakeshore we went — to the Streatham Post Office and the home of the Billy Rist family — to ask where the teacher would be staying. We were told that I would be boarding with the Fred Talbots so on we went to the school-house, turning up a little rutty road behind it. Mrs. Mabel Talbot came out of a small log cabin to greet me. That left Dorothy and the driver to go on to Wistaria. We bade each other an emotion-charged farewell. What lay ahead for us in this isolated, sparsely populated lake country? We both felt very homesick.

Mabel showed me my room, which was in the lumber-built part of the house attached to the cabin. It had been wall-papered (the log cabin had newspapers on its ceiling and walls to help keep it warm). She brought me a cup of tea, but as I drank it, it was diluted by large salty tears that welled up in my eyes, despite my efforts to keep my composure!

Fred and Mabel Talbot proved to be wonderful folks, originally from London. I remember Fred singing 'Pale Hands I Loved' in his fine voice, and Mabel's delicious Yorkshire Pudding, and her ability to sew. It was a very different experience living with no running water, coal oil lamps, no central heat, and lots of snow!

Later on in the year I moved in with the Billy Rists, and their daughters, Monica and Jessie. Now I was boarding with another wonderful family — and with a phone, and post office — so life was a little lovelier! I could talk on the phone to Dorothy in Wistaria and Vera at Bennett's hotel.

Because I had only five regular pupils: Monica Rist, grade 6; Wilton Taylor (Barker), grade 5; John, Doris (grade 4) and Alma Anderson (grade 2); four-year-old Dennis Talbot, who lived with his aunt and uncle, the Fred Talbots, filled in. Also, every so often, a pupil from Ootsa or Wistaria would be 'borrowed.' It was disheartening to receive, every month, from the Department of Education in Victoria, a notice that the school would be closed because there were too few pupils. Somehow we survived. The next year a lady teacher with school-age children was hired.

I remember lovely musical evenings in the Olaf Anderson home, with Mrs. Anderson at the piano, and *Etude Magazine* scattered about. I'll also never forget the dances and gatherings at the Jim Harrison home on their bay. They dispensed such cordial hospitality — they seemed to love young people. And there were dances at the Wistaria Hall.

I remember a morning in the spring when my pupils and I heard a great clamour on the road below the schoolhouse — the Clarkes had arrived from the U.S.A. They had a sort of covered wagon and several family members were on horseback. They made quite a procession!

About December 20 after a dance at Wistaria, I went up to Nadina River to visit Mr. and Mrs. Jim Harrison, who were cooking for a settlers' road camp. Dorothy Howes couldn't go at the last minute. The Harrisons had sent an Indian's car for us. Then a big snowstorm a few days later snowed us in. I finally returned to Streatham by horsedrawn sled, and found a mail sack, all for me, nearly filled with packages and Christmas letters, etc. Such a thrill!

All in all I have a great many wonderful memories of that year on Ootsa lake. All three schoolmarms did considerable horseback riding, and so visited around, at the Mohrs, the Shelfords, etc. When the Rist barn caught fire, I remember the helpless feeling I had. There lay the lake, but there was no way to get the water to the fire, except by bucket. Frustrating!

When I ordered a trunk from Eaton's, Mr. Rist uncrated it and told me to open it. Out popped Jessie! She was about four years old. I remember seeing a full moon over Ootsa Lake from the Hotel. Such serenity! I introduced the Talbots to canned corn. They thought of corn only as a food for animals. I was only at Ootsa Lake for ten months but it was quite an experience for a city gal! And mostly a delightful experience. People were kind, friendly, helpful. Many had interesting backgrounds, and broad experience.

One time I went out in the rowboat with Mr. Rist to check the fishing nets. A wind came up and we couldn't head back to the house. We had to go with the waves to keep from sinking. I was frightened, and also concerned, because I had a date coming to pick me up, and I knew he'd be kept waiting. The waves were high and menacing — it was horrible! The weather had changed so quickly! We were finally able to get shelter in a little bay a mile down the lake and were then able to come ashore and leave the boat for the night and walk home. Needless to say, I was late for my date.

Each year just before Christmas, the school teacher would put on a Christmas concert with all the kids taking part. It was something the whole community would turn out to see. Once the concert was over and Santa had been, the small kids were put to bed on the cloakroom floor; then the dance would begin and last all night.

There was always a lot of competition to see who in the community would board the teacher. Nearly everyone wanted to get the board money in order to pay for a few groceries. The first teacher I remember got $30 a month and paid $20 for board — teachers certainly didn't come into the country to get rich. One thing they did enjoy in nearly all communities, however, was the deep respect of all the settlers. The teachers were looked upon as the best source of information and advice. Together with the ministers of the churches, the teacher enjoyed a position of very high prestige. Many young teachers ended up getting married in the district as there were so many eligible bachelors around. If the teacher didn't get married, it was because she didn't want to, not because of lack of opportunity.

And that reminds me of a story about two brothers who came to the Ootsa lake area together to establish their farm. They worked hard to clear a few acres of land with only an axe and pick. It was a slow, laborious task. One night, while sitting around after dinner, they came to the conclusion that they could do far more work if only they didn't have to spend their time cooking meals, washing dishes, and cleaning and mending their clothes. The solution seemed simple enough. After a lengthy discussion they decided that one of them should get married. But, as neither would volunteer to go out and look for a bride, they ended up tossing a coin; the one who lost the toss was the one who would get married. And they stuck by their bargain. The next winter the "loser" took a wife. And that's were the story usually ended. But I wouldn't be at all surprised if the "winner" didn't come to see what he was missing and go after his own mate. It's surprising how many marriages like this worked out well, the husband and wife enjoying each other's company and raising a fine family.

It would be interesting to know the number of hours spent by the many pioneer families in clearing land so they could feed a few cattle and horses through the winter. The scarcity of winter feed was always the limiting factor for my dad and uncle when considering how many animals could be kept. In contrast, summer feed on the range was always plentiful. By today's standards the cattle herds found in the area in those early days would look very small; the larger producers would seldom have more than thirty or forty head. During the time when the cattle were driven out to the rail line, it often took four or five owners to get enough for one carload — around thirty-five head depending on size. Most of the animals were fairly big as they were always kept until they were about two years old before being sold. There is no comparison between the steers in the early years and those of today. Today they are as large at one year as they were at two years in those days. The main reason for this is artificial insemination which brings in a far superior strain. No one could afford the good bulls that are used today.

It is interesting to note that very few cattle cheques for an entire year's work were ever more than $700 or $800. In those days beef prices were a half-cent a pound for cows and three-quarter cent for choice steers. This money had to last many families for a whole year for clothing and whatever food had to be bought. My uncle and aunt were always extremely upset every time the federal government came out with figures indicating the poverty level for Canadians. Even though their income went up over the years, they never did get above the federal poverty level. The poverty level was never very realistic for the rural areas of Canada where so many people worked extremely hard and were pretty well self-sufficient.

# 4. A Visit to the Stikene

The area around Telegraph Creek and Glenora along the Stikine River has always fascinated me. Now a ghost town, Glenora was at one time a major settlement with a population of more than one thousand people at the turn of the century. It was one of the major supply centres for the rapidly growing prospecting and mining industry in the north of B.C. and the Yukon. Hundreds of miners from many countries of the world flocked to Glenora and Telegraph Creek en route north to the goldfields of the Yukon.

Although everyone was out to find their fortune, many never got further than the comfortable surroundings of the major supply centres. Some built hotels and bars to attract the lonely miners returning from months and sometimes years in the wilderness in their search for gold. In many cases this turned out to be a very lucrative business — often much more profitable than prospecting. In fact, it was often those who spent their time in the gambling houses and saloons who ended up with the gold that some prospector had worked so hard to find. Those who had been lucky in their search for gold, spent their hard-earned money freely in the bars. They had spent months working hard, now they wanted to play just as hard. Some would sit all night in the poker dens or wild crap games frequented by professional gamblers, who could spot a greenhorn in any crowd.

The gamblers' first approach was to get very friendly and make the victim feel his new-found friend was out to help him. Most of the pros would coach a new player and let him win to gain confidence so he would gamble freely with his hard-earned gold. Many greenhorns lost everything they had. Then, as likely as not, they would be loaned enough for a grubstake to go back and find some more gold so they could pay their debts to the professional gamblers. The latter hung around supply centres like the leeches that cling to a fish until all the blood is gone. Every major gold strike, even today, has these people around. Most of them will take away more money than any of the miners, even those who strike it rich. Those who don't gamble spend their money on drinks, especially for the dancing girls who either come in for adventure or who join in the world's oldest profession of prostitution.

Other people came to the supply centres in search of more honest pursuits. Many worked on the supply trails and at Glenora there was work surveying a rail line to the Yukon. In spite of the fact that it was never built, a great deal of time and money were spent searching for the best route. Some spent months and even years in this search. Most of this work had to be done in the summertime as during the cold winters it was difficult to operate with the dangerous blizzards that often sweep through the mountain passes. These storms force everyone who travels to seek shelter — either in heavy timber if any can be found, or if one can get into a canyon that breaks up the wind. Those who can't find this type of shelter often perish before the storm is over. During the worst storms that come in from the north, the temperature will drop to forty or fifty below zero. Those with experience who see the storm coming and understand how severe they can be, aim to reach an area that has an abundance of dry wood and a wind break and wait out the storm without too much danger. Many others who haven't learned to recognize the storm signals and start out over the open country where the storms hit with all their fury, are lucky to survive and get a second chance.

The Ball family were among the early pioneers to the Glenora area. George Ball spent most of his time freighting supplies up the Stikene River from Wrangle, Alaska. The latter point was where the supply ships came in to unload their cargo and passengers heading upstream to seek their fortunes. Those who had tasted the harshness of the country and decided that it was not for them often headed back down the river on the first ship.

Bobby Ball, George Ball's son, learned the art of river freighting and guiding during his teens and got to know every rapid, log jam, sand bar and other hazard along the river. I met Bobby Ball on numerous occasions, mainly at Guide Association conventions. However, I didn't really get to know him until Barbara and I and our good friends from Terrace, Bob and Edna Cooper, decided to go up and visit the area. We'd heard so much about the place over the years that we were finally determined to see the country for ourselves. The four of us travelled with the Cooper's truck and a twenty-three foot trailer, a very comfortable way to travel.

At that time there was no pavement after we left Kitwanga. We spent the first night alongside the Nass River below Meziaden Lake where the federal government built a fish ladder so that the salmon could get up into the lake and spawn in the streams coming into it. It was a lovely sight to see the big salmon trying to jump up the falls, which are over eight feet tall. They seemed to try many times before making their way up the ladder.

The next day we drove up to Morcheau Lake, seven or eight miles before we crossed the upper Stikene River. This was a lovely place to camp and the lake was full of pan-sized rainbow trout. We soon caught enough for a good dinner. The next day the weather was lovely and warm and the gravel roads were good as far as Dease Lake. However, from there on there was very little gravel and the road bed was mainly clay. The clay was as hard as cement in dry weather and as slippery as glare ice during and after a rain.

It's a very interesting drive from Dease Lake through to Telegraph Creek, crossing two major rivers which are in the bottom of very deep valleys. The dirt road wound down one side and back up the other. At the top, you could look down over a mile to the river below and see the road winding down the hill below. Some of the bends in the road were so steep that it was hard to get the trailer around without going in the ditch and so steep you wondered whether the brakes would hold. However, in the dry weather it wasn't all that bad. We passed the Indian village of Tahltan and watched the young boys catching big spring salmon that spawn up the Tahltan River. The oldtime village was built on a lovely piece of land where the Tahltan River joins the Stikene River below the falls.

In the old days before the white man arrived, the Indians would all get together in the fall and drive the cariboo from the nearby mountains into the narrow neck of land where the two rivers meet and where other waiting natives would hide behind rocks and spear the cariboo as they came by. The meat would be dried like the salmon for the coming winter.

We camped at the Telegraph Creek Airport, which had a lovely view of the Stikene River and the mountains to the south. The next day we went to visit Agnes Ball, Bobby's mother, who is one of the most interesting people you could ever hope to meet. She made tea and told us a great deal about her life on the river in the early days. We were also able to contact Bobby, who lived on the farm across the river from the location of the old town of Glenora, downriver from Telegraph Creek. He agreed to meet us at the river after we came across.

Bob Cooper had a canoe with a little motor. The river was quite swift, so we went upstream a hundred yards or so, then cut across. The current carried us down as we went across, but with Bob's good judgement, we managed to land where Bobby's wagon road came down to the river. When we landed and all were out, we pulled the canoe up the beach some distance. When I tied a rope from the bow to a willow bush, one of the others asked me why.

"The river might come up if it rained," I said. At that moment it looked very unlikely, as the weather was so nice, but you never know about the weather in the north country. I worked on the assumption "better safe than sorry." Bobby Ball soon turned up in his Jeep with a wagon behind. In the wagon he had hay bales for us to sit on. The ranch was four miles from the river landing. Once we were away from the river, where the wind kept the black flies, mosquitoes and deer flies at bay, the insects came in by the thousands. We swatted flies all the way to the ranch, which was beautifully situated on the side of a big hay meadow with lots of horses grazing in the pasture.

Our intention was to visit for the afternoon and then head back to the trailer we had left at the airport in the evening. Soon after we arrived, Bobby's wife Nancy had the coffee made and we listened with interest to the stories about life in the area. You have to be independent and ready to look out for yourself to live in that country as it was very isolated at some times of the year. In the early winter the river froze over so you couldn't use a boat and yet the ice was not thick enough to travel on. The same thing occured in the spring at break-up when the ice got unfit to walk across. Boat travel was impossible for several weeks if it was a late spring and the ice stayed on. We got so interested in comparing stories about the early days and discussing the future of the guiding business that it was soon dinner time.

Nancy and her three girls had prepared a lovely dinner — better than anything you could get in downtown Vancouver. They had a nice garden, and grew all their own vegetables. We continued to enjoy ourselves and the pace of the conversation didn't let up at all. After dinner the Balls insisted that we stay the night.

Just before we went to bed the clouds began to roll in from the coast and it started to rain. However, we were nice and comfortable in the cabins that Bobby had for the hunters that he guided in the fall. The next day the rain was still pouring down, and we stayed in the house all day, still swapping stories about guiding and life in the wilderness in general. The Balls insisted that we shouldn't try the river as it was probably coming up very fast. The rain was swelling all the creeks and rivers coming into the Stikene. The whole Ball family were excellent hosts, so we enjoyed our stay very much. We talked about coming back the following year so that we could go up into the mountains to take pictures.

The next morning the rain had let up and travel was possible once again. We left by Jeep and wagon for the river, and once again battled the flies once we got into the timber where the wind couldn't blow them away. When we we saw the river, we wondered whether we still had a canoe. It had risen over fourteen feet and was up over the shore and into the bushes along the banks. At first there was no sign of the canoe. But when Bob and I waded out to where it was tied to the willow, we discovered that the boat was still there but had sunk to the bottom. The engine was still on, and, amazingly enough, the gas tank was floating and still attached to the motor. We pulled the canoe in and tipped the water out. We thought the motor would never run again after being under water so long, so we didn't try to start it. We decided to paddle across the river. The crossing didn't take long with the river in full flood. We used the current and we went at an angle so that the speed of the river helped push us over.

The road back to Dease Lake was a sea of mud and Bob couldn't use the brakes to hold the trailer back or the truck would slide like a toboggan down the hills. At times, looking over the banks on a turn, we could see the road three hundred feet below. I know the three passengers were uncomfortable and wished we were walking; however, Bob did an excellent job of driving under such conditions — it was raining again. Once down, we wondered if we could get back up the mile-long hill on the other side. The climb had six switchback turns so we couldn't get a good run at it. I volunteered to walk up to the top to try to assess if it was possible. Others had obviously tried the hill as there were ruts cut a foot deep in the roadbed. Someone had even broken up bales of duroid roofing in an attempt to get traction under the wheels. They must have thrown out over a thousand dollars worth of roofing, plywood and boards trying to get up that grade. Bob's truck was four-wheel drive and it looked to me like he could make it, so I signalled that he should give it a try. The girls weren't so sure, though. When Bob started up, Barbara and Edna asked him whether they should walk; they thought that a lot safer. However, in a very serious voice, Bob said, "No! Just shut up so I can drive." And drive he did. He did a superb job and we were soon over the crest and out of danger. From there on we knew we would have no further trouble so we camped for the night.

The next day we had no trouble driving back half way to Terrace. One thing for sure, we all made up our minds that if we ever went back we wouldn't take a trailer along. We'd only take a four-wheel drive truck.

Bob and Edna Cooper and ourselves decided early in the year to book a five-day trip with Bobby Ball to see a little more of the country and his guiding area in particular. Bobby had asked us to visit his guiding area several times over the years. We decided when we started out that we were going to see as much of the area as possible, providing the weather was a little kinder than the first time we were there. On this trip we arranged to stay in his hunting cabins rather than try and bring the trailer into Telegraph Creek again.

During dinner Bobby outlined the various options we might take during our stay. The river boat trip sounded very interesting, so we decided to start with that. Early next morning we were off to the river with supplies for an overnight trip. The boat was an open, eighteen-foot river boat, so there wasn't much room to move around with the five of us and sleeping bags and food. The day was lovely, without a cloud in the sky. We ran downstream all day. We passed through some beautiful country, heading west with the coast mountains rising high all around us. During the late afternoon the wind got up and blew sand from the bars into our faces. With the hot sun as well, most of us got a good burn before the sun went down.

On the way down the river we saw something white hanging on a stick on a tiny log jam in the middle of the river. It looked like a distress signal so we went in to see what had happened. The river was swift so Bobby had to go past the log jam and come in from downstream, where there was a little quiet water to get the bow of the boat up to two big logs where we could get out and see what it was all about. A fellow had hit the log jam and sunk his boat. However, he had managed to get out on the log jam but couldn't get to shore due to the fast water.

The man was more than a hundred yards from either shore so he spent the night and most of the next day on the small log jam. In the middle was an area about ten foot square that was dry, but there was no grass, moss or bushes to make a comfortable bed; however, he had gone to a lot of work laying small pieces of wood together so he could at least lie down on these carefully placed small logs and sticks. The white thing on the stick was his underwear shorts, which he had put up to signal help. All he had on to spend the night (which gets cold even in good weather) were his pants, t-shirt and underwear shorts. When we arrived he was gone and we learned later that he had been picked up just before we arrived and taken down to the fisheries camp near the U.S. border. By sunset, we were all getting tired. We all had burns on the face from the sun and cutting sand driven with such force by the wind. At near-dark, Bobby said, "I know where there is a cabin that the owner won't mind if we use." This sounded like a pretty good idea as everyone was ready for some dinner.

Once the sun went down the flies were terrible and we didn't have mosquito nets. As a result, I was thinking we'd be making up the fire all night to keep the flies away. An old cabin sounded good. It was situated in a quiet bay and there the boat wouldn't be in any danger. There was also a lovely view of the mountains and glaciers from the cabin window. As soon as we got inside the cabin, we were in for a surprise — there were mice running everywhere. We could see five behind the stove at one time. There were mouse droppings in all the pots and pans. In the frying pan, they covered the bottom. Bob Cooper and I decided to make a mouse trap and catch them all as quickly as possible. We cut the top out of an old five-gallon oil can and put a small soup can on a wire so that when the mouse jumped on the can to get the bait it would spin around and then fall in the water below. We put a board up on each side of the oil bucket so the mice could run up and jump out for the bait. Both of us had made such traps before so we knew they worked well. While we were doing this Barbara and Edna were trying to defend themselves from the mosquitoes and black flies so they lit a mosquito coil, which burns slowly and keeps the flies away. The women also helped Bobby by getting water boiling to wash all the utensil, pots and pans with lots of soap; we hadn't brought many utensils along with us. We couldn't understand why our mouse trap wasn't working as mice were running everywhere but they weren't interested in anything to eat. We only caught one.

Bobby had brought along five big moose steaks, potatoes, and carrots, so once things were cleaned up we had a good dinner, even though the ladies were not too keen on all the mice around. There was a little bedroom that had no door but which contained two fair-sized bunk beds, on which the four of us slept. There were straw mattresses on the bunks and the mice had been all through them. When we went into the bedroom there were six mice trying to get out of the window. I took a swipe with a stick and didn't get any. Edna said to Bob, "Come in here and take a look." He came in and smiled and said, "Hickory, dickory, dock, the mouse ran up the clock." I don't think Edna appreciate his humour at that point. Barbara and I had a big sleeping bag so we crawled into that and the mice didn't come near all night. Next morning there wasn't a mouse in the place. Apparently, the mice didn't like the smell of the mosquito coil burning and were desperate to get out and that was why they were running around like mad and weren't interested in our mouse trap.

There was a sack of flour with mice holes into the sack. I'd volunteered to make hot cakes in the morning, which no one took seriously until I started to get things together. Barbara said to Edna, "Do you know what Cyril is doing? He is using that flour." I'd found that on one side of the sack the mice hadn't chewed a hole, so I got two cupfuls out of there for my hot cakes. Bobby sat drinking coffee and said, "Do you think your friends in the Health Department would approve of this?" Everyone seemed to like my hot cakes and came back for more. Next morning we went down river into the U.S. and visited a fish plant on the Canadian side before heading back up river. Barbara's face and eyes were all swollen up by this time from the sun and blowing sand. It looked as if she wouldn't be able to continue on the rest of the trip; however, she braved it out all the way and didn't miss anything.

The weather was still good and we all enjoyed the boat ride. As we were going with the wind, the latter didn't bother us any. Bobby was giving a running commentary on the names of the mountains and streams coming into the Stikene River. All together we travelled nearly 200 miles before we got back to the landing and the tractor and steel-wheeled wagon which were waiting to take us back the four miles to the ranch. If it got too rough bouncing on the rocks, roots and stumps, we got out to walk a lot of the way. When we arrived just after dark Nancy and their girls had another lovely dinner ready. Because Bobby was away a lot of the time guiding, Nancy and their son put up most of the hay. Nancy could run a tractor as well as any man. The three girls — Tammy, Heather and Moyia — did the rest of the work, looking after the horses, cooking, etc. When we returned it was getting close to hunting season so Nancy wanted the machinery repaired as they raked hay with the Jeep and its radiator had a bad leak. Therefore, after breakfast I took the radiator off and soldered the leak while Bob did some welding on the tractor and hay-mower so that they could start haying while we were away up the mountains. The girls were rounding up the horses to take up the mountain. There were quite a few to choose from and we needed seven saddle horses and four pack horses.

Bobby was getting all the equipment together.

Once they had the horses saddled, around 2 p.m., Bob, Barbara, Edna, Tammy and Heather left for the mountain cabin with some of the supplies so they could get dinner ready for when we arrived later with the rest of the supplies and the bedding. It was eight miles up to the cabin and very steep most of the way. The climb was over 3,000 feet, so the horses had to walk with care as it was nearly solid rock in many places and, therefore, the others didn't get up to the cabin very early.

To my surprise, as I thought we were ready to go, Bobby came to me and said, "Let's go out and break Joe Clark." (Most of his horses were named after politicians.) I never did find out which one was named after me, but it must have been on the range as we didn't have it on the pack train or as one of the riding horses. Bobby decided to tie Joe Clark to Trudeau, as the latter was well broken and wouldn't get excited. The first thing we had to do was to get horseshoes on him, which was no easy task as he never stayed still for a second. The front feet are easy as you can tie one foot at a time with a rope over the back. The hind feet are far harder to do and the only way you can do it without throwing them flat on the ground with their legs tied together. This is something good horsemen don't like to do as it scares the horses so much they remember it for life. You have to throw the horses every time a shoe comes loose — which can happen two or three times a trip in rough country, such as that we were going into. The best way is to get one hind foot up and straddle it, one leg on each side with your backside against the backside of the horse. The horse can move his leg back and forth but not down if you are strong enough. Usually, the horses give up after a while and stand still. The only real danger is when you have the horseshoe nails driven through but not cut off and bent over. If the horse starts to struggle at the wrong moment, he can pull the horseshoe nails into your thigh, as the nails are about an inch through the hoof before they are cut off. If this happens, you can hear the swear words a mile away. Fortunately, old Joe Clark stayed still while I did one foot and Bobby did the other. We then proceeded to shake out Joe Clark, which simply means you shake a saddle blanket behind their heels and in front of their face. Once they quit kicking and jumping, they are ready to stand still while you put on the pack saddle. We took it in turns, as it took nearly an hour before he settled down and to know that we weren't going to hurt him. Bobby said, "Old Joe Clark is an ornery critter and you had better watch his heels." I took this to heart, as he sure could kick. Trudeau stood quietly by, as much as to say, 'What's all the fuss about?' The horse named Bill Bennett was very quiet and stayed away from the other horses as much as possible. Once Joe Clark settled down, it was easy to get the pack saddle on and cinch it down. He never moved when we put on the pack. Once all were packed, we left for the mountain about 4 p.m. However, we didn't make very good time as the packhorses soon got tired because it was their first trip of the year.

Not far out of camp we met Heather on her way back to the ranch to help her mother. Bobby and Tammy stayed on the mountain with us. I'm sure we were all a little concerned because Heather wouldn't reach the ranch until well after dark. One thing the kids in the remote areas such as this soon learn is independence and how to take care of themselves. Our main concern was the fact that grizzly bears were in the area and if the horse she was riding got spooked by one of the bears, anything could happen; however, all went well and Heather got home safely.

Again, just before we got to camp Bobby looked at Joe Clark as we were resting the horses and he was standing with his head down. He shook his head and said, "He sure can't stand these tough trails like old Trudeau." Trudeau still looked as if he could go another eight miles. Once we arrived in camp, we unpacked and put the horses out to pasture in a nice meadow close to camp. Bobby had a fence on the home-side of the meadow. This was so that if the horses wanted to go home they had to come through camp and someone would hear the bells on four of the horses. Dinner was waiting as soon as we got the horses away. Tammy was extremely efficient under such difficult circumstances with only an old tin wood stove to cook on. This stove had several holes in the side where pieces of tin were stuffed in to keep the hot ashes from falling out. After dinner we pitched a tent and slept out there. Barbara's eyes were still nearly closed after the boat ride on the river, but she didn't miss a chance to go horseback riding. (She had done a lot of riding in her earlier years when she used to round up the milk cows every evening before dinner.)

The next day while Tammy was cooking the breakfast we went out to round up the horses. Some of the horses had gone a mile or so from camp in an attempt to find the very best feed as there was lots of it in the many meadows just below the timber line. All the trees in the area were in patches and easy to ride around. They were all of poor quality and very few were over thirty feet high. Nearly all the trees had broken tops because of the severe winds that hit the mountains on a regular basis. The things that impressed us more than anything else were the forget-me-nots that grew all over the mountain. In the clear mountain air, they were just as blue as the skies — as the good weather continued to last. We rode up a valley which was like a dream world — with all the flowers of different kinds. We came across the mountain marmots. (These animals are commonly known as whistlers, because they make a whistling sound as anything approaches to warn the other ones to get under cover. They are very pretty animals and will come to get a good look at you if you stand perfectly still without even moving your head.) We saw and heard more than fifty as we rode up the valley. Every mile we would stop and watch the mountains on all sides with field glasses for cariboo, sheep, goats, and with luck, a moose or grizzly bear; however, nothing was seen in one of the best areas of the province for all these animals. Bobby was very concerned as hunting parties were coming in soon. The problem was the same as that in most areas of the province — where the wolves get too plentiful they destroy the game population. There weren't even game tracks on the once well-travelled game trails. There was only the beauty of the mountains and flowers of many species wherever we went. The only tracks we saw were those of either wolves or grizzly bears.

We rode more than fourteen miles up a mountain pass and could look over the whole country from there. Telegraph Creek was below us to the north, with the Stikene River winding its way to the sea. To the east was Mount Eziza, known to all the local people as 'Pink Mountain.' On a clear day, like the one we had, you could see thirty or forty miles in any direction. The last four miles were fairly steep and we started to get held up in the snow at an ele-vation of 8,000 feet. In most areas, the snow was hard enough for the horses to walk on top of; however, they would suddenly break through and get stuck. We walked and led our horses in order to take the weight off them, but this didn't work completely. Therefore, we tied the horses to a rock, as there were no trees, and walked the rest of the way. I'm sure we all thought the trip worthwhile as we stood on a mountain peak looking down on the country below. There were mountains as far as the eye could see in all directions.

On the way back to camp we travelled slowly as the horses and riders were getting tired. Edna had never been on a horse before this trip, but what she lacked in experience she more than made up for with courage and determination. She walked the last three miles into camp, as she was getting stiff and sore from riding. One thing for sure, Bobby sure picked the right horses for a beginner, as it was so quiet and carefully picked its way wherever it went. We crossed dozens of mountain streams coming from the snow patches and cut a ditch about three or four feet wide and two or three feet deep. Our horses were frightened and didn't want to cross. Eventually, when they did cross they would take a big jump; however, Edna's horse would just plod in one side and out the other. Most of the streams had rock bottoms; however, some would be in muskeg and a horse could easily get stuck going across. It's likely that our horses had been stuck some time in the past and were frightened of all streams.

When we got back to camp we were all ready for a good dinner. We sat around the campfire telling stories and listening to Bobby playing his guitar and singing songs. He could keep singing all night, especially with the help of a glass of rye once in a while. He was very good and could have travelled with a western musical group had he wanted to. However, he chose to stay on the ranch in the most peaceful environment you could find anywhere in this troubled world in which we live today.

The next day it was back to the ranch and the end of a most enjoyable holiday. We also left the mice and the flies to their peaceful world in the valley of the Stikene. Bobby took us back to Telegraph Creek and we all enjoyed a visit with his mother, Agnes Ball, who lived most of her life in the Stikene Valley. Today, she is over eighty years old and still as sharp as a tack. She can discuss nearly any topic from guiding boating on the northern rivers to politics and even city life. Every winter she goes out of the valley but anxiously wants to get back to the land she loves when the snow goes in the spring. She is like the Canadian Geese — when the warm spring winds start to blow across the valley of the Stikene she can't wait to get back to see the flowers pop out of the ground only days after the snow leaves. It's wonderful how they can come up along side of a melting glacier and flower, seed and die all within a month — in warm areas, such a cycle takes months.

On leaving the valley we took something with us that will last forever — the memory of a valley largely untouched by modern society. When we left, the rose and saskatoon bushes were turning red for the coming fall. This is what the Indians call 'Dog Tears' for the coming winter. It's the signal for the Indian braves to leave the river that supplied them with food all summer and go to the mountains to hunt for game animals to supply the tribe with meat to dry and animal skins for clothing to carry them through the coming long, cold winter.

Our visit to the Telegraph Creek area made me appreciate more than ever the spectacular country that we are blessed with here in British Columbia. The wonderful hospitality that we experienced at the hands of the Ball family also reinforced my belief that the people of this province are our greatest resource. British Columbia has long had the reputation of attracting those with the pioneer spirit and I think that that tradition continues. My uncle Arthur Shelford was certainly a good example of a man who set out to build a lifestyle that suited his own particular wants and needs. His story is a great example of the true pioneer spirit that has built this province. But I will let him tell his story for he will tell it far better than I ever could.

# Uncle Arthur's Story

# 1. Canada Calls

Near the end of March 1908, after a long day at the office, I decided to emigrate to Canada. I was twenty-two years old at the time. This news came as quite a shock to all those with whom I worked at the Post Office Savings Bank in London. I decided it was not my ambition to spend the rest of my life catching the 8:10 a.m. train run to be at the office at 9:00 a.m.; then, to spend seven hours of routine, monotonous work, day in and day out, until I got a pension at 65 — and this without knowing what the rest of the world was all about. I had spent my short working life in London — employed most recently by the Post Office Savings Bank, but before that the Ministry of Agriculture and Fisheries and the Department of Defence (both for a short time). None of these positions did anything to help me prepare for a life in the wilds of Canada where there would be no roads or railroads, running water or electric lights, and where the closest store for supplies would be close to two hundred miles away. No doubt, the encouragement from my brother Jack in letters relating his experiences in Buffalo, Chicago, Hayoe City, Kansas, San Francisco, Vancouver and Alaska stirred my curiosity for life in a new country where adventure would be a daily event.

I spent most of April getting ready to travel and saying farewell to my many friends and my family who didn't think I was well suited to a life in the wilderness of Canada. Nevertheless, on April 24th, 1908 I sailed from Liverpool on the old Allan liner *Virginian* with my sister there to see me off. Well, other people might be worrying about my departure, but amongst that gay crowd of 2nd Class passengers there was no opportunity for me to start worrying.

Those were the days of mass emigration to Canada, both from Britain and the European continent, and all the boats were filled to overflowing. Our crowd on the *Virginian* was mostly composed of young men and women between twenty and thirty years of age, with a sprinkling of older people and a few younger ones. A finer cross-section of British it would have been difficult to find, and I think that security was the last thought in the minds of most of them. They felt that they were going to a great new land of adventure. They didn't know where or to what they were going, they were simply on the way. And that is the only spirit in which to embark on an adventure of this kind.

Life was bound to be different and, for that matter, I think that most of us wanted it to be! Hand-picked jobs were not going to be waiting for us at our destinations. It would be up to us to take any job we could get to get started in the new life. Very soon a newcomer gets acquainted with new conditions, new opportunities, and, most of all, new people. If he is a likeable person, these people help him to get better and more suitable jobs, but he must have a willingness to work, even to the point of wanting to do a little more than he is expected to do.

The only persons who were a bit inclined to put a bit of a damper on these feelings of high expectations were a few returning Canadians of British origin, who had been home for a holiday. They would say that, for many aboard, the balloon would burst when they came up against the hard reality of life. But these were mostly from Eastern Canada, where life is very similar to life in Britain, and just about as parochial. They knew little of the West, and certainly had not got the spirit of the West.

The voyage, for most of us, was just one big, happy party. The food was, as is usual on most liners, most excellent and, at sea, one is always hungry, unless sick, and, if sick, one is doubly hungry afterwards. We had one very rough day, and I fed the fishes for the only time in all the voyages I have made.

But all good things come to an end and, on the tenth day we entered the St. Lawrence. What a lovely entry into Canada lay up that beautiful river, with the shores dotted with the white houses of the Quebec habitants, and the innumerable islands in the wide expanse of water, while the Laurentian hills rose gently in the background.

During the last leg of the voyage, from Rimouski to Montreal, Immigration officials and doctors got busy with us. The former wanted to see that we had the regulation amount of money to be allowed to land, and to ask a few questions as to reasons for our particular destination and what we intended to do when we reached it.

To these questions I could only answer that I had just picked Calgary, that I had no friends there, and that I figured on getting any job at all that was going.

The doctor's examination, a more or less perfunctory one, was mostly confined to the eyes, to be sure that we were not suffering from trachoma, a disease that was not common in emigrants from Britain, but more so in those from European countries.

Then came the bustle of landing, of numerous goodbyes, the Customs examination, and the checking of baggage unwanted on the train journey that lay ahead. Trains were ready to take everyone on the start of their land journey but  as an old London friend, a bank clerk who now worked in Montreal, met me there, I decided to spend the night in Montreal. I also assumed that on the train the next morning there would not be the same crush that there was at this point. My friend took me and a young English boy, whom I met on the boat, to a hotel near the Windsor Station and, after a short trot around the city, we were left on our own.

Next morning, before train time, we went shopping to stock up on food for the journey, as we were travelling "colonist," and so did not get our meals in the dining car; mostly because prices charged there were far too high for the ordinary emigrant. Sure, travelling was tough, with hard board seats and only what bedding you had of your own, but I was figuring on taking the rougher kind of life in Canada and, this being the case, it was just as well to plunge right into it. It is just like entering a cold stream, plunge right in and it is all over, and you hardly notice the cold; but enter with a toe or two first and then the rest of your body gradually and you get lots of shivers and misery.

I think every Britisher coming to Canada in those days was first impressed by the huge locomotives with their clanging bells and the loud, raucous whistles, and the long, commodious railway coaches, so different from the small British-type locomotives with their piping whistles, and the small British carriages.

The first bit of Canada that one sees on the rail journey is not exactly impressive, for the best part of Ontario lies to the south of the CPR main line. All the country traversed north of Lakes Huron and Superior is of the most desolate nature, indescribably rough and hilly, strewn with huge boulders, and with a poor growth of timber on it. For miles the track winds along the rocky shores of Lake Superior, with curves so sharp that, sometimes, when I saw an engine rounding a curve ahead of us, I wondered what other train it was, only to discover that it was the front end of our own snake-like train.

Ice was still on the lakes but the creeks were all full of the dark brown water so typical of creeks in the spring run-off all over Canada.

One incident on that journey through Ontario I will always remember. Late one night, when we were all nicely asleep, my friend and I being in an upper berth, a horde of noisy, vivacious, swarthy-looking men boarded the train at a small wayside station and, after that, sleep was quite impossible until they left us at some later station. It might have been a bunch of Sicilian bandits for all one could tell but, in reality, it was just a bunch of French-Canadian lumberjacks returning from a winter's work in some remote logging camp. Naturally, they were in high spirits at the thought of getting home, and most of them had a good load of other spirits, too. Though very noisy, they turned out to be quite good-tempered. That night I got my first experience of the tobacco chewing habit and its vile spitting accompaniment, and I relived Martin Chuzzlewit's same experiences and reactions on his journey to Eden.

Taken by and large, this first part of the trip over Canada, until one reaches Winnipeg, is not in the least impressive. Outside of the few big towns, the population appears very sparse and scattered, while the smaller places seemed to be built-up in a very haphazard style, with a woeful lack of paint. However, I soon discovered that this was just one of the growing pains of all new communities.

From the neighbourhood of Winnipeg westward, the vastness of the prairies could not fail to impress anyone. But in those early days, with the land on each side of the CPR belonging to the railway as a land grant, very little actual settlement on the land was seen, for most immigrants had little money, and so took up the free homestead land outside of the railway belt.

At Regina I lost my last travelling companion from the *Virginian*, the young boy just out of school in England. And now, I, myself, was getting near my destination at Calgary, having traversed practically the whole breadth of the prairies, and now within sight of the foothills of the Rockies. But I never had a feel for the prairies. I just was not the type to farm, or even live, on that vast, treeless expanse, with their brazen skies in summer, and their bitter cold, biting winds and drifting snow in winter. As a place in which to make good money in times of good crops, the prairies would be hard to beat, but my desire in life was not to make a pile of money, but rather to live my life and do my work in some place which I could really love.

# 2. Pick and Shovel

The chief item on the program now was to get a job, and this, as it turned out, was not very easy. In the fall of 1907 Canada and the USA had been hit by a fairly heavy financial crisis. I remember reading in the English papers of the collapse of the Knickerbocker Trust Company. But, though England also had her unemployment troubles, with large parades of unemployed in London, a person living there never realized just how a new developing country like Canada could be hit when money was tight. Besides all the incoming flood of immigrants, there were thousands of men just starting to build up farms all over the prairies who had to work part of the year in order to finance their home activities for the remainder.

First of all I went to the Immigration Office, which was supposed to help newcomers to get jobs, and to give them any necessary advice. The only staff there was an old Englishman who, quite cheerfully, told me that he knew of no jobs at all and that, as regards farm work, the opportunities were small, as it was the off-season between seed-time and haying and harvest. He stated flatly that it was too early to come to Canada, and that I should not have arrived for another month. However, he was very cheerful about it all, because he himself had a good job and, as far as one could tell, mighty little work to do.

About the only other way for a new arrival to connect with a job was to contact one of the several private employment agencies, but, on their boards, the only jobs offered were pick and shovel jobs on the railway construction work and maintenance, and there were not a great many of these. There was, however, one big undertaking on which most of the labourers in Western Canada at this time worked at one time or another. This was the Field Tunnel, a wonderful operation near the summit of the Rockies. Previous to the construction of this tunnel, trains had to put on a second engine to hold them back on the long, steep grade, going towards Field, the first station in British Columbia, and, likewise, to pull them up the hill when going east. By the project on hand, instead of going down the hill, the railway entered into Mt. Stephen and, by a wonderful tunnel in the shape of a figure 8, right inside the mountain, came out at the lower level so that now, one never realizes that there is any hill at all.

Jobs as labourers were advertised on the boards at $2.00 a day. I paid my dollar to the agency, and was told to be there at a certain time. At the time I did not know that I was applying for a job in the Field Tunnel. Soon after this, a chance acquaintance on the street told me grim stories of the wet, miserable work in the Tunnel, and that it was quite dangerous, too, with many men being killed there. So, back to the Employment Office I go and asked if the job I was hired for was the Field Tunnel, as, if it was, I did not want it. The fellow there said that it was, but that I did not have to work in the tunnel if I did not wish to, but could work in one of the grade camps. And so, I agreed to go on the job. At the agreed time, one of the bosses from the camp who happened to be in Calgary at the time rounded us up at the Employment Office. A bunch of men from half the nations of Europe, we were herded to the train for our trip to camp.

That journey took us right into the heart of the Rockies, first through the rolling foothills, and then, into the mountains proper. Banff, the famous summer resort, was passed and from there to camp, over the Great Divide, we were really in amongst the big fellows. As the train steamed down the big hill towards the camp, we were told to get near the exit platform of the coach, and then, without the train being brought to a halt, we all easily jumped to the ground, and, there we were.

Soon we were divided up into different lots to go to the various camps and later, our group arrived at a grade camp. It was Sunday evening and we were just in time for supper. The food, like everything else around camp, was on the rough side, but, if one kept one's eyes off the roughness, it was quite good. The bunks, too, were rough and you brought your own blankets, but since then, I have slept under a great deal worse conditions, and always slept the sleep of the just.

Six o'clock next morning came breakfast, and at seven we were off to work. Our job was filling small dump trucks with dirt and rock, to be taken to fill up low places in the grade. As we each had our own trucks to fill, it was quite easy to check whether you were keeping up with the others. Mine was filled just as quickly as anyone's. But at ten o'clock the foreman called to me with a "Hi, Jack!" and when I went to him he continued, "You're not used to this kind of work, are you?" I said that I wasn't and he said, "Well, I guess you had better go get some work that you are used to."

And so ended my first job. I was soon to find out that I was just the victim of a racket that used to be run in those early days between the Employment Agents and the bosses on big jobs. The Employment Agent got his dollar commission for each man he hired, and so the more he hired the more dollars he got. In those days, when men were plentiful and jobs were scarce, unscrupulous bosses would go in "cahoots" with the Employment Agents, firing men fairly steadily, and getting fresh ones hired. They would then split the commissions with the Employment Agent. It was a common saying in those days, about jobs of this kind, that there was always a gang working, a gang going, and a gang coming. The abuses of this system got so bad at last, that, at any rate in British Columbia, the private agencies were suppressed, and the whole employment system run by the government, or directly by the employers.

However, I can say quite truthfully, that I was one very happy fellow fired, for my soft hands, only so far used to pushing a pen were by this time sporting quite a few beautiful blisters. This taught me "Lesson No. 1" on the "Hard Labour Front" in Canada. This lesson was to get a pair of leather gloves, and use them. This practice of wearing gloves was a most common practice with everyone doing rough work, both to keep the hands from getting sore and also to keep them looking decent.

I had made one mistake when coming to this job. I had paid my own train fare from Calgary, instead of letting the contractors pay it. If I had done this, they would, at least, have kept me until I had done enough work to pay it off.

After picking up my belongings at the camp, I "hoofed" it along the track to Field in order to get the train back to Calgary, where I had left my trunk. That walk was through some of the finest mountain scenery in the world, and, from a tourist point of view, I really got my money's worth on this trip. However, at the time I was not so much interested in playing the role of tourist, but in getting a job.

Back in Calgary, prospects seemed no better. I made a brief trip south of the city to look for work on a farm, but I really did not look for work seriously and was soon back. There was one very decent

Employment Agent, a Scotsman, on Eighth Avenue, and, as I wanted to get some kind of a job, I went and asked him to get me on a railway section job, or plate-layers' gang, as we would call it in England. But he did not want to do this, and said, "Look here, are you up against it?" I said that I wasn't. "Well then," he said, "I don't want to get you on a section gang; the pay is the smallest going, and you will probably be in a gang wholly composed of Europeans, the boss included, and, quite likely, none of them speaking English. But if I get a chance to put you on an extra gang, I will do it. There, you will find lots of men speaking English, and will be quite at home."

For the uninitiated, an extra gang on a railway is composed usually of about fifty men, who live in box cars fitted with bunks, etc., with kitchen and dining-car attached. They are stationed on sidings near where some special job, too big for the small section gangs, is necessary. When that job is finished, your "home" is hitched to an engine, and you are moved to the next job on hand. This time luck was with me for that same afternoon, the agent hailed me as I was passing, and said that he could ship me to an extra gang job. So I once again paid my dollar, and was booked for Job No. 2, at the great wage of a dollar and a half a day.

Next day, in company with another English boy and some others, I arrived at the gang at a siding halfway between Calgary and Banff. A little Scotsman beckoned me and the other English boy to the car occupied by the English-speaking portion of the gang and, after dinner, we started work shovelling gravel on to high flat-cars, with a big, fine-looking Norwegian-American boss on top, looking down your collar, to see that you worked. I had gloves this time, and so my hands did not suffer, and I was able to hold up my end.

When loaded, the train was taken to where it was needed, and there unloaded by the engine pulling a blade along the length of the cars. However, it was 2:00 a.m. before we got back to our quarters, as we had to wait for both east and west-bound passenger trains to pass. I will always remember that trip on those flat-cars that night. It was about the first of June. The sky was clear and, in those mountains, that means that it is frosty, even in June. Believe me, that was cold, for we hadn't even any coats on. However, I was beginning to get wise to the ways of the world and, when I saw a few of the fellows slipping along the cars toward the caboose, I soon followed suit, and spent the rest of the journey in warmth and comfort, as the train-crew were decent enough to let us in.

We were up again at 6:00 a.m., for breakfast, and work at 7:00 a.m., so you really had no time to get tired. I must say that I enjoyed working on that extra gang. In our car were several Scotsmen, a few English, and a Norwegian. In the other cars were mostly eastern Europeans, the majority from Austria, but all called Galicians, with a few Russians.

That was my first experience of being amongst a bunch of men of mixed nationalities and I must say that it was a healthy one. I soon got to appreciate the many good qualities of most of these men, who were mainly from the lower classes of eastern Europe. They were a merry bunch, not a bit hard to get along with, and any national pride and prejudice one possessed to an extra degree soon began to shrink and, finally, to disappear. Most of them had homesteads on the prairies, and were out working to get money to enable them to improve their holdings. It was not hard to visualize how quickly most of them would fit into the Canadian way of life and that the next generation would be so well molded into it that the vast majority would not readily be distinguishable from the Canadian and British-born population.

And, certainly, in the years that have since passed, this has been amply proved, for many of our finest citizens at the present time are descendants of this European emigrant stock. In most cases, if it were not for the typically European names, it would be difficult to even guess at their national origin.

Most of these Europeans on the gang were Catholics and the only time they let themselves go was on some religious festival. At such times they would all stay in the cars and let the work go hang. If they were in a siding near a small town or village, where there was a saloon, they would send a delegation to get buckets of beer, and really have a rousing time. The boss was wise enough not to interfere when they took these holidays and so, there was never any hard feeling engendered.

Two of these men have always stuck in my memory, in the fifty years that have passed since — Nick, the big fine-built one, and Shorty, as his name denotes, a small, stocky fellow. Both were fine workers and fine dispositioned, and were looked upon as leaders by the rest of their nationals.

Getting back to the subject of work, I don't wish anyone to get the idea that I was now a natural pick and shovel artist, with no aches and pains. With my gloves my hands did not bother me any more as regards sores and blisters, but gripping the pick and shovel for ten hours a day had its effect. Each morning, on rising, I would have to gradually get my fingers straightened out, and, likewise my back, unaccustomed as it was to long hours of toil.

However, I soon found out that I was not the only sufferer, for, on exclaiming about the state of my back to the other fellows, I was met by the remark, "Don't worry, young fellow, we who are used to this work, also get a sore back." The fact of the matter was that, in this time of job shortage and labour surplus, workers were kept pretty steady at it, and ten hours is a long stretch. Those five hours, from 7:00 a.m. to 12:00 p.m., seemed to stretch out like a bit of elastic and, in the mountains, though cool at night, it could often be pretty torrid in the daytime.

Another lesson I learned soon from the other men and that was to drink very little water while at work. There was a water-boy with a bucket of ice-cold glacier water always patrolling up and down, but I soon got to know that there is no surer way of playing oneself out than by taking frequent drinks of cold water.

However, I soon got inured to the work and then most of these troubles faded away. The life was varied, for we were continually on the move to different parts of the division, and to different kinds of work — a stretch of track to be lifted, a mud-slide to be removed, a near-washout to be fixed, and so on. Often the hours were long, when some pieces of work had to be completed between trains. One such day, we were at it from 7:00 a.m. to 10:00 p.m. and just completed the work for the passenger train going west to get over it on time. I say that it got over it with reservations, for often-times I watched a heavy train pass over some of our new work before the track was properly tamped and the way the track would sink about a foot under the weight almost brought my heart to my mouth. But the trains would go very slow over such stretches, and nothing ever happened.

One day we were loading rails onto flat-cars. Men stand close together, along the length of the rail, raise it first, belly-high, and then, at the word of command, all do a sort of double shot-put, and the rail is hurled onto the car, behind the fish-plates put in the sockets along the car to prevent the rail coming back off. This day, the boss said, "English! You're a big strong fellow, get on to the end of that rail and see that it goes over the fish-plate." Well! English and the boys at his end of the rail got it over O.K., but the fellows at the other end did not, and the rail came back at their end. Was there a scattering? Many dodged under the car, but I took a backward jump that would have qualified me for an Olympic team. "My God, English," said the boss from the top of the car, "I bet you never made a jump like that before in your life." Next time, however, the rail went up quite O.K.

Sunday was usually wash-day, and one Sunday, when we were at Banff, I decided to try and bathe in one of the mountain streams. I had been used to all-winter bathing in the Hampstead and Highgate ponds, and I didn't think that any water could be any colder than it was in those frozen ponds. Little Scottie came along also to have a dip, but I had to try it first. I found a nice pool in "Forty-Mile Creek" and in I either jumped or dived. I've been cold many times since then, but I think that those few moments in that glacial stream before I could struggle to land were the coldest in my whole life. It was just instantaneous refrigeration, accentuated, of course, by the warmth of the outside air. That was my first, and last, bathe in a glacial stream. Needless to say, Scottie did not indulge.

Altogether, I spent about a month on this gang, and then, while we were still parked in the Banff yards, an old English soldier, who had been quite friendly with me, got jobs for himself and me on a road gang in the Banff National Park. So, having served my apprenticeship in pick and shovel in a pretty tough school, I moved up a step to considerably better wages, and more congenial life and work.

Before leaving the story of my life on the extra gang, I feel that I must pay tribute to our good boss. He saw that you did a day's work, but he was never mean. Just after we left the gang, an incident occurred which showed one of the fine sides of his character. A pay-day came along and the Scotties on the gang celebrated by going uptown and getting good and drunk. So much so that the Royal Northwest Mounted Police, who were in charge of law and order in Banff at this time, picked several of them up and put them in jail. I never saw the jail myself, but it appears that there were outside cages of steel bars attached to the jail, where the prisoners could take exercise.

Sandy MacIvor, who had not been picked up by the Mounties, went up to see his pals in the "jug." Whe he arrived, he found the keys to the cages hanging on the nearby wall and, as he himself was a little under the influence, he promptly opened up the cages and released his friends, all except one to whose cage he could not find the key. They all managed to get away without being seen, but when they reached the cars, the boss at once asked what had happened. When he heard the story he took Sandy to the office car, had the timekeeper take Sandy off the roll and enter up a new man, Jock Scott. Then, he said to Sandy, "Look here, Sandy, the bulls will be down here in no time at all, and you can really be in trouble. Remember, Sandy MacIvor has left and gone down the track. You are a new arrival, just put on the gang."

Very soon the police came roaring in and wanted Sandy MacIvor. Unfortunately, the man who had not been freed, had been forced by the police to divulge the name of the man who had freed the others. The boss said that Sandy had gone down the track. "Line all your men up!"

demanded the police, and when this was done, the Sergeant went straight to Sandy and said, "What's your name?" "Jock Scott" came the reply, and, in the end, the police just went away with their former prisoners.

However, as soon as they were gone, the boss said to Sandy, "Look here, Sandy, I hate to lose you, for you are my best man, but if you stop here they will be bound to get you, so you had better beat it right away." Sandy did just that, and I have never learned whether, in this case, the Mounties fulfilled their boast of "always getting their man."

The road work in the Banff National Park lasted all summer, and was most enjoyable, as we saw all the fine scenery that tourists pay so much to see and worked at our job meantime. First, we joined a small gang near Bankhead, a small coal mining town. Here, I got my first experience of "baching," as the size of the gang was too small to warrant having a cook, and so we had to provide and cook our own meals. However, it was not as our tent camp was right close to a store where we could get everything we wanted. When you can buy bread, meat, eggs, vegetables, in fact everything, there is not much to baching. To know what real baching means, as I found out afterwards, you need to be way back in the brush where you have to bake your own bread, rustle what wild meat you can, and generally make meals from a small variety of supplies.

But I had my trials in this case of baching, for friend Tom went on a bender soon after we hit the job and, like most men after spending all they have on a "good drunk," he was very mean with himself afterwards, and unwilling to spend anything, even on the most necessary food items. Anything in the food that I suggested he would at once veto, so I just told him that he could starve, if he liked, but I was going to eat. As I had to do all the shopping and cooking, it meant a lot of separate bookkeeping but that could not be helped. As it was, he did nearly starve himself but, fortunately, after a couple of weeks, we went to a different part of the Park, where we had a bigger gang, with cook-house attached. When we were moving, Tom said to me that, if we had not moved, he would have had to quit, as he could not work on the grub he was getting. "Small wonder," said I, "for you have been so darned mean with yourself, and spent nothing for food." "What has it cost me for the two weeks?" he asked. I told him that his bill was just over two dollars, for he had eaten nothing but bread and eggs. After that he kept his mouth shut about baching being starvation.

Our next camp was in the Lake Louise area where, even at that early date, there was a splendid CPR chalet. Our tent camp was in the bed

of a pretty little mountain creek, and we were making a new road to
Moraine Lake and the Valley of the Seven Peaks. I think Moraine
Lake was probably the prettiest of all the lovely mountain lakes that I
saw that summer, with a splendid campsite where the road hit the lake,
and, on the opposite side of the lake, the precipitous walls of the Seven
Peaks and the bluest of blue water in the lake.

The men in the gang were at nice bunch, nearly all English, even to the
boss, with about three Canadians, and one Swede. We were a motley
crew, but that only added to the interest of things — three old soldiers,
two machinists, carpenters, homesteaders, two London milkmen, and
the boss, a typical bearded Dorset man, who had been in Canada since
the days of the Riel Rebellion. With many good singers, as one usually
finds in a bunch of Englishmen, the days and evenings were never dull,
and, as everyone had travelled, and most had been in many different
kinds of jobs, there was always plenty of interesting conversation and
tales. The two London milkmen would compare notes and describe
the ways and means by which they diluted the milk in order to have as
much as possible to sell on their own. A young Kent farm labourer told
many stories of his poaching efforts, while "Cockney" had plenty to
tell of life in London.

Perhaps the worst thing was the food, not that it was bad, but often
it was not too plentiful. The government let the feeding out to a
contractor, and I guess he figured that the less we ate, the more he
made. We did not starve, and the Chinese cook did the best with what
he had, but we could have eaten more. However, there were lots of
fish, good trout, in the lakes, and we often supplemented our diet with
them. Our fishing was mostly done on our Sunday jaunts, and I am
afraid we did not use good sporting methods. We wanted fish, so we
used the bait that brought in the most fish, and that was some nice red
meat. For that matter, we had no tackle to indulge in flyfishing, for a
willow pole had to suffice for a rod. I have spoken of the cold glacier
water; one Sunday we set out for Consolation Lake, as we heard that
the fishing was good there. To get there, we had to wade over Moraine
Creek, and on the rough pebbles, with the water so cold that it almost
felt as if it was cutting off your feet, it was far from pleasant, even on a
hot summer's day. But the fishing paid for it. I fished from a snow-
back reaching right down to the water's edge, with a huge rock-slide
close by. In the crystal-clear water, fish were quite visible and easy to
catch, but we did not take home all we caught. Unnoticed by us for a
long time, marmots, or whistlers as they are often called, quietly
slipped out of the rock-slide and packed away our trout. When we

spotted the thieves, we tried to get them, but had no luck — they were too smart for us.

In August, we got a nice change from road-making. The summer had been very dry and, to the south of us, on the British Columbia side of the Rockies, the little mining town of Fernie had suffered badly from a forest fire which laid waste quite a bit of the town. So, when a forest fire started up in the Spray Valley, several miles south of Banff, the citizens of that town got very worried, and our gang and another one were called in to go and fight this fire. I don't think there was any real danger to Banff itself, but if the fire had really got out of hand, it could easily have wiped out the big Banff Springs Hotel.

As a matter of fact, we had quite a nice time for the weather favoured us, with no wind, except one day, and it became more a matter of guarding the fire and stopping it from spreading in the moss and undergrowth. The evenings were very jolly, for we all sat round a big campfire, like a bunch of Boy Scouts, sang a great deal and otherwise amused ourselves.

But all good things come to an end, and after a nice free bath in the Government Hot Springs at the Cave and Basin, we once more went to the road camp and worked there till nearly freeze-up.

In those early days, Banff was not a great winter sports centre, as it is now, all the tourist business being confined to the summer months, with its mountain-climbing, trail-riding, fishing, and swimming in the different hot springs. Skiing and tobogganing had not yet become popular in Canada, but there were two winter sports in which the townspeople indulged to their hearts' content, skating and curling. There was a fine open-air skating rink on the river, with warm dressing rooms, and a curling rink close by. We all spent many enjoyable hours, either skating or watching those engaged in the "roaring game," with their brooms and tam-o-shanters.

The first winter in Banff I came across a custom which greatly impressed me, and which I do not think is at all prevalent in England, the Community Christmas Tree. In a large hall a concert, at which most of the performers were children, was first held; then Santa arrived and distributed gifts from a huge Christmas tree to all the favoured ones, both young and old. Supper was then served to everyone and the rest of the night spent in dancing.

Altogether it was a most joyous gathering at which practically the whole population was present, and everyone had the opportunity of meeting everyone else. In the years that have passed since then, I have found the custom quite general in most rural communities and, in this district, most of the younger generation take in several of these Christmas trees.

During that winter four of us rented first a cabin, and later, a three-roomed house, and bached. But again, baching was no hardship, as all necessary provisions could be got at the stores. Sunday morning was baking day for the next week and, as Mother had given me quite a few lessons in cookery before I left, I baked enough pieces and cakes to last us the coming week. Since I was never thrown out of the job, I must have proved fairly satisfactory, unless no one else wanted to do it.

The real jewel of the party was "Scottie," the Glasgow longshoreman. He wasn't very talkative, but everything he said was very much to the point, and he had a real fund of dry humour.

In spring, Bill and Scottie left and went to Vernon in the Okanagan Valley in British Columbia. Soon after they got there, the hotel in which they were staying burnt down during the night. They had to flee hurriedly and, in the rush, Scottie grabbed his new pair of overalls which he had bought the previous day, a poor choice, for in the old pair was all his ready cash, a couple of hundred dollars. Scottie always used the right cuss word, in the right place, and I imagine that the right words would not fail him at this tragic moment.

At Christmas Mother had sent me a delicious Yule pudding, which arrived in fine condition, but brother Jack was not so fortunate with the one which she sent to him in Alaska. In those early days, there was no parcel post to Alaska in winter time, and so the pudding was held up at Seattle, a letter being sent to Jack advising him of the fact. He did not get this letter until he came in to Fairbanks in the spring from his trapping grounds. He at once sent off a letter to the Post Office at Seattle, the first part of which I still remember, and which read as follows: "Dear Sir, Maid, or Madam or who the devil reads this, I am informed that you are holding a bale at my risk, at the Seattle Post Office; let me inform you that, if I was in Seattle, you would be holding it very much at your risk. I would have you know that the contents of this bale are not just ordinary plum-duff, but fifteen-hours-boiled real English Plum Pudding."

As the parcel was also overweight for shipment at any time to Alaska, he authorized them to open it and cut the pudding in half, sending half to him, and keeping the other half for themselves. They replied in the same vein and said that they just could not deprive him of any of the toothsome morsel. In due course, the parcel arrived and Bill, Jack's partner, came home holding it at arm's length, saying, "Here, take your stinking old pudding." Alas! it had been too long in transit and, not being in an airtight container, had gone absolutely rotten.

As the cold of January came to an end, and the weather warmed up, I got a job as rough carpenter on the new hospital, and later helped with the shingling of the roof. Our boss was of the "rusher" type, and one morning when I got to work, there were about two inches of snow on the roof. I got the broom and proceeded to sweep snow off the roof and foot-plate on which I had to work. Along came Sam, the boss, who shouted at me, "Now, Arthur, throw that broom down and get on with the shingling. I'm not paying you to sweep snow."

About ten minutes later, Sam was again in the vicinity when I slipped on the snow, and it was just luck that I grabbed the bottom foot-plate as I was going over the edge of the roof. Sam rushed and helped to pull me to safety and then bawled me out, saying, "You go and get the broom, Arthur, and sweep that snow off. You ought to have more sense than to work on that." And that was that.

After the shingling came lathing and, as I could not make a fortune, as it was by piece-work, I again went on to the ditching work when it started again. But I only worked at this for a short while until I was ready to move on to British Columbia, as soon as work opened up well in the spring. There I intended to try work in the coast logging camps among the big coast timber. At that time most of the hauling of the logs was done by donkey engines and, as I intended to try this engineering job, I had taken a correspondence course in steam engineering during the winter so as to have some little idea of the subject.

About May 1st, I boarded a CPR train and went to Vancouver and I must admit that, as we neared the coast it was very nice to see real green grass again after the winter snow and the brown grass it left behind when it disappeared.

# 3. In Coast Logging Camps

Vancouver, even in 1909, was a very nice city, and it was very enjoyable just to walk through the residential sections, where all the houses were detached and had nice gardens. Every house was built to a different pattern, and this struck me very forcibly after the monotonous row upon row of houses in most English towns. Vancouver was really only just getting out of short pants, but every man and his neighbour were filled with the feeling that the city was really going places. In the business section every second building was a real estate office, and almost the sole topic of conversation was the buying of town lots, many of them miles from nowhere; some of them, in fact, have only been built upon in very recent years. But everyone was happy, buying one day and selling at a profit a short time later. Many made good money if they managed to unload before the bubble burst when World War I broke out in 1914.

Once more, what I was chiefly interested in was in getting a suitable job and so, after a few days of sightseeing, especially wandering around that unsurpassed of all natural parks, Stanley Park, I again sought the "slave market," in other words, the employment agencies of Powell, Cordova, and Water streets.

I have stated before that I had a notion to take up donkey engine work in the logging camps. To get an engineer's job, you first had to pass an examination and be licensed and you could not sit for this exam until you had put in six months time as a fireman. So, seeing a fireman's job advertised on the boards, I went in and asked for it. "Have you ever fired a donkey?" I was at once asked. Not being a

64

good liar, I had to say that I had not. "Well, I am afraid that I can't ship you out, then." But then, he went on to advise me to take any ordinary job in a camp, and I would soon get a chance at a fireman's job. So, I went to a camp on Vancouver Island as a skidroad labourer.

At that time practically all the logs were hauled in long "turns" of a dozen or more logs by a "roader" donkey to either water transportation or a logging railroad. The skid-road was like a railway track, without rails, except that the ties were large logs set in the ground, and having a groove in the centre for the logs to run in. It had to be well "engineered" by the skidroad boss, so that the logs drawn over it would not butt against the skids and knock them out of position. If the skidroad had to cross a depression, long trees were laid endways in the form of a trench, to take the logs until the depression was passed. These were called "fore-and-afters."

The Employment Agent proved to be quite correct in what he had told me, for, in less than a week, I was told by the boss to go and fire the donkey which was being used to break up a log jam on the Courtenay River, our camp being quite near to the little town of Courtenay.

When speaking of the donkey in a logging camp, I am always reminded of the story of the Cockney who went to a camp and was told by the boss on the first morning that his job would be to carry water to the donkey. "What's wrong?" said the Cockney. "Cawn't the bleeder walk?"

I can't say that I learned much about firing on this job, for the amount of steam required on a spasmodic job like pulling logs out of a jam in the river is very different from the amount needed to pull a heavy turn of logs continuously for often about a mile. The job did not last very long, as a small forest fire did some damage around the camp, and we were laid off and went back to Vancouver. I was not very sorry for this was the only camp on the coast at which I worked where both the food and general conditions were not up to the regular coast standards.

As soon as I got back to Vancouver, I found another fireman's job advertised at the same agency as before, so I went and asked for it. "Ever fired a donkey?" said the agent. "Sure," said I. "What camp?" he said. "Chemainus outfit at Courtenay," I replied. "Who is the boss?" he asked. "Kaye," said I. "O.K.," said he, and that night I went up coast about ninety miles to a camp on Powell Lake. The old tub *Cassiar* landed us on a raft anchored in the bay at about midnight, and after being taken ashore in a small boat, we slept the rest of the night at the beach camp. Next morning, a mile journey on a logging railway and then fifteen miles on a small steamer owned by the company, took us to our camp on Powell Lake.

Then followed nine of the nicest months which I have ever spent. The boss, Jim Springer, who had been in Vancouver at the time of the big fire in 1886, was one of the finest. He ran an excellent camp; the food was as good and as varied as in a first-class hotel, and the men of the crew were a splendid bunch. Several came from the Maritimes, a few were French-Canadians, some British, Americans, and Scandinavians, plus a few odd nationalities such as Syrian, Spaniard, Filipino, and a South African Boer. A good outfit always feeds well and pays good wages, so that the crew stays put and no efficiency is lost by continually breaking in new men.

The weather at Powell Lake was ideal, with only about one rainy day a month, and almost no mosquitoes or other pesky flies. The work was not hard as, oftentimes, there were not many turns of logs coming in. I just had to split the wood which was sawn into proper lengths by the wood bucker, and keep a good head of steam in the donkey. Very occasionally, I was kept hopping, and that was when there was a good supply of logs handy to the "yarder" donkey, which pulled them out to the skidroad.

The only dangerous time was in very wet weather in winter when the logs slipped too easily. A few times we had runaway turns which came loose from the cable and came down the hill to the lake on their own in a real hurry. All signals were given by means of a wire stretched on stumps into the woods and attached to the donkey's whistle, and on such occasions of danger, we would have a succession of short toots on the whistle and we would scurry to safety away from the donkey and from where the logs could possibly rush in their mad race. We never had an accident of any kind; the logs just rushed into the lake, dogs and all, and the men in charge had quite a job disengaging the dogs from the logs in the lake and fishing them out with a pike-pole. Meanwhile, we on the donkey could just sit and watch.

The main cable was hauled back to the woods by a haul-back cable, the dogs and other necessary tools being taken on the "pig," a small hollowed-out log, like a very flat dugout canoe. The men in charge of the turn, or pig men, also rode back on it.

All the buildings of the camp were built on rafts made of huge cedar logs — the bunk-houses, the cook-house, the office and store, and numerous small buildings. In this way, when the timber in one area was logged off, all the rafts could be strung together by short cables and towed to a new site by our little steamer, the donkeys likewise being loaded on to spare rafts and also taken along.

I think that Powell Lake is just about as nice a lake for a summer holiday as one could wish for. The water gets nice and warm for swimming, there are plenty of deer for the hunter in the open season, and the trout fishing, right off our rafts, would have delighted Isaac Walton. McBride, a big man from Northern Ireland, was our chief fishing devotee. He and others had fishing poles fixed on the rafts, and often the fish caught themselves at night. McBride would be up first in the morning, and most fellows thought that he was not a bit particular whether the fish were on his lines or someone else's.

McBride had another accomplishment besides fishing — he was a most persistent and sonorous snorer. Being big and fat, he liked to lie flat on his back in bed, and so of course, he was going full blast almost as soon as he got to bed. Boots, curses, and any objects at hand, were hurled across the bunk-house at him, but in the main had no effect.

Another man from Northern Ireland, however, solved the problem for us. McBride's bunk was just inside the door and the water bucket and cup were right at his head. One night, when we were being subjected to a particularly violent display, I saw a stealthy figure slip from his bunk just across the corner of the room and silently move to the water bucket. A good full cup of water was emptied into McBride's wide-open mouth and Charlie was back in bed before the spluttering victim could gather his wits. It wasn't snores that now filled the bunk-house. McBride scrambled from his bed, put on his heavy logger's caulked boots, stamped around the bunk-house and, in lurid language, told all and sundry that if he only knew who had done such a dirty trick, he would surely wipe the floor with him. I think he really knew who the culprit was, but was scared to call the turn. Charlie was about half his size, but a real tiger-cat, and I would not have bet on McBride. Soon after this, McBride went and housed himself in one of the small cabins in the camp, and so we were rid of the nuisance.

The loggers of those days were almost to a man unmarried and would work for about six months, then take a trip to Vancouver, and blow their stake. For many that did not take very long. Dan Munro, a most likeable fellow from P.E.I., inevitably went to sleep as soon as he got a few drinks in him. Result: he was rolled almost as soon as he hit Vancouver, and all his money taken from him. At that time saloons were running wide-open and, in the loggers' hotels along Water and Cordova Streets and that vicinity, there were plenty of sharks awaiting their victims, while others dressed in loggers' clothes, as if recently down from the woods, continually hung around these haunts and just helped those who had worked to drink up their stakes. I'm not saying that all loggers drank up or otherwise wasted their earnings, for there were many who worked hard to better themselves in one way or another, some to invest in Vancouver real estate, others to set themselves up in some other line of business, but still the percentage who wasted their earnings was far too great.

In camp, no drinking was allowed. Anyone coming from town was allowed to bring back just one bottle to give his friends a drink, but that was all. Discipline was fine, there was no fighting, and regular hours were kept just as if one was in the Army.

All had travelled a great deal and had had many and varied experiences so that interesting conversation was always possible, and one got a real education of the lives of people in all parts of the world. There was the inevitable clique of gamblers, but the number was a small percentage of the crew.

About the most interesting of all was a middle-aged South African Boer, who, like myself, fired one of the donkeys. Even in the warmest weather, he always wore a sweater and a coat and, when ridiculed for it, he would exclaim, "Well, you use lots of clothes in the cold weather to keep the cold out, so why not do the same in summer to keep the heat out?" But firing a donkey in summer did not seem exactly the place for heavy clothes, and I still stayed with just my undershirt and trousers, as did most of the rest of the men.

Towards the end of July I was busy doing my washing at the donkey, where I could get lots of hot water, one afternoon when trouble with one of the donkeys had kept us idle. I was singing away at the top of my voice and did not notice anyone approach. The first intimation I had of anyone's presence was a voice which said, "Why don't you sing in tune?" I was about to ask how the deuce it was any of his business when the voice continued, "Don't you know me?" "Sure I do," said I. "It's Jack."

And sure enough it was Brother Jack. He had been in Alaska for about six years, engaged in trapping, and hunting and fishing for the markets in the mining camps. He was on his way home for a holiday and when at Vancouver, had cabled home for my address. Needless to say, we talked a streak for the rest of the day, though he also found time to have quite a pow-wow with "Raffles," the Boer. Jack had been in the Yeomanry in the South African War and, as they had fought against each other on the same fronts, they were busy comparing notes about the different actions in which they had been engaged.

Jack also came across other men who had been in Alaska and the

Yukon and found many common interests in talking with them. But perhaps the greatest pleasure I got from Jack's visit was the fact that he could see that I was hale and hearty and content, and therefore, when he got home he could reassure Dad and Mother that there was no need to worry about me, for I think it was very likely that they were still worrying that the baby of the family might not be too able to take care of himself in the rough and tumble of life in Canada.

Life went on quite uneventfully until Christmas, except for one rather exciting episode. On Friday and Saturday of one week in October, British Columbia experienced two of the wettest days on record. It just rained and rained, and then rained some more. On Sunday morning, some of us had just come into the bunk-house from the cook-house after breakfast, when the cats there began to act in a crazy manner, rushing around as if demented. Almost immediately after, one of the men rushed in shouting "Slide!" and at the same time we heard a loud roaring noise. We all rushed out and could see a huge mass of logs and water rushing towards the camp. We ran along the different floats to get out of the way, and some even jumped in the lake in their hurry. But it was all over almost as soon as it started, with no damage done.

The camp was at the mouth of a small creek which entered the lake at this point, and from which the camp's water supply was piped. The area around the creek had been logged off and the ground was strewn with short chunks of logs, tree-tops, and other debris. The great amount of rain gradually floated a lot of this debris together and formed a dam which had kept increasing in size. A large head of water was built up behind the dam and, at last, the dam could not stand the pressure and the whole bunch came hurtling down the creek-bed, sweeping along more debris as it progressed. The only thing that saved the camp was the fact that the bed of the creek opened out as it got to the lake, and so the pressure behind the debris was greatly reduced. As it was, the huge pile was only stopped by a few big cedar stumps about ten feet from the camp office and quite close to the main camp itself. The rush of water had cleaned out the creek-bed as if it had been swept by a broom, but the only real inconvenience caused by the slide was the fact that, every day, we had to clamber over that huge pile of rubble as we went to work.

When Christmas came the camp closed down for the holidays and we all went to Vancouver, each spending his holiday in the way that suited his taste. Many spent it quite quietly; however, many spent it in quite a different manner. One little incident serves to show the attitude of some of the loggers towards money. It was Saturday afternoon when I met McLeod and Myers on the street, and McLeod at once hit me for a loan. "Sorry," said I, "but I have only enough to tide me over the weekend, and all the rest is in the bank." "In the bank!" cried McLeod. "That's no place to have money, drag her out, fireman, and we'll help you spend her!"

The weather was lovely all the time we were down, and Vancouver was truly "The Evergreen Playground," as it liked to style itself.

We made the trip back to camp on the old *Cassiar* on New Year's Eve, and what a trip it was! The *Cassiar* was a regular old tub, with few staterooms, and she was loaded to capacity with loggers, a large percentage of whom were, as could only be expected on New Year's Eve, very, very drunk. Almost every foot of available space was covered with men bedded down in their blankets, but, even so, a few of the drunks would manage to wander around in their caulked boots, and I can never understand why some of the sleepers' faces were not trampled on. Of course, as long as the bottles lasted, there was little chance of sleep, and then, we had one final diversion before settling down for the night. As chance would have it, the stewards had left the pantry door unlocked, and someone happened to stumble in there. In a very short time, all the milk and much of the food that was to last for the trip up the coast to the numerous camps and tiny settlements, was despatched by the crowd that assembled. Finally, one of the stewards happened to come along and, though he got mighty mad, there was little he could do about it with a bunch of cheerful drunks.

When we got back to camp I was shifted from the "roader" donkey to the "yarder," the donkey that pulled the huge fir and cedar logs out of the woods on to the skidroad, where they were assembled for the "roader" to pull them down the long haul to the lake. This work was really more interesting, as one saw all the operations necessary to get the logs through the maze of stumps, trash, and any standing timber that was left.

The hook-tender was the man in charge of these operations and was usually a man of unlimited energy, while his lurid vocabulary was, I am sure, quite equal to that usually attributed to Varsity rowing coaches in England. Under him were the rigging-slingers, chasers, etc., whose job it was to handle all the cables and chokers, often a pretty dirty, dangerous job, and they really earned the extra money, especially in view of the amount of gloves and clothes which they wore out.

Once or twice while on the "yarder" I got short spells of driving the donkey when an engineer would quit and there was no one else available to run the donkey. This gave me some real practical experience in handling a donkey, and a donkey engineer has to be able to do a lot more than just run a steam engine. All directions were given by whistle signals from a wire stretched through the woods and attached to the whistle on the donkey, and, with hand always on the throttle, one had to continually move it back and forth according to the amount of power needed throughout every pull. A man may be a first-rate engineer, as far as qualifications go, but at the same time, he can be a rotten donkey driver, if he has not got the right temperament.

When spring came I had put in sufficient time as a fireman, and so applied to sit for my exam as 5th Class engineer, papers which would entitle me to run a logging engine, or a farm engine, up to a certain horsepower. The winter I spent at Banff I had taken correspondence lessons in steam engineering, and so with my educational background, I had not trouble in passing the exam. In fact, the examiner told me that I could get 3rd Class papers if I liked to sit, but I had to tell him that I had not yet put in sufficient time to be allowed to sit for 3rd Class papers.

And now, just as I had qualified to follow up engineering in the woods, in that peculiar way of humans, I decided to take a trip with my friend Sammy up to Graham Island, the largest of the Queen Charlotte Islands, to see what the prospects were of farming there. I suppose it was something in line with my decision to quit the Civil Service in England after I had studied hard to get into it and come to venture into the unknown in Canada. But, after all, it was probably just my inward nature searching for the mode of living which would best suit me.

This really ended my work in camps in British Columbia, a year which I shall ever remember for the companionship of the fine men who worked in the camps at that time.

# 4. More Wandering

The first part of the trip to Graham Island in April 1910 gave us what I consider to be one of the most delightful sea voyages that can be indulged in anywhere in the world. This is the inside passage route from Vancouver to Prince Rupert, a distance of around 500 miles, practically all of it in sheltered waters, with Vancouver Island and innumerable small islands forming a shield against the sweep of the Pacific Ocean. Queen Charlotte Sound at the north end of Vancouver Island and Milbank Sound are the only two stretches of open water but, if the weather is bad, these two can give one all he wants of the open Pacific.

Starting from Vancouver harbour the voyage is just one of continuous scenic splendour between rugged tree-clad islands and an even more rugged mainland, on which the mountains in most places, especially in the latter half of the voyage, come right down to the shore, often in the most precipitous fashion. Countless small waterfalls are seen, and the whole trip was one of wild beauty. In those early days very little settlement was visible, especially north of Vancouver Island, and the fine steamships on the Vancouver-Prince Rupert-Alaska run had no other ports-of-call. Still they were loaded with passengers going either to Prince Rupert or further on to Alaska and the Yukon, for in 1910, the gold-mining in these two latter places was still very much alive.

After a day and a half on the water we arrived at Prince Rupert, which was just beginning to emerge as a town. The Grand Trunk Pacific Railway was at that time under construction between Winnipeg and Prince Rupert and the latter was the headquarters of construction from the western end. As a result, it was full of construction workers of all nationalities. The railway was then being built up the Skeena River between Prince Rupert and Hazelton. Accommodation was mostly of the rougher type, but we were not exactly of the millionaire tourist variety ourselves, so that did not worry us. Sammy had worked on the survey of the Prince Rupert townsite and ran across many old acquaintances, so we soon got to know what was going on.

Prince Rupert, like Vancouver, was in the midst of a real estate boom, and everyone was buying and selling town lots in the full expectation that the city, as the terminus of a transcontinental railway, would soon be a thriving metropolis. To me, at the time, it looked like piles of rock strewn over a very rough piece of terrain. It was difficult to imagine how a reasonably level town-site could be made out of such a rough beginning, but now, after 50 years, a pretty town is emerging. However, I am quite sure that a great many of the original investors in Prince Rupert in those early days never got their money back.

We were not interested in either construction work or in real estate, but rather in farm land, and so we soon found ourselves on the steamship *Henriette* bound for Masset, a little settlement on the north end of Graham Island. The town was situated near the entrance to Masset Inlet, which is a considerable arm of the sea, reaching right into the centre of the island.

On one of her trips a month or two before we sailed in her, the *Henriette* had developed engine trouble and had been blown a long way off her course, finally ending up in Ketchikan, Alaska. On our trip, the weatherman tried his best to duplicate that incident, for soon after we started out a violent wind sprang up and forced the captain to take shelter in Refuge Bay, on Porcher Island. Even there, the refuge was not really dependable for the wind was so strong that the ship started to drag her anchor. However, after a rather worrisome night, we woke up next morning to find ourselves still afloat, and, in due course, we reached Masset — or New Masset, as it was then called to distinguish it from Old Masset, which was the Indian village about a mile to the north. It was not a very inspiring place at which to be dropped off, for there was just a small new hotel, still quite in the rough, and a few other cabins.

The Indian village gave us quite an interesting visit. On the road to it, we ran across one of the old Indian customs, that of "burying" their dead up in the hollowed-out trunks of big trees, or in holes in the back of totem poles, of which there was a very fine array on the shoreline. Age had been at work on some of the tree burials, for in several cases, the "remains" were strewn around at the foot of the tree.

In the village itself I saw my first Indian cemetery, "new style." Here, each grave had a little house built over it, and inside were placed many of the treasures of the departed, such as gramophones, special ornate dresses, musical instruments, hunting equipment, and many other interesting relics.

The village itself was far ahead of the new settlement; it had well-built houses, a good store, and an Anglican church. Those Indians are of the Haida tribe and are both progressive and industrious. In former days they had been famous for their war-like tendencies, which often sent them on expeditions against other coast tribes in search of both booty and prisoners. Their huge dugout war canoes were famous. In a special boathouse was the prize specimen, a beautifully made craft, cleverly carved and nicely painted, which had been sent as an exhibit to the Alaska-Yukon-Pacific Exhibition held in Seattle in 1909. Altogether, I think those Haida Indians of Masset were about the finest specimens of B.C. Indians whom I have come across on my travels, but I expect that there are many tribes in different parts who are just as good.

We fixed ourselves up with necessary food, etc. at the Indian store, and after hiring a boat we set out next day to row up the Inlet, which takes one right into the heart of the island. This was before the day of the out-board motor and so, it was just a case of rowing or not going, as there were no craft making any regular trips. It was a nice holiday, and we met many interesting settlers, but the type of land, on most of which there was very little natural vegetation, did not appeal to either of us, and so we wended our way back to Masset.

There were reports of land with better natural vegetation in the northeast corner of the island, where a herd of wild cattle were reputed to roam at will and make their own living, being the remnants of a tame herd which had been abandoned by an early settler; however, as neither of us was favourably impressed with the general outlook, we decided to return to Prince Rupert when the *Henriette* came again on her weekly trip. The matter of transportation was another thing that influenced our decisions, for the poor boat service did not recommend itself very highly to us.

Aboard the *Henriette* once more we were not to sail straight back to Prince Rupert, for she went first to Queen Charlotte City and Skidegate on the south end of the island, and then to several small ports on Moresby Island further to the south.

Some of the crew used to try and boost the stock of the *Henriette* by telling us what fine lines she had. She may have been a good sailing ship, but her poor engines did not make her a good steamer and, to add to our troubles, her propeller got loose and she had to be beached at Pacofi, a small fishing station, so that it could be fixed, and this delayed us some more.

However, there was one bright spot in the old tub, and that was the German skipper, Captain Schmidt, who did his best to while away the tedium of the slow motion voyage. He was a real card enthusiast, knew lots of good tricks, and was also a good raconteur. So, on the whole, we had quite a nice holiday, saw quite a bit of country, and satisfied ourselves that we did not want to settle on Graham Island. From reports I have had since, I think our decision was a wise one. The island had quite a boom in World War I, as it supplied a lot of airplane spruce which was in great demand and so a lot of logging was done there. There is still considerable logging carried on on the island but, as far as I can learn, it has not advanced much in agriculture.

Having arrived back in Prince Rupert, we looked over one or two construction jobs, but such work had no glamour for us after life in the coast logging camps, and so we sailed back once more to Vancouver. There we found the Vancouverites still busy peddling real estate lots back and forth to each other and having a whale of a time, but after our holiday we decided we had to get another job.

At this time the Powell River Pulp and Paper Company was just starting to build its big mill. This was right on the coast, at the mouth of the river which is the outlet of Powell Lake where I had previously worked in the logging camp. In this mile of river there was a waterfall of considerable height, and so with Powell Lake over twenty miles long for a reservoir, all the requirements for a real good hydro-power site were really made-to-order.

As the chosen site had once been virgin forest, it was still covered with huge stumps of fir and cedar and all the other mess left by logging operations. On enquiry at the company office in Vancouver, I found that they wanted a donkey engineer, and so I hired myself out for the job, while Sammy got a job as rough carpenter at the same place. My wages as engineer were really quite good for those days. I was now making $85 a month and board. On the other jobs the board cost from $4.25 to $5.50 a week.

The work was not really logging work, as it consisted mostly of pulling out the big stumps after they had been split up with powder and hauling the bigger chunks left from previous logging. A very big force of men was working on the different kinds of work at the site. The dining room could seat 400 men at once, and even then two sittings had to be held to feed the whole crew. And what grub! I had been used to splendid food in other camps, but the food here excelled everything I had ever had. At every meal there were several different kinds of the very best meat and vegetables, pies, cakes, fruit of all kinds, both canned and fresh, and all the usual extras. It was worth working there just for the food.

There was just one jarring note in connection with the food and that was the terrific amount of splendid food wasted and thrown into a huge garbage pile. The work had not been in progress very long, but that garbage pile was already sending out a stench which could cause serious sickness in the camp, and I felt sure that something would have to be done about this menace before very long. However, I was not there to see what happened about it, for after I had been there a few weeks Brother Jack again appeared on the scene. He had spent the winter at home in England and had then come back and visited some old school friends who were farming in Alberta. With him came an elder brother of the boys who came to see if life over here would benefit his health. Bert was an Oxford graduate, who had been working as a scientist with an engineering company. Soon, having found that the life and work were too rough and tough for him, he returned home. Jack was highly amused at one little episode.

Bert had been given the job of harrowing a newly-ploughed field. Only someone who has done this job in a field of deep, black soil, on a warm day when one perspires a lot and with just enough breeze to raise a thick cloud of dust, can realize what Bert looked like when he came home to supper. When Jack asked him what he thought of things, Bert replied, in a most tragic voice, "Jack, this is the worst thing that ever happened to me."

The two brothers were also highly amused, but Bert saw no funny side to it and the next day he set out for Red Deer and purchased a nice big bathtub for use in such emergencies in the future. He stuck it out for the summer, but when a freakish early snowstorm flattened their grain crops on August 24th, he decided to return to his old way of life in England. However, the country appealed to him enough that he has been back there for a couple of holidays since. Farming in Alberta did not appeal either to Jack, and so he came once more to British Columbia and hunted me up at my job at Powell River. I was just getting steam up on the donkey before breakfast when he appeared from the newly-arrived steamer, and about the first thing he said to me was "How'd you like to come with me and look for land in northern B.C.?" "Sure," said I, and, as there was another engineer around looking for a job, I was able to quit as soon as the office was opened that very morning.

Soon we were on our way to Vancouver once more. However, we had to wait long enough for the next boat which allowed Jack to have a few meals in the big diningroom and to wonder anew at the quantity and quality of the food provided. We had to wait a few days in Vancouver for the boat going to Prince Rupert, during which time we did some necessary shopping and I got posted up on all the news of Jack's trip home and of his stay in Alberta. Then, once more, I was on another phase of my changing way of life.

# 5. Land Seekers

The trip to Prince Rupert was once more in beautiful weather and it was even lovely when we arrived there, though Prince Rupert has the reputation of being a very wet spot. In those days of busy railroad construction up the Skeena River, a person seldom had to wait long for a river boat, the only means of getting up to Hazelton. And so, soon after arriving there, we boarded the *Port Simpson,* a well-appointed flat-bottomed sternwheeler owned by the Hudson's Bay Company. Jack had had lots of experience in travel by riverboat on the Yukon and Tanana Rivers in Alaska, but this was my first trip of this type. It was most interesting and educational. As always on such trips, our fellow travellers were a motley crowd from all parts of the globe, and life was never dull.

Most of our companions were, like ourselves, going to seek land in the north-central part of British Columbia, which was being opened up by the new railway, and all of us had different ideas of what we should find and what we should do when we got there. The trip up the Skeena certainly opened up no vistas of wide stretches of farm land, for it is a fast flowing river, running between high, steep mountains on either side. But we were not expecting to find land there, and so were not disappointed.

The first hundred miles, as far as Kitselas, was quite uneventful and just a quiet, pleasant voyage. However, from Kitselas on to Hazelton the river changed its type completely. At Kitselas there is a very rugged canyon about a mile in length where the river runs through a narrow gorge bounded on both sides by upright rock walls. To anyone

78

unaccustomed to such places the canyon looked absolutely impassable for a boat of any kind for the water just boiled up and raced on among the rocks. At medium height of water the riverboats did get through, but could not do so at either high or low water. In early June the river was just about as full as it could be, so we had to disembark and walk overland to the upper end of the canyon, our baggage being taken by wagon.

There we found the steamer *Hazelton* waiting for us, and from there to Hazelton we really learned what travel by riverboat was like. The river was much faster and narrower and so our progress was slower. Many times in the swifter reaches the boat seemed to make no progress at all, at times hardly holding its own. In some stretches it was too fast for the boat, and some of the crew had to take a small boat and pole up the edge of the river, taking a cable with them which they attached to a "dead-man" fixed on-shore above the fast water. Then, with its paddle-wheel churning at full speed and its winch winding in the cable, the steamer literally hauled itself through these tough reaches.

But even with all the care and splendid seamanship of the captain, such was the turbulence of the Skeena that on at least three occasions we could easily have met with disaster from the swift cross-currents, especially where fair-sized fast-running streams entered from the mountains.

One of these incidents still remains vividly in my memory. One moment we were on a perfectly straight course, the next the bow of the boat was swinging to the right and we made a complete about-turn. There was a nice rock-bluff coming right down to the water's edge, just ready for the boat to wipe its nose on, but luck was with us and we ended up in a nice quiet eddy, a little down-stream, ready for another attempt.

I remember too that Jack was at the time beguiling the hour talking to a pretty nurse en route to the Hazelton Hospital, but directly the boat swung, I am afraid the nurse was quickly deserted as he rushed to see what would happen for, having been in similar incidents on rivers in Alaska, he was well aware of the danger. Some boats had been smashed up in similar cases on the Skeena, but I am not sure whether any of the mishaps occurred at this same rock-bluff.

Very few stops were made on the journey except for occasional stops at wood-cutters' camps to take on a supply of fuel. The boat had to tie up at night as it was quite impossible to navigate in the dark. One night we stopped at an Indian village but did not go ashore.

At length, Hazelton was reached. At that time it seemed to be composed mostly of hotels and stores, plus a government office, the bank, a few ordinary residences, and one or two churches. This was only to be expected, as it was definitely more of an outfitting centre than anything else. Pack trains loaded up there with supplies to be taken over many miles of lonely trail to different points in the area and new settlers, either looking for land or going into land previously located, got their supplies here; men from construction camps gravitated here as it was one of the few centres where liquid refreshment could be obtained, while numerous Indians were always around town, interested in all the bustle and happenings.

Hazelton is very prettily situated at the confluence of the Skeena and Bulkley Rivers. The latter is the Skeena's largest tributary and drains a large part of the district through which we were to travel. All round the town are mountains of various heights, and valleys stretching in all directions. As the new railway was to run along the opposite bank of the Bulkley to that on which Hazelton is situated, the town did not get quite as much of the business of the men in the camps as it would have done if the line had passed right through it, but still it benefitted plenty.

Any description of Hazelton would be incomplete without mention of the Indian village of Hagwilget on the opposite side of the Bulkley, about four miles south of the town. This village was at that time the headquarters and meeting place of all the Interior Indians from distances up to one hundred fifty miles and they used to congregate there in the summer months to catch and dry salmon for feed for themselves and their dogs in the winter.

Hagwilget was situated at the head of a long, deep canyon with high perpendicular rock walls through which the Bulkley River ran, and it possessed one of the most interesting tourist attractions in the whole northern part of British Columbia. This was a fine specimen of a primitive type of cantilever bridge, constructed over the canyon by the Indians, the only materials being poles cut from the neighbouring woods and telegraph wire which the Indians had ''salvaged'' when the telegraph line to the Yukon was constructed through the district. It was most ingenious in its construction and gave very definite proof that the Indians possess good brains for practical craftsmanship.

We had decided by this time to go into the district around Ootsa and Francois Lakes, distant about one hundred fifty miles from Hazelton. Many people have since asked us just why we fixed on that district, especially as it would have been quite a long way from the railway even when that was constructed. And the answer is that we were mainly influenced by a booklet put out by the Department of Lands, Bulletin No. 22, which gave write-ups and pictures of all the different areas in the province, and I suppose the description of the Ootsa Lake area appealed to us most. I don't think we quite realized what the distance from the railway would mean, but I can say this, that even with the apparent handicap of distance from the railway, we never regretted our decision, or even felt that we had suffered any great drawbacks from such distances.

When we arrived in 1910, most of the best land near the railway had been picked over and taken up by earlier settlers and, even if it is near the railway, poor land is not worth consideration. A lot of the really fine pieces of land had been taken up by persons who had worked on the telegraph line which had been put through the Bulkley Valley and continued on to the Yukon just after the Klondike gold rush. A great deal of the remaining best land had been staked by professional land-stakers and purchased from the provincial government at very low prices by persons from all over Canada, the U.S.A. and Britain just for speculative purposes. In later years when no great profits were forthcoming, most of this land went back to the government for arrears of taxes, and consequently, many later settlers got better land than did we early arrivals.

As we were to follow the usual procedure and walk in with just one horse to carry our food, bedding, tent, etc., our next job was to get a horse. But this was not a hard matter in those days, for all the Indians had ''cayuses'' and there were also lots of other pack horses in the district. We went up to Two-Mile, the regular camping grounds for persons coming with horses into Hazelton, and soon picked up our first horse, from persons who had come right up from Ashcroft up the Cariboo Road and through the same country into which we were going; they also had been looking for land. This was one of the routes used by settlers coming to look over this huge country. Another route was the one from Bella Coola on the coast and then over an old Indian trail.

Next requirement was a pack-saddle, and therein lay a lot of future grief for us. Jack knew quite a bit about horses, but neither of us knew anything about pack-saddles. On enquiry at the Hudson's Bay Store, Johnny Boyd, the manager, said he hadn't the ordinary cross-tree pack-saddle but had a Mexican-type or ''aparejo.'' It looked a funny kind of contraption to us greenhorns, as it consisted of two flat leather cases hinged together at the top and filled with straw. When we hesitated Johnny called in Charlie Barrett, an old packer and one of the telegraph line builders mentioned previously, who now had one of the best ranches in the whole country. Charlie was to convince us that it was a perfectly satisfactory type of pack-saddle. And indeed it was for anyone well used to it — but not to us greenhorns. On this type of pack-saddle, the pack had to be secured in quite a different method from that used with the ordinary type; it was almost impossible for one man to use it satisfactorily.

Having made our grub-box and got everything necessary for the journey, we proceeded to pack our horse Tom. The stableman at the Omineca Hotel gave us what help he could, but that was not very much, and we were not very proud of our finished effort.

The road out of town passed right up the main street and in front of the Omineca and Ingineka Hotels. There were always plenty of spectators sitting on the verandahs of these two hotels. We decided we did not want to parade our effort in front of this critical audience, so I went that way with our two small packs for our own backs and Jack was to go by a back-way and meet me on the road, a little way out of town. Unfortunately, however, Jack's route led up a very steep, little hill. After waiting for Jack and Tom for a considerable time at the appointed rendezvous, I saw Jack coming along; he was looking very crestfallen. He said that coming up the hill the whole pack had slid right off the aparejo, over Tom's tail, and had rolled down the hill. So that was that. We decided to pack the stuff up the hill ourselves and make a new start at the top.

You are not supposed to know anything about packing until you can throw the "Diamond Hitch," which is universally used to secure the pack on the pack-saddle, and we were to hear a lot about this famous hitch before very long. However, in the meantime, we used the good old "Shelford" hitch; but please don't ask me what it was like! We got loaded up once more and this time we got as far as the hospital, about a mile and a half from town, when the pack once more began to show signs of uneasiness. But a good Samaritan turned up in the person of a very friendly Indian, and noting the wobbly state of the pack and evidently seeing the word "green" written all over us, he smilingly hazarded the guess that we didn't savvy the "diamond hitch" and offered to fix up things for us. So, in due course, we went on our way, but as it turned out, it was not the "diamond hitch" that was needed for an aparejo, and soon we were back to the "Shelford" hitch, which, on the whole, did not work too badly now that the going was fairly level. But we still got the occasional lesson on the proper way to fix a pack. The next time it was from a settler who was already located in the Ootsa Lake area — Bill Eakin, who himself had come in by the Bella Coola route. We got acquainted with him when we both stopped for lunch at one of the numerous creeks and when we repacked he opined that "you boys don't savvy the 'true Diamond.'"

*Packtrain on the move, 1911.*

We confessed our ignorance and, once again, had the proper hitch applied. But again, it was not right for the aparejo, and very soon it was a case of "as you were."

That journey up the Bulkley Valley was just a lovely trip, full of interest of every kind, construction camps dotted along at different points, settlers and would-be settlers coming and going, stretches of pine and spruce timber, and then open patches, often partly covered with poplar timber. In the open and poplar country the vegetation was truly wonderful with grasses, peavine, and all different kinds of weed growth up to a man's shoulders. It was beautiful feed for the horses but not so pleasant for a man when he had to hunt the horse in the dewy mornings after he had been loose all night with his clanging bell and in hobbles to keep him from straying too far. That rank vegetation was just sopping from the heavy dew, and so was anyone going through it unless he had oilskin leggings reaching to his hips.

Usually we travelled fifteen to twenty miles a day, and the walking worried us not at all. I fancy that poor Tom was the only worried one. His green English masters did not understand that the stuffed pads of the aparejo had to have the stuffing of straw altered to fit the shape of the horse, and so poor Tom walked day on day with the equivalent of two wide boards tightly cinched to his ribs. No wonder that his progress was marked by a continuous "ugh-ugh-ugh . . . ugh-ugh-ugh" for the whole of the journey. What suffering ignorant greenhorns can unwittingly inflict on poor long-suffering animals!

Our diet would be termed rough and monotonous by most people — oatmeal with bacon and bread for breakfast, beans and bacon and rice for lunch and supper, with occasionally dried apples for dessert. Of course, there was always plenty of tea. Our bread was baking powder "bannock," baked in a frying-pan before a specially built camp-fire, and most men prided themselves on their ability to bake a really good bannock. That fare might seem rough and monotonous to some people, but let them walk all day, up to twenty miles, fix camp every night, cook their meals and do all the other odd jobs, and I am quite sure that, if their appetites are normal, they would deem it fit for princes.

Our journey took us eighty miles up the valley of the Bulkley River, and just near the end we passed through the ranch owned by Charlie Barrett, the Gloucestershire man who had allowed us to saddle ourselves with the aparejo. This ranch was probably the largest piece of open land in the Interior and was a real gold mine to its owner during the construction period, as it produced enormous crops of hay, every pound of which was eagerly bought by the construction camp, as in those days all the heavy work was done by horses.

At what is now the thriving village of Houston, but which in those days was just the small store and post office of Silverthorne, we left the Bulkley Valley and struck across-country on a pack-trail which was really the slightly improved old Indian trail, as indeed were most of the trails in those days. On this part of the trip we saw very few people, but about twenty-five miles out, we were overtaken by a settler in the Ootsa Lake area, Hank Raymond by name, and, from there in, we travelled with him, as he was anxious for us to locate near him. When we set out next morning from our camp at Trout Lake, Raymond said he would put the "true diamond" on for us, and he did; but again, it was not for an aparejo and we even ventured to say that it was not right, but he avowed that we should find it quite O.K. Less than a quarter of a mile from camp we had a steep, little descent into Trout Creek, which we had to ford, and, right there, the whole pack slid forward onto Tom's neck. Hearing our exclamations, Hank took one hasty look around and kept going, and, once again, the greenhorns had to put on the "Shelford hitch"; and that was our last lesson on the "true diamond" during the trip.

When we reached the head of Francois Lake we had to swim our horses and raft ourselves and our belongings over the Nadina River, which enters the lake at this point. Francois Lake is a splendid lake running for about seventy-two miles almost due east and west with a width from one to two miles. At that time there was no means of transportation on the lake, and all travel to the south side had to come in by this same trail from Silverthorne.

Another trek of about eighteen miles took us within sight of Ootsa Lake, but as Raymond lived near the east end of the lake, we still had quite a distance to go, as Ootsa Lake is about forty-five miles long. The government bulletin had not exaggerated about the charm of the country and the vegetation in the district, which we found to be similar in most respects to that of the Bulkley Valley. However, it did differ very much in one important respect. Whereas the Bulkley Valley is in most places fairly narrow with high mountains on either side, the Francois-Ootsa country consists of a wide stretch of land, which could be termed a rolling tableland. As we journeyed, we crossed numerous creeks, which flowed from chains of small lakes dotted all over the countryside. These same numerous small lakes, coupled with the many large lakes, have given the district the name of the "Lakes District" of central British Columbia.

Every step brought a vista of new beauty, either of lake or stream, timbered hillside, or grassy slope; while everywhere was the luxuriant weed growth, with bright-flowering larkspur, fire-weed (willow herb), yarrow and numerous others (of which, perhaps, the most interesting is the "Indian Paint-Brush" which, with its top leaves appearing as if they had been dipped in different shades of red paint, gave a nice touch of colour to the landscape, especially on the drier and less fertile soil). And, of course, added to these nearer views were always the distant ones of hills and the snow-covered peaks of the Coast Range to the west.

But we had not come to admire the beauty, but to look for suitable land, and so, with Raymond as our guide, we plodded on until we came to his place, which was on the lakeshore several miles from the east end of the lake. On the way there we had not looked at much land, as he wanted us to locate near him so as to give him more neighbours. In his locality, he showed us around quite thoroughly, and we staked one or two pieces of land in case we might wish to record them.

Staking land in those early days was quite a chancy business. There were few houses in the district at that time and almost no people at all there in the summer-time, as most of the people already located there were outside earning a grub-stake; some worked on roads being built everywhere through the district, while others worked on survey gangs or were packing in supplies for them, or for stores or for themselves; others worked in mines or on railway construction. In all our wanderings through the district we only saw the Nelson cabin at Wistaria and the Bennett and Ellison cabins at Ootsa Lake. There were a few other cabins, notably the Morgan, Mitchell, Olaf Anderson and Brennan homes, but we never saw them. Actually, the only persons we saw in our whole land-hunting wandering were Mrs. Eakin and her young son, Sammy, who were living in the Ellison cabin at the time.

To get land, you just searched around to find a suitable piece and then, if there were no other stakes visible on it, you put in your own stake, which was usually a growing poplar tree cut off about five feet from the ground and squared with an axe for the top foot, whereon a notice of staking was written. The wonder of it all was how you came across the stakes put in by other persons. I suppose it was that they chose to stake the land, describing the boundaries of the land which they desired in the same most suitable spot which you yourself would choose. Anyway, the fact remains that very few stakes were missed, but even if land had a stake on it, other persons would also stake on it, as many stakings were never recorded at the Land Office in Hazelton.

In the end we did not see any land which took our fancy in the vicinity of Raymond's place, and so retraced our steps towards the west end of Ootsa Lake. On the lakeshore at what is now Wistaria, we left our horse Tom in a pasture naturally surrounded by windfalls, made a raft, and poled up towards the west end of the lake. Then we trudged across country, climbed hills overlooking different parts of the country, until finally from one hill we looked down on two sizeable beaver meadows with a fair amount of upland around them.

Here we felt that we had reached the "promised land." We planted some more stakes, although we found some already planted on the land, and decided to make tracks for Hazelton to record our land at the Land Office. Altogether it had been a most enjoyable trip. We were young so the journeying worried us not at all, with perhaps one exception — the flies — the mosquitoes, the black flies, and the tiny sandflies or "no-see-ums," as the Indians very graphically term them. The mosquitoes were always with us, especially in the sheltered timber where no wind could get at them, and day or night made no difference, but fortunately, as we had mosquito tents with us, we could sleep in comfort. The blackfly is a more vicious type of beast and really chews one up, but even he has his good points, for he doesn't worry in a house, and quits at sundown. The "no-see-um," weight for weight, can probably give one the most discomfort, but he only bites when weather conditions suit him, and that is not too often. Anyway, we used to get this fellow in the Old Country in the evenings in suitable spots, calling it the midge, so he wasn't really new to us.

Game for fresh meat was not very plentiful, but there were lots of two types of grouse and, though they were not exactly in season according to the Game Laws, I'm afraid we did not carry a .22 in one hand and a copy of the Game Laws in the other; as a result, we did not come off too badly for meat. Fish were plentiful in most of the numerous lakes, and so, here again, we could get some variety in our food.

After about six weeks of wandering we finally got back to Hazelton, there to record our pre-emptions of 160 acres each, at the Land Office. Altogether, we had travelled at least 400 hundred miles, which is a fair little jaunt for even an able-bodied youngster. And right to the end of that return journey, poor old Tom, though now only loaded with tent, bedding, and an almost empty grub-box, kept up his never ceasing "ugh-ugh-ugh . . . ugh-ugh-ugh." The unfortunate part of Tom's misery was that he developed no sores of any kind to give concrete evidence to any trouble, and so he just suffered, but not in silence.

I believe that altogether we staked about a dozen different pieces of land on our trip, and now we had the problem of deciding on which of them we should finally try to get our Records. In the end Jack recorded on the largest of the two beaver-meadows which we had discovered, but since there did not at first appraisal seem to be enough land for two places, I recorded on a place on the shore of Ootsa Lake about two miles below the Bennett place, the centre of a small settlement, which later took the name of Ootsa Lake. The only unfortunate thing about these stakings was that the two pieces of land were twenty miles apart, but I suppose at that time that distance seemed nothing to us.

Recording land was by no means a simple job, for many of the people who had previously recorded had but a very hazy idea as to where their land was actually situated; some didn't even know whether it might be on the north or south end of some small lake. There were no survey lines at all in our district in those days, but, strange to say, when the land was later surveyed there were practically no conflicting stakings.

And now, with our land recorded, we had to prepare for our next step, that of purchasing an outfit of food and all other necessary supplies to carry us through the coming winter, and getting them in to our new "home," a little matter of 140 miles away.

# 6. Preparing for Winter

It was fortunate indeed that Jack had had lots of experience in buying outfits during his five or six years in Alaska, for I am afraid I would have left out a lot of very necessary things and when your nearest well-stocked store is about one hundred fifty miles away, you can't just pop in for something you may have forgotten.

Our grub supply was entirely of staples and, as far as I remember, was about as follows: 600 lbs. of flour, 200 lbs. of beans, 200 lbs. of rice, 200 lbs. of sugar, 100 lbs. of bacon, enough rolled oats and cornmeal for breakfast cereals, with dried apples for the only fruit, and then the odds and ends, such as baking powder, baking soda, and salt. Last, but by no means least, there was a good supply of tea, with a limited amount of condensed milk, and a little canned butter. Bacon grease comprised the greater part of our supply of fat, and candles were our only source of light. Not a very varied diet, and when I think sometimes of the grumblings of many people about their monotonous diet during World War II, I rather wonder what they would have thought of our diet. But when you are working hard and have a purpose in mind, your appetite is ready and willing to take on any diet as long as it gives a comfortable feeling under the belt.

For other supplies we had to take in a good supply of traps for Jack had done a lot of trapping in Alaska and this was one means we intended to use to bring in a supply of ready money. Jack had sufficient carpenter's tools, but we had to take in cross-cut saws for cutting firewood and that never-to-be-forgotten whip-saw for cutting lumber, of which much more later. Enough cooking utensils for three or four camps, plenty of good winter clothes, moccasins, rubbers and mitts, a good supply of different sizes of nails for building purposes, with a couple of knock-down sheet-iron stoves and a few odd tools of different kinds just about completed our outfit. Altogether, it made a goodly accumulation. Then came the matter of getting it transported. We decided to buy two more packhorses and so, we soon became the owners of Billy and Romeo. Billy we purchased from Round-Lake Tommy, an Indian, who gave him the rather strange recommendation that "He all-time pack 300 lbs. iron." But he was dead right. The answer to the old riddle "which is the heavier, a pound of lead or a pound of feathers?" may be true, but try packing 50 lbs. of lead and 50 lbs. of feathers, each for a fair distance, and you will soon find that the lead soon feels a lump of lead as it sits on one small spot, whereas the bundle of feathers is at least soft, spreads over considerable space, and is really much "lighter" to carry.

Whatever his character, Billy did yeoman service for us, being just as wise as his years, which were considerable. Romeo was a little gem of a packhorse, with big liquid brown eyes, a real Roman nose, and a personality which, when he wanted anything such as sugar, salt or nice hay, was quite irresistible. But three horses were no good for our load of stuff, so we hired an Indian, Tom Campbell, with several packhorses, to travel with us and take the greater part of the load for the first ninety miles, where we branched off from the Bulkley Valley, at what is now the thriving little village of Houston. It cost 5 cents a pound for this transport, which made such things as flour, salt, sugar, etc., pretty valuable at the journey's end.

While we were at Hazelton the big salmon run was on in the Skeena River, and so we really went to town on fresh salmon. Too much so, in fact, for it upset my tummy so badly that Jack and Tom Campbell had to leave town without me, as I had to pay a brief visit to the doctor and then make forced marches to catch up with them. One good thing we learned from Tom Campbell was that an aparejo needed to be shaped to each individual horse by altering the straw packing inside it, and so after that poor old Tom was saved a lot of misery. We also, of course, learned the correct way to fix the dear old "diamond hitch" on an aparejo. For Billy and Romeo, we fortunately got the regular cross-tree pack-saddles.

After Tom Campbell left us we had to relay three times with our three horses for the last fifty miles, and so, altogether when we reached "home" with the last load, we had knocked off another three hundred miles on this trip. It was now September 7th, and so we had to hustle to get everything in shape for winter. First, we had to put up enough slough hay with a scythe to carry our horses through the winter. Fortunately, the weather, which had been quite wet on our trip, turned to a beautiful period of Indian summer, and for three weeks we had cloudless skies and warm weather.

With the hay up we had to build our log cabin, and so had to use one of the horses to haul the jackpine logs. We had only one set of single harness and could only use one of the horses. We decided to use Billy, but it was not a wise choice for he was too old and light for the job and we had many toils and troubles before we got them hauled.

The straight jackpine logs made a fine cabin, and chinked with moss between the logs, it was really snug and warm. But the cabin was really spoiled by the roof, which was made of small poles with a good covering of dirt over them. This made a fine, warm roof, but when we had heavy rains or when the snow melted in the spring, that roof leaked like a sieve, and often we had to pitch a canvas "fly" inside the cabin under which to park ourselves and our goods, in order to keep dry. For five years we endured these periodical drenchings without getting enough sense to cover the roof with boards or split "shakes," either of which would not have taken a great deal of time and which would have saved us a lot of misery and inconvenience.

About this time we got our first experience of whip-sawing. We had to have a certain amount of lumber for doors, windows, the floor, and to make a small boat which we needed for net-fishing on Ootsa Lake. The nearest sawmill was over seventy miles away in the Bulkley Valley.

I had seen several saw-pits in our village in England but only one of them was used, and that by the village carpenter and undertaker for cutting wide elm boards for coffins. In this country pits are not used but a stand about seven feet high is made right in the timber with trees as posts. The saw-logs were rolled up on it after being squared on opposite sides for lines to be made with a chalk line. Then with one man on top and one underneath, you very soon got a notion of what purgatory may be like. In frontier countries it is commonly said that whip-sawing has broken up more partnerships than anything else.

One of our neighbours, a droll Irish-Canadian, told us of his experience with the whip-saw. Kelly said that he was working a placer-gold claim with two other men in one of the western states of the U.S.A. They had to have a flume to bring water to their claim to wash the pay-dirt, and as there was no sawmill within reach, they decided that the only thing to do was to whip-saw the necessary lumber.

Kelly's two partners started in first, but before very long they came to loggerheads and Kelly was called upon and got the berth on top of the log. "Well," said Kelly, "everything went alright for a little while and then the saw started to come up hard, and the harder it came up, I know the harder it went down. At last, it got so I couldn't stand it any longer, so I stopped and said to the other feller, 'Say, feller, I don't know if you can pull me down any longer, but I can't pull you up any more. What say if we talk things over?' Well, we talked it over and both agreed that each had been bucking the other. Then we agreed to have another go and not to do any bucking, with the agreement that if it went hard it was really neither's fault but just the tough sawing. And we never had a bit of trouble after that and soon got the job finished."

And that was the spirit in which Jack and I started on our task. Even so, at times, it almost broke our hearts, not to mention backs. The trouble mostly comes from the kind of log you happen to choose. When sawing the boat lumber, the first log was a nice spruce, which cut just like cheese and on which we would move an inch at a stroke; however, the next log was just as tough. It was a mean, miserable, stringy affair which you couldn't cut straight to the lines and it took a dozen strokes to go half an inch. We did finish it at last, but after a little of such toil we should have used our heads and tossed it off the stand and got a new one, in spite of all the work we had had in getting it ready for sawing. However, experience soon taught us which logs to choose — a nice, quick-growing tree and not a tough, old, slow-grown one, however nice and straight and clean it looked.

But however nice the log, whip-sawing was never easy, and not a job one would choose for relaxation. It was commonly said that the man on top had the easier job, as the man underneath had to make the pull which did the actual cutting; however, I always noticed that Jack, who was on top, had to shed his garments, while I hardly warmed up at all. Nevertheless, the underneath man does have one disadvantage — and that is sawdust — for, whichever way the wind was blowing, the sawdust seemed to come right into my eyes. That is where the English pit method has the advantage, for in the pit there would be no wind to affect the sawdust. It was several years before a sawmill came into our district, and in those years, we whipsawed quite a pile of lumber.

Jack soon got our boat made, and the fish from Ootsa Lake helped out our diet a great deal, though the lake at this time was not a good fish lake and most of our catch consisted of coarse fish, such as squaw fish and suckers, with a few trout, white-fish, and ling. Most people do not consider the coarse fish very palatable, but put them on a diet of bread, beans, bacon, rice and mush and they will soon change their tune.

At this time, the district was poorly off for game, deer being the only large game, and they were not very plentiful. We spent time each week hunting for fresh meat and got quite a few grouse, while squirrels were not despised for stews. The snowshoe rabbit, which usually went through a seven-year cycle, from nothing up to millions and then down to nothing again, was just about at its scarcest, but we got lots of ducks of all kinds. When the fall migration was on, many of the small lakes were literally covered with them; but one can get very tired of wild duck.

We had brought in two bear traps, but we caught no bear that first fall. However, I found a small grey animal in one of the traps one day and brought it home for inspection. Neither of us knew what it was, but as it had the teeth of a vegetable eater, we decided to try it. After we had boiled it, Jack tried a spoonful of the liquid to taste what it was like. Even today I can see him spluttering that liquid out, and it took a lot of other grub to take that taste out of his mouth. But fresh meat was fresh meat in those days, and so I said that we would boil it in some fresh water, and after doing so, the little "critter" was quite good eating.

The trouble was that this animal, like many others such as mink, weasel, skunk, etc., had two scent glands under its tail, and we had failed to remove them. What was the animal? Just the common bush-rat or pack-rat, which comes around the buildings a great deal just before winter and is a real nuisance as he delights in packing away all kinds of odds and ends into his nest. He is certainly not an animal one would include in one's diet, after a little acquaintance with him, for wherever he hangs around the smell from his scent glands is always very much in evidence. Incidentally, I have been told by several people that the odoriferous skunk, if you carefully remove its scent glands, is really quite palatable. But though I have caught several, I have never felt quite hungry enough to try one.

But I have eaten many of the smaller animals at different times. The porcupine doesn't make too bad eating though, of course, he has his own "porky" flavour. However, he is a very useful animal in the woods, as he is one of the only animals that a man can kill with a stick if he is out of grub and really up against it. Muskrats and beaver are both quite palatable, each with its own special flavour. I didn't dislike the former and have eaten many of them, but I was never very fond of beaver, though Jack was quite partial to them. I can't say that we used a great deal of any of these animals, but when you are short of fresh meat you will try anything once. Yes, even a bush-rat.

By the time we had got our cabin in shape for use, it was about the end of October and as, on thoroughly looking over the land in the vicinity we had decided that there was plenty of suitable land for both of us, it was therefore necessary that I make another trip to Hazelton to abandon my first pre-emption, which was twenty miles from Jack's, and stake on one almost adjoining his land.

And so, away I went on another little jaunt of three hundred miles the round trip. I have wondered since why I didn't use one of the horses, but I didn't, and just hoofed it the whole way, and probably made as good time, for none of the horses could be called a real saddle-horse. Averaging about fifteen to twenty miles a day, it took me about three weeks and by the time I entered on the last fifty miles from home, there was nearly a foot of snow to trudge through. Fortunately, three of our future neighbours — Kelly of the whip-saw story, Jim Nelson, and Mark Brennan — were a little ahead of me with a bunch of pack-horses, and so the trail was fairly well-broken. But even so, it was pretty tough going, and by the time I got fairly near to an unused trapper's cabin, where I planned to spend the first night, I was just about all in, for I was carrying a pack of over fifty pounds besides two blankets. There were several articles which we had overlooked in our shopping list, and so I had to bring them in now. However, I had a reviver in my pocket — and very glad I was to have it. When I was trading at the Hudson's Bay store at Hazelton, Johnny Boyd, the factor, had invited me to go with him to the well-known "Stone Hoose," a tiny house built of rocks taken from the bed of the Skeena River, where the supply of liquor was kept. I didn't accept the invitation, but said that I would be glad to accept a small flask of whisky or brandy in case I might need it on my long journey home. A sip or two from that flask was real lifesaver, and I made the cabin O.K. Next day I had to make about twenty miles to the cabin of old Bill Watson, a real old character who hailed from Cumberland. It was quite a trip, but I made it and found that my three neighbours had stayed there the previous night.

The real joke of this trip in the snow was that I was packing a pair of snowshoes I had bought in Hazelton, but didn't realize the labour they would have saved me. I also didn't know the way to fix them on my feet. Ignorance was not bliss in this case.

By mid-morning of the following day, I caught up with the three who were to be our good neighbours in the years to come. They were just breaking camp on the further bank of the Nadina River, which runs in the head of Francois Lake. Before reaching them I had already made the acquaintance of another man who was also to be a good friend and neighbour of ours, old Indian Sam of Nadina. I was to get from him a new pair of snowshoes that Jack had ordered, but he hadn't made them and palmed off an old pair on me at the same price. However, we needed them, and so I had to take them, but Sam heard more about them later. The Indians in those days would always try to put one over on you at first acquaintance, but after a good reprimand and if they found that you treated them fairly, they would usually be quite fair and square with you. Sam did just that and was in later years one of our real friends. He always impressed me by his dignified bearing on greeting you: "Ah, good morning, Mr. Shelford. How you do?" After removing his gloves, like the real old gentleman that he was, he would give you a fine handshake, and then don his buckskin gloves again.

The last short lap of the journey was quite uneventful, though my companions shook their heads in a worried manner when I had to leave them and strike out towards home with no trail of any kind. Fortunately, Jack and I had a good measure of "woods' sense" and, though the country looked very different with a foot of snow covering everything, I had no trouble in getting home. Thus ended our season's preparations, and we were ready to go into the winter.

During the return journey from Hazelton I met up with just one more primitive mode of pioneer transportation. Mike Gallagher was a big, raw-boned Irishman who had put in many years of hard work in the gold-fields of the Yukon. He had made good stakes there, but they had all vanished by the old method of "wine, women and song," and now Mike had come to spend his remaining years on a small homestead on the trail about two miles past the head of Francois Lake. Mike had probably done much wheelbarrow work in the gold-fields, and so he used this method of transportation when he came into our district. He took all his meagre belongings in on a wheelbarrow, a distance of over fifty miles over very rough trails.

When he decided to move out to the Bulkley Valley to get work for the winter, he again used his barrow, but this time it was not a wheelbarrow, for such was unusable in the snow. Mike had replaced the wheel with a small sled and pushed it ahead of him. Each to his taste, but I think that my back-pack was the better method.

# 7. A Winter's Trapping

With the advent of the snow, all was now ready for our winter activities, and Jack soon put me wise to the proper use of snowshoes and also to the general methods of trapping the different animals, which consisted mostly of marten, mink, weasel, and muskrat. His trapping lore was most useful, but there was one part of his Alaskan experience which was very much the reverse. In Alaska the country he travelled was mostly flat and over muskeg with very little timber on it. He, therefore, used a dog-sleigh or a hand-sleigh for all his winter transportation. On my return I found that he had already made a very nice hand-sleigh, and as I was to do most of the trapping away from home, I had to start in and cut out a sleigh trail. This was quite a job in itself, as the timber was often quite thick together; but the trail cutting was nothing compared to the pulling of the sleigh over the rough, rolling country, heavily loaded as it was with stove, traps, tent, bedding, and grub.

My first tent camp was at Peaked Hill, about five miles from home and surrounded by five or six small lakes. From there I cut more trail and did what trapping there was to be done. I got my first taste of winter muskrat trapping. We had a nice little cold spell early in January when it got down to 55 below zero and, believe me, playing around with traps in the water at that temperature is not exactly a picnic. I had to carry a towel and use it at every muskrat house, but it soon got wet and frozen. I am glad to say that the Game Commission now prohibits muskrat trapping before March 1st, and I am wholly in favour of it for it is just cruelty to trappers to allow them to trap them in winter. Even walking across the lake at this temperature with a brisk east wind blowing was no joke, and some nights when I returned home from cutting trail I would go right into the tent in my snowshoes and light the fire, and then look around for something to eat, only to find everything frozen — bread, beans and such-like. Even the condensed milk was too stiff to spoon out of the tin, and so the only available thing was sugar. However, a tent soon warms up, and it would not be long before I could eat.

Some people might think that life in a tent in such temperatures was a great hardship, but it is not so. A thick layer of spruce boughs keeps your bed and the rest of the floor from the snow, and your bed and stove are so placed that you can light the fire in the morning whilst lying in bed and get the tent warm before getting up. A tent soon warms up. But it also soon cools off, and when the fire is out at night the temperature in the tent quickly becomes the same as outside. I am not saying that life is joyous at such temperatures, and anything below -40 can be quite chilly, especially in bed at night. When it got too cold for a candle to burn properly, then it is just about cold enough. In a tent when it gets below -40, the heat of the candle cannot melt the outside wax and the candle just burns down the centre until it goes out for lack of air. Fortunately, our cold spells seldom last over two weeks, and usually less than that.

I finally got my outfit about another six miles further, and then I had had enough of the sleigh and from then on did all my moving by packing on my back; as my stove was too big to pack, I just camped under spruce trees and cooked on a campfire. With suitable bedding, this is no hardship in moderate weather.

Jack used to tell an amusing story of an acquaintance of his in Alaska. Jack was telling him about getting turned around and lost on a dull day, but the man, who was from Wyoming, said that he never got lost. He went on to say that, anytime he was in doubt, he used a sense he had of the direction in which his old home lay. Said he, "I just say 'Wyoming east' and then I am able to get my bearings from this homing sense."

Some time later, Jack came across a real mess of circling tracks and then ran into "Wyoming East," as he always called him afterwards. Wyoming was in a pretty explosive humour, and the remarks he made about getting lost on a sunless day were quite unprintable. It remained for Jack to touch off a real explosion when he mildly suggested that he should say "Wyoming east" and all would be well.

I have been temporarily lost in summertime when quite close to home on such bad days, when the only thing to do is to try and get to some elevated ground to get a glimpse of some landmark, or climb a good tall tree for the same purpose. You have a very funny feeling when you get that glimpse and find that the hill or mountain that you see is stuck in exactly the opposite direction to where you felt it should be. You have to stay on that hillock or up that tree until you get it firmly fixed in your head that your home lies in a certain direction and get yourself thoroughly oriented before you start off again — and then you keep in that direction by lining up trees ahead of you.

The only danger when you get thus lost is if you get rattled or panicky, for then you can really be in for it. Otherwise, you ultimately come across some creek which you can follow, or a small lake or other landmark which will give you a correct steer for home.

To get back to trapping, everything was pretty much routine after I got the lines laid out and different camps established. After that, it was just a matter of jaunts in snowshoes up to fifteen to twenty miles a day. Was it lonely or monotonous? Not a bit to a person of the right temperament. You are never lonely if you have lots of work to do, and that you certainly had, in running your lines, extending fresh ones, skinning and stretching the pelts of any animals you had caught when you reached camp, with always some cooking to do or firewood to cut, and often snowshoes to be repaired. I had absolutely no reading matter on the trapline, unless you reckon the English and French directions on the condensed milk cans, which actually did get read and re-read a great number of times.

But you do not miss the literature, and there is something refreshing as you sit on your bed-log and gaze into a nice, bright campfire, with a good canvas fly to reflect the warmth. There is plenty of time for meditation and deliberation on things past, present and future, and you are certainly far removed from the rush and tear of present-day city life and from the "madding crowd."

At times, I used to bring to mind a little verse I had written in the autograph album of an Irish girl on whom I was a trifle sweet during the end of my life in London. Considering that I had absolutely no idea of what I should be doing in Canada, I really made a pretty good delve into the future. Here it is!

I am sitting by my fire in the forests of the West
A-thinking of England and all I love best,
When amongst the flames many faces I see,
And right in the forefront is one from Kilkee,
Then above the sighing and the moaning of the trees,
Old sounds, old voices are wafted o'er the breeze,

> But by far the clearest and sweetest of them all,
> Is one that is singing 'The Auld Plaid Shawl.'

Well, Kathleen Mavourneen, that probably happened, but man being the volatile and impressionable being that he is, I would not swear that it was always your face and voice that came to me.

Everything went more or less smoothly that winter except that we lost our first horse, Tom, who fell through the ice into a hole in the creek, which fitted him too snugly and he couldn't get out.

It is a real study in patient effort to see the little horses pawing continuously in the deep snow to get their feed, and until a violent thaw and heavy rain came early in March and put a thick crust on the snow, they did splendidly and kept quite fat. But when the crust came they had to be fed and Jack had quite a time prodding with a pole in the deep snow to find our oversize cocks of hay, for they could hardly be called stacks.

I didn't see Jack very often that winter as I only went home every three weeks or a month, and even then, sometimes he himself was away on a trapline of his own. We did not get any mail all winter, as our nearest post office was fifty miles away.

With spring and the opening of the creeks and lakes came our friend, Indian Sam, and his whole family to hunt beaver, for we had located on part of his "illahey" or hunting-ground, a fact that he sadly bemoaned when we first met him. In those early days, the Indians had the whole country divided up into individual hunting-grounds, but I am afraid that this system went by the boards in the years after the advent of the white man, who trapped anywhere and everywhere that he took the notion.

Sam said that he didn't mind us trapping marten, mink, lynx, fox, etc., as these animals ran over a lot of territory, sometimes being on one man's hunting-ground, sometimes on another's. "But beaver," said Sam, "he all-time stop my hunt-ground, all time stop my lake, he my beaver and I don't like you touch him."

As a matter of fact, we did not touch Sam's beaver very much, and I believe that I myself only took two of them through all the years. Sam had a fine hunting-ground all around us with the innumerable small lakes all well-stocked with beaver, and he really "farmed" it, only taking the surplus, and usually leaving them entirely alone every second year. But this year, he did hunt, and he and his family usually got about forty in our vicinity.

As I said previously, the old Indian hunting-ground system went by the board when the white man moved in, for the Indian reasoned to himself that if he didn't get the fur the white man would, while the white man reasoned the same in reverse. Consequently, the fur population, especially the beaver, went almost to the disappearing point.

I consider it a very great tribute to the Indians and their hunting-ground system that, some years ago, the provincial government had to set up exactly the same system in order to preserve the trapping industry, and now all trap-lines, for both Indians and whites, are registered, with no one but the registered owner allowed to trap on them. In this way, a trap-line is just a large fur-farm, where the owner can have his well-established cabins and it is up to him to always leave enough breeding stock of all kinds in order to perpetuate the line.

To return to our friend, Sam, who, like most Indians, was forever short of white-man grub, especially at the end of winter. In due course he came to us and wanted to buy anything that we would let him have, but, unfortunately for Sam, we also were getting very low in supplies, and so we had to turn down all his pleas.

However, Sam evidently went and put his brain to work, for some little time later he returned and, after the usual opening remarks, he said, "Little Mary awful sick." Little Mary was his infant granddaughter about two years old. "She awful sick, she won't eat fish or deer meat or nothing, she just wants white-man glub." With difficulty concealing our smiles, we asked what "glub" Little Mary wanted. "Oh," said Sam, "Little Mary like a little bean, a little 'lice,' some 'plour,' some 'thugar,' and some milk."

Needless to say, the amounts that Little Mary seemed likely to need were quite considerable, and it looked probable that Sam's own "Little Mary" might be the ultimate recipient of the food rather than his little granddaughter. However, we will give Sam credit for a large measure of truth, for Little Mary was undoubtedly sick and she died a little later. Whether it was from eating too much white-man "glub" or not, we will never know.

So ended our first winter and now we had to start a real busy summer's work. Incidentally, we did not see any of our neighbours all through that winter, although we were only about ten miles from them; we were just too busy to spare the time. Jack was quite used to such loneliness, as in Alaska he had spent all one winter trapping on the Kushokwim River in the shadow of Mt. McKinley without seeing a single person until some Indians appeared in the spring. It all depends on temperament — some folks can stand it and some can't.

# 8. The Ride of the Cowboys

Work for the summer resolved itself into trips to the outside for supplies by Jack, and for myself, mostly clearing land until it came time to put up hay. But first we had to dig up a garden patch and put in a good quantity of all different vegetables.

May 15th was the earliest that one could take horses on the trail, as any earlier they could not get enough feed. Therefore, about that date Jack set out with our two horses and hired a couple from our friend, Sam, for which he was to be paid with grub. This trip was just made to the Silverthorne store, at what is now Houston, and so, being only fifty miles, it did not take very long.

The next trip, however, was to be to Hazelton, and when Jack again wanted Sam's horses, Sam agreed but said that this time he wanted money. Jack asked how much he wanted, and Sam said, "I think maybe ten cents a pound alright." "Ten cents a pound!" echoed Jack. "Why, Sam, for ten cents a pound I can get the stuff brought in by somebody with their own pack horses, and I don't do any work but just sit at home and wait for it." "Yes," said Sam, "I guess that's right." "Well, then," said Jack, "how much you think now?" To this question, Sam blandly replied, "Oh! I think maybe ten cents a pound alright." Laboriously, Jack went through the whole explanation again, with Sam agreeing to it all, but still, "I think maybe ten cents a pound alright." Which all goes to show that the province missed a great Minister of Finance when it overlooked Sam for the job.

Financial arrangements with Sam thus being deadlocked, Jack had to make other arrangements and got the use of two horses from one of our neighbours. He left me to clear land, tend and fence the garden, and to build two small hay-sheds, roofed with wooden shakes, which really should have gone on our cabin.

Just after Jack's return from this trip and when he was starting on his next, he met one of our neighbours on the trail who said that Cousin Bert was somewhere on the trail looking for our place. After a little trouble, Jack connected up with him. Bert had had quite a time of it for Jack had given him very scanty directions by letter on how to find our place, and when he reached Hazelton, he didn't know whether he was two miles or two hundred miles from us. However, he finally landed up at Silverthorne's store, and who should he meet there but our old friend Sam, who was on his way to Hazelton to take in the salmon run. Sam pricked up his ears when Bert said he wanted to find the Shelford boys and said that he knew us well, that we were friends of his, and lived near him. He gave Bert good directions as to our approximate location, and Bert bought some grub for the trip. However, not being used to feeding himself, he did not buy enough and ran out of food after crossing the Nadina River at the head of Francois Lake.

Finding our place was something like searching for a needle in a haystack, for we were two miles off the main trail and there was no notice as to where our trail branched off. For two or three days Bert slept in an old trapping cabin with a stone fireplace at Nadina and each day made the round trip to the Nelson cabin at Wistaria — over thirty miles in all. This was quite a hike on a full stomach, and Bert's was anything but full. Fate was a little kind to him in one respect, for someone had gone along with a sack of beans which had a hole in it and beans were scattered thinly along the trail. What he collected were quite a help but, unfortunately, he had had no experience of cooking beans and boiled them only about twenty minutes, and so they were something akin to eating rocks. Bert said to us later that after eating them he said to himself that if the people up here ate such grub as that they must be pretty tough customers. Subsequently, however, he ate and enjoyed many, many meals of well-cooked beans.

At the time no one was in residence at the Nelson cabin, and, with no other house along the trail, prospects of finding us seemed pretty dim. However, he happened to run across Jim Nelson on the trail and then Jim met Jack, and that was that. After some discussion, I took Bert down to the Ootsa Lake settlement for him to stake the piece of land which I had given up. After this Jack and he went out to Hazelton where Bert recorded the land at the Land Office.

When they reached home again it was time to start haying and, as we planned to make a trip to Bella Coola on the coast to get some cattle, we had to put up quite a bit of hay. With our available machinery this was no light job, for two scythes and strong arms were our mowers and all the hay had to be raked by hand.

As we still had old country ideas of hauling, Jack made a rather wonderful little cart with an axle of birch and wooden wheels, and forty-seven years later the axle and wheels were still intact and on exhibit at the Centennial celebrations at Wistaria. However, sad to relate, they met disaster there for someone sat down on the axle, and it collapsed.

The cart was not a real success for hay-hauling, though little Romeo did his gallant best in it, for the loads it could take were too small. The following year, we used the method which was then general in the district — that of a go-devil, consisting of a rack on wooden runners, and this was much more efficient. With haying finished about the end of August, we started on the real trip of the summer—the hundred eighty mile journey to Bella Coola to bring in more supplies and some cattle for the start of our herd.

So away rode the three gallant cowboys with our two plugs, Romeo and Bill, and Bob and Ginger, the two borrowed horses. The latter was rather a mean beast and hard to catch and had to be picketed every night. The first thirty-five miles to the east end of Ootsa Lake was a lovely ride through alternate stretches of pine and spruce timber, poplar timber with rank vegetation amongst it, and many patches of open grassland. Along the entire length of the lake we only passed three habitations — the Nelson cabin, the Bennett home at Ootsa Lake settlement, to which Harold Bennett had recently brought his bride, newly arrived from England, and the Ellison cabin a little farther on. There were about another half a dozen settlers' homes in the first twenty miles, but these were all off the main trail. After the Ellison cabin all the way to the Bella Coola valley, we only passed one Indian cabin in the Cheslaslie valley and the small Indian village of Algatcho, about half-way to Bella Coola, which was quite deserted, as all the Indians were at Bella Coola for the salmon fishing.

Our first spot of trouble came at the foot of Ootsa Lake where we had to swim our horses and raft our bedding, grub and horse gear. The swim was quite considerable and, led by Bob, the horses refused to face it and broke back to land. What to do next? Well, the only alternative was to raft the horses over, one at a time. But making a big enough raft was no easy task for we had no nails of any kind and, therefore, had to make the best job we could with our pack ropes. Our first effort

*You can lead a horse to water, . . . but you can't always get him to cross the river. Sometimes it took a group effort!*

completed, we led Bob on to it first, since he was the cause of all our trouble. We had scarcely pushed off from land when the weight of the horse caused the logs to spread apart and, the next thing we knew, Bob had all his legs through the raft and was standing on the bottom of the lake. Fortunately, Jack steadied the raft and I hastily got Bob on to dry land once more. Then we had to put a second deck of small poles on top of the raft and, as these were not in the water, they did not move apart and on our second attempt we got Bob safely across. But it was no easy job for it was more than two hundred yards wide and the water being too deep to touch bottom and use the pole, Jack had to use the pole as a sweep, which made progress very slow. By this time, it was dark and we just had to leave Bob tied up by himself on the far shore.

The next morning we took Romeo across and nearly met with disaster for the slight current drifted us down so that we were just getting into the swift current of the Ootsa River when Jack struck bottom with his pole and was able to get us to shore just in the nick of time. It was very fortunate for us that Jack was a good poler for he had done lots of poling on the Tanana, Kantishna, Kuskokwim, and other rivers in Alaska.

With two horses over, we decided to give the other two a chance to swim, and this they did without any further trouble. Ignorance is not always bliss for, had we but known it, there was a comparatively easy ford a little distance down the Ootsa River and a boat there that was used by Harry Morgan, one of the Ootsa Lake settlers, who made several trips to Bella Coola each summer, packing in supplies for survey gangs.

The Cheslaslie River, at this season of the year, was very low and the horses could wade without any trouble, but the Teta-chuck was another swimming proposition. However, it was not nearly as wide as the Ootsa Crossing and the horses swam it without any trouble, but we had to make another raft to ferry our gear over. This crossing was at the foot of Teta-chuck Lake, about a mile above the beautiful Teta-chuck Falls, and later we learned that there was a good ford a little above the Falls, but even had we known that we should have hesitated to use it, as it was so near the brink of the Falls.

From the Teta-chuck to the mountains flanking the Bella Coola River, the country was of a desolate nature, having been burned over several times by forest fires, and there was no horse feed except at beaver meadows, which were fortunately well spaced along the trail. Just before we reached the mountains we met the only traveller we saw on the journey — Harry Morgan with his pack train. We were very glad to get information about how far we had to go and other details of the trail over the mountains.

One very nice thing about our journey was the fact that we got plenty of fresh meat, for grouse were numerous all along the trail and, being on horseback, we saw them every time they flew up at our approach. I think that the grouse congregate along the horse trails as the ground is uncovered on them so that they can easily get their supply of grit.

The journey over the mountains was a very welcome change, as it was mostly wide open, with only a few belts of spruce; the flowers and vegetation were all of the alpine variety, while the numerous rills and tarns and the succession of terraced pools, held up by little moss dams, were really picturesque. It was on this mountain plateau that we saw our first bunch of ptarmigan with their plumage in the transition stage between their summer and winter garb. This is a most interesting sight, with the white plumage of winter partly replacing the brown of the summer.

But the mountains did not seem quite as beautiful towards evening, for it was getting late when we arrived on the far steep slope and saw the little blue ribbon that was the Bella Coola River winding along the bottom of the valley thousands of feet below us, and it looked as if it would be a case of rolling down the mountain-side.

And, indeed, it was almost that, for the trail wound hither and thither to get any possible grade, and in many places it was so steep that the horses almost seemed to stand on their heads. To add to the joy of things, it started to pour with rain and, long before we reached the valley, it was pitch black. There was one bright spot and that was the gleam of a campfire by the river, which at least told us we were getting somewhere. Even after getting down to the river we had some distance to go before reaching the ferry, a cable contrivance which worked by the front end being winched until it pointed upstream and then the force of the current forced the boat across the river. We were very fortunate that the old ferryman, who lived across the river and some distance upstream, had heard us coming down the trail and was good-hearted enough to turn out and oblige us, though there was no obligation on his part to do so at that time of night.

I don't need to say that that night was not exactly a picnic, for it is no joy pitching tent in the pouring rain, with the extra difficulty of lighting a fire and fixing up the horses for the night. But the next morning was fine and sunny, and when we heard later from Bill Eakin, who was a day behind us on the trail, that instead of the rain which we got it had snowed heavily on the mountain, we really counted our blessings for, with the trail covered with snow on a bare mountain which we had never travelled before, we could really have been in trouble.

Riding down the Bella Coola valley was a very pleasant contrast to the first part of our journey, though that had its own joys and thrills the whole of the way. The valley is mostly peopled by Norwegians who first settled there in the latter part of the nineteenth century. Evidently, the similarity of the valley made them feel as if they were back in Norway, for the whole set-up is so like their native land, with the narrow valley flanked by high mountains, big timber in most stretches, and ending up in the fiords of the rugged British Columbia coast.

Even in this old settled valley there were considerable stretches with no habitations. But half-way down the valley there were many farms in the vicinity of Hagensborg, all with well fixed-up houses and farmsteads. Coming from our more open country, the clearings seemed pitifully small to us and this made us wonder where they could grow enough feed for their stock. Also, in some places the valley was so narrow there seemed only enough room for the river.

Camping at Hagensborg for the night, we struck a little diversion in the form of a political meeting. It was during the campaign for the "Reciprocity" election of 1911 and, though we had previously heard nothing of the election and really knew very little of the issues at stake, it was enough that the speaker was a Liberal and we were Conservatives. Therefore, we waded in with considerable heckling, enjoyed ourselves, and, I believe, made the meeting entertaining for the rest of the audience.

Next day brought us to the sea at Bella Coola and the end of our outward journey, which had taken us altogether about ten days. There was not much to see at Bella Coola, for, as far as I remember, there were few residences other than the two well-stocked general stores and a hotel, with an Indian village at the mouth of the river and another store on the far side of it. It took us about two days to purchase our supplies and to buy another couple of horses to help pack everything on the long trail home.

Bella Coola is far off the main sea route between Vancouver and Prince Rupert, being about fifty miles up Burke Channel, one of the innumerable winding inlets off the B.C. coast. A coast steamer called about once a week in those days and was the only communication with the outside. But, compared with our isolation in Ootsa Lake, Bella Coola seemed to be almost in the midst of "civilization."

One other little bit of business was done before leaving. Jack had been greatly bothered by an aching tooth and so, as there happened to be a travelling dentist there, he had the tooth extracted or, at least, he thought he did. For a time, all was well and the pain vanished, probably owing to the released pressure from the extracted tooth, but soon he discovered that friend dentist had taken out the wrong tooth and he suffered agonies from toothache for the greater part of the winter until the very pain burnt out the nerve in the tooth. But what could he do but grin and bear it with the nearest doctor at Hazelton, and being all by himself with horses and cattle to attend to. One little point about this toothache has always amused and mystified me. We had a lot of lovely wild blackcurrants growing hear to us and so we got busy and put up a lot of jam. When Bert and I returned home in the spring after a winter's trapping with our mouths just drooling at the thought of what we were going to do with that jam, about the first thing we mentioned to Jack was the jam. His face fell to about 50 below zero as he told us that he had eaten the whole lot. He said it was the only thing that relieved his toothache, and so you will all know what to do to relieve the pain in toothache — eat plenty of blackcurrant jam!

To return to our journeyings; we now set off with our loaded packhorses up the valley as far as Hagensborg, where we camped while we searched around the farms for any likely cows. Hagensborg is the centre of the best farming portion of the valley. The people were friendly, and it was a real pleasure visiting the different farms. We were, of course, looking for cows, but there were other things which we really didn't have to look for, for it was impossible to miss them — and that was the fine bevy of good-looking Norwegian lassies who were everywhere in evidence. I rather imagine that if our stay in the valley had been a little longer, we should have been wanting to bring back something besides cows.

But, alas, in about three days we had arranged to purchase our seven cows and a young bull, mostly of the short-horn breed, and so had to drown our amorous thoughts and get on our way. However, we have always remembered those fine families around Hagensborg: the Gordons, Svisdahls, Lauritsens, Hammers, Oussits, and the fine family of girls with their widowed mother, the Nordskogs, whose father had been Fish Commissioner.

We then moved our horses up to the ferry landing where we could get lots of horse feed as well as farm food for ourselves, and Bert stayed and looked after the horses while Jack and I went back to bring along the cows. And quite a time we had! First we tried to drive them loose, but those cows decided that they didn't wish to leave home and go to they knew not what, and so they took off along the innumerable trails in the woods around their homes. I still remember Briggsey putting her head down and her tail up and disappearing so suddenly that we never expected to see her again. However, she went home at night and we picked her up again the next day.

Finally we had to lead a couple apiece and then come back for the other four. Did you ever try leading a couple of unwilling cows for several miles? It's a job. As with our horse-packing, we got lots of gratuitous advice from persons we met on the road, and I well remember the mailman, Sam Gledhill, who, seeing our troubles, asked us if we had tried "tying them snug," that is, tying two heads together so that they can't travel in the timber and so drive better. When asked if he had ever tried it, he smilingly said that he had not but that he had heard of it. We did not try it, and decided to proceed as we were. Years later, we did try it on some difficult cattle of a neighbour in driving them off his place to the railway. Quite definitely, it did not work.

However, all things come to an end, even griefs, and we got the cows all joined up with the horses at the ferry. Now that the cows were off their home range they caused us no more trouble in the valley and we drove them all together up to Advent, a small Seventh Day Adventist settlement several miles up the valley, since we had decided to go home by the Burnt Bridge trail, which was not quite as steep as the one on which we had come down the mountain. One little scare during that drive up to Advent still remains very vividly in my mind. Suddenly, out of the blue, four or five big bulls came at a gallop and appeared as if they would eat up our little herd and ourselves as well. Jack and I always agreed afterwards that they appeared to be the biggest (and fiercest) bulls we had ever seen, but I guess the circumstances magnified them in our eyes. For a short while, there was a lot of roaring, snorting, and pawing of the ground, and then the bulls must have come to the conclusion that we were of no interest to them and they disappeared just as fast as they had come.

Having arrived at Advent, we arranged that I should stay with the cattle at an Adventist farm where the father had recently been killed by a tree falling on him as he was running a mowing machine. The Kivets were a kindly family and I enjoyed my short stay there, especially as it was Friday and, at sundown, as the Adventists retain the Jewish sabbath, their sabbath commenced and I was invited to join in their service. Mrs. Kivet played the organ and, as they had hymns that I knew well, I could really join in the singing. I always remember what Mrs. Kivet said to me after the service. "Well, sir, you have a fine voice if you use it to the glory of God." Perhaps on the whole I have, but I rather think there may have been a few lapses.

The following day Jack and Bert struck camp at the ferry landing and came up with the packhorses. I imagine that the American family who had the farm at the ferry was very sorry to see us depart for we had been very good customers to them for horse and cattle feed and farm produce of all kinds for ourselves — all at pretty stiff prices. Undoubtedly, the farm produce which we enjoyed the most was the fresh fruit — mostly apples — of which none was available to us in our district in those early days.

And so ended our stay in the Bella Coola valley, and we were almost sorry to leave, for the people were so kindly, and I think it will bear repeating that the young Norwegian girls were just "tops." As the colony had been established for a number of years, the homes were all of good size and well built, and the small farms as well established as could be expected in a valley where the timber was of great size and natural clearings very small. The chief drawback of the valley was its narrowness and the fact that the high mountains on both sides kept the sun out of many parts of it in the winter.

The steep mountains, coupled with the heavy coast rainfall, often caused extensive flooding owing to the rapid runoff and, occasionally, the flash floods had been really disastrous. Just one other sour note on the pleasantness of the valley, at this time of year, was the stench of dead salmon along the river and up all the creeks. We were there just after the salmon run had taken place. After spawning, the salmon die and rot. The resultant stench did not add to the joy of life. It was difficult at this season to get any water fit to drink without boiling.

But, all in all, it is a very pleasant valley and at that time was quite old-world owing to its comparative isolation. I very well remember that many of the settlers wondered whether they really wanted easier communication with the "outside." One of the Nordskog girls said that, if they lost their isolation, a lot of the charm of life would go, and with the advent into the valley of persons of unsuitable character to fit in with the old way of life, the distinctive Norwegian way of life would largely disappear.

# 9. Another Winter Further Afield

We had been told that the Burnt Bridge trail was not nearly as stiff a climb as the one by the trail from the ferry, but when we started the climb we were inclined to doubt the fact. The packhorses went ahead with Bert behind them and then Jack and I, with two Adventist boys, one a Kivet and Walter Hober, driving the cows behind. But right at the start of the climb there was a real zig-zag trail that wound like a snake up the hill. The cows went along the trail O.K. but when the ones ahead were on a zig and the later ones on the lower zag, the ziggers said, "Why, there are cows down there!" and promptly went the shortest cut to the zaggers. And so it continued. We were just in a vicious circle. In the end, we had to put ropes on the cows and each of the four of us led the alternate cows. In this way, we managed to get past the zig-zag.

It was still a very stiff climb and it took the efforts of all four of us to urge those critters up the mountain. By now, the cows had quite lost their bearings and knew of nowhere to go except on the trail ahead. I have never seen cattle so exhausted; their tongues hung out like those of panting dogs as they struggled upward. At last we got over the steepest climb and were able to let the boys go back home. Once up the mountain we had no trouble on the trail except at the swims, though Lucky, one of the cows, persisted in walking in the timber instead of taking the easy way on the trail. One of us had to keep an eye on her all the way, though I don't think you could have lost her even if you had tried to do so.

After passing Majuba Hill, Algatcho, the Indian village, Coal

**110**

*Packtrain on the Bella Coola trail.*

Meadows, and other stopping places, we arrived at the Teta-chuck River or rather, at the foot of the Teta-chuck Lake. Here, we had quite a spot of trouble for the water was cold; in fact, there was some ice on small bays and eddies and the cows were thin and felt the cold. Directly their feet touched the cold water they decided they did not like it, and just refused to face the narrow crossing. It brought to my mind the verse of a well-known hymn.

> But timorous mortals start and shrink,
> To cross the narrow sea
> And linger shivering on the brink
> And fear to launch away.

I should have told them that the first line of that hymn was:

There is a land of pure delight.

Once again, we had to use a raft, but this time it was easier to make one as we had plenty of spikes which we had bought at Bella Coola. We didn't try to load the cows on the raft; Jack poled it, I led the cow with a rope, while Bert urged the cows into the water.

First, we tried Reddy, the thinnest of the bunch, but she told us very emphatically that she was not going to swim and cavorted around and plunged every old way but the right one. Next, we decided to try Lucky and she behaved quite nicely until halfway across when she got the idea that if we could ride on the raft, why couldn't she? Up came a front leg onto the raft, down went the raft and we nearly took a ducking before I managed to beat her off. Then she decided that we were going too slowly and so she went ahead of us, which made it difficulty to pole the raft; in the end, we made it and tied her up on the shore. Next came Beauty, a really lovely Shorthorn, and all went well until we got quite close to the other side. Then things got balled up. First she thought she would swim to Lucky and started ahead of us. I threw the rope over her back, whereupon she promptly turned right around and went back to the bunch. We then had to repeat the performance. The rest gave us no trouble, and when it came to Reddy's turn, we just turned her loose and she swam across to the others without any bother. By this time, I think the cows were enjoying the change from the Bella Coola conditions where a lot of their feed consisted of leaves from the luscious shrubs growing on the coast and where they looked like a bunch of giraffes as they pulled down the branches with their long tongues. On the plateau of the Bella Coola mountains, when they saw their first lupin plants, or wild beans as we called them, they really made a bee-line for them. I believe they began to wonder why they had stopped so long in the valley. The nearer we got to Ootsa Lake the better the feed became, and as they were now getting used to river crossings, they gave us no trouble at crossing the Ootsa River.

Another forty miles, up the length of the lake, and we were home. But my wanderings for the year were by no means finished for we still needed more supplies and I had to take Romeo and Billy and set out for Hazelton once more — just another little walk of three hundred miles. On the outward journey I had the company of George and Peter Lawson, two Scotsmen, who were going out to work in a railway construction camp for the winter and, as the weather was fine all the way, though a bit cool, camping out was quite pleasant.

On the journey home I had to stop at roadhouses in order to get feed for the horses, for snow had fallen, and, since the horses had to be hobbled in order to prevent them from wandering too far, they could not paw for their feed. However, from Houston homewards, as there were no stopping places, they had to rustle their own feed. On the second night, when I camped at Trout Lake, they somehow sneaked past me during the night, even though they both had bells on, and next morning, I had to walk seven miles to get them. After this fourteen-mile walk, I still had to go ten miles to get to Francois Lake and, as the horses were now very weary after their summer's work, they only went a little over a mile an hour. It was, therefore, very late when I reached Francois Lake. Moreover, it had turned colder and was well below zero. But the temperature took a sudden, pleasant rise when I knocked at the door of our old friend Sam to ask for feed for my horses. Directly Sam opened the door he exclaimed, "Ah, Mr. Shelford, come right in. The boys will unpack your horses and fix them up." Being cold and very weary, I was more than glad to accept this invitation and I really had quite a night of it. The little cabin was just about full of Indians of both sexes, and all sizes and ages, and I hardly knew any of them. But it was warm and friendly, and after I warmed up and cooked a good supper, which the Indians were very willing to share with me, I felt at peace with the world.

Towards bedtime Sam came to me and said, "Mr. Shelford, I think we maybe pray a little, perhaps you like go to sleep." "No," I said, "I think I pray a bit, too." All the Indians in our area are Roman Catholics and, as the service was said in Indian, I knew nothing of what transpired, but it was a very pleasing experience. Sam appeared to act as a kind of precentor and intoned a sentence, which the others then repeated in unison, and so it proceeded.

Then we all rolled in our blankets and just about filled the floor of the cabin, and I expect we all slept the sleep of the just. Next day we reached home quite early, and it was very amusing to watch those mile-an-hour plugs, directly they were turned loose, galloping around and acting like a couple of kids as they played with Grey and Pinto, the two other horses that we had bought at Bella Coola. I imagine they all joined in singing "There's No Place Like Home."

While I was away Jack and Bert had put up a log barn for the cows, and so they were all fixed up for the winter. As they cut the trees for the barn and trimmed the logs, they burnt up the brush and they related how, on cold days, and even on days not so cold, those Bella Coola cows stood around the fire like a bunch of kiddies round a bonfire.

Well, it might look like a restful winter for the cows and horses, but such was not the case for the men folk — Bert and I were scheduled to go trapping up the Tahtsa River, while Jack stayed home to look after the stock. Unfortunately, by this time, the end of November, considerable ice had formed on Ootsa Lake and on the Tahtsa River and so, getting our supplies of food, traps, stoves, cooking utensils, and bedding up the river was made very much harder.

First, we took the supplies by boat about four miles up Ootsa Lake until we struck ice at Windy Point. From there we had to pull both supplies and boat on a hand-sleigh to the mouth of the Tahtsa River, a matter of about a mile and a half, and then by boat again to the forks where the Tahtsa and Whitesail Rivers join. From there it was all a matter of sleighing, and we had to relay several trips while gradually moving camp nearer to where we had decided to trap. Fortunately the frozen Tahtsa River made a nice level road, but even so, a nice level road means a steady pull with no relaxation of a little downhill. We both pulled the sleigh and, here again, as in the whip-sawing, it is a case of both pulling together, but we never had the slightest trouble in that respect.

As we freighted up the river we trapped and got quite a few muskrat and several mink and marten. The muskrat carcasses gave us a little variation in diet, but otherwise, it was straight bacon, beans, rice, sugar, flour, rolled oats, dried applies and tea. We were still moving our supplies to camp at Christmas and tried to get something for Christmas dinner, but there was virtually no game. One day I came across a hawk, which had just killed a rabbit. I ran shouting towards it, and though he managed to get airborne with the rabbit, he was in the end forced to drop his prey and we figured we had at least something for Christmas dinner. But "the best laid plàns of mice and men aft gang aglee," and the Fates decided against us. While the rabbit was lying outside our tent, a weasel came and beat us to it — there was no Christmas dinner left. However, we had plenty of food to give us full tummies, and work enough to give us good appetites, and so we didn't grieve too much over our lack of a banquet.

It was January 7th when we finally finished moving up the river, after a steady five weeks grind which could all have been done in a couple of days or so if we had been able to get it done before freeze-up and taken it all up by boat. Then we had to build a small log cabin for our main headquarters and break trail for about ten miles out and build our second cabin there. In the meantime we were also setting traps where fur signs showed on the snow at suitable spots. Later, we set up two tent camps. By branching out in different directions from all these camps, we covered a great deal of territory. As the area had been trapped very little, we got quite a good catch by spring. In the diet line we had the good fortune to find a nice fat bear in her hole a little after she had borne her cubs about March 1st. She had only had her cubs for a day or two, not long enough to pull her down in flesh, and she was lovely eating. A fat bear is easily the equal of good pork or mutton, that is, if it has not recently been feeding on rotten meat or fish.

I'm afraid that Bert ate a little too heartily on this fresh meat, and really got himself a dandy nightmare. Dreams seldom occur in the actual place where a person is, but in this case, he was actually in the second cabin when he was attacked by a big pack of wolves. It was so realistic and gave him such a scare that he got up and never went to bed again that night.

As spring approached, I ran lines from a tent camp near Huckleberry Mountain, and it was here that I ran into trouble with that dread of all trappers, a wolverine. A wolverine is a heavy-set animal of somewhat similar build to a bear, but, of course, much smaller. In his make-up the wolverine has a lot of the very devil himself. Very definitely, he is well endowed with brains, and his love of mischief goes much further than ordinary mischief on to plain devilment, for he revels in doing all the senseless damage he can. If he gets into camp or cabin, he seems to take a delight in tearing sacks of food, breaking boxes open with his powerful claws, and mixing up all the contents into one glorious mess; he ends up fouling everything with his unpleasant wolverine smell.

Fortunately, the wolverine never got to my camp that spring. My first knowledge of him was when he got into one of my marten traps, which had not been strong enough to hold him. After that, he ran my lines systematically, going the full length of one, and then cutting across country until he got to another, and then running that. If a set trap was in the trap-house, he never ventured in the front way, but went to the back of the house, pulled out a couple of the small poles of which the house was made and then reached in and helped himself to the bait. If a marten or any other animal was in the trap, he ate it up and if the trap had been set off without catching an animal, he was wise enough to know that the trap was harmless and went in the front way. On any line that he ran, I never got any more fur, for he either ate the bait or the captured animal. By good fortune it was near the end of the season when he appeared and so he did not cause too much loss.

Trapping in late spring is not a bit pleasant for the warm days cause the snowshoe trails to break down, and it was a case of getting up very early and travelling on the crust from the night's frost, or not travelling at all, while the foot-filling in snowshoes was continually needing repair as the melting snow caused the rawhide to rot and break. And so, about April 12th, we were glad to have everything collected in the main cabin once more. We then struck out for home with our fur on our back, the trip taking us two days.

We found Jack and all the livestock quite O.K., but he had seen absolutely no one all winter, though he was only eight miles from the nearest neighbours. After a period at home to allow the ice in the river to go out, we again sallied forth, only to find that the ice had not gone out when we arrived at the Forks, where we had left the boat.

Instead of waiting till the ice did go out, we foolishly decided to go up to the cabin on foot and do the little bit of beaver hunting that we expected to do. That was about the most miserable trip that I ever made, for we were either walking in deep, soft snow or deep, cold water, with lots of willows to make it real tough walking. When we got as far as our cabin we were on the wrong side of the river, so we made a small raft; however, it was not big enough for our combined weights and we got a good ducking — the latter proved that the water was neither deep nor fast, and so I decided to try walking across. Though I was in water up to my waist and the current was quite strong, I got across O.K., and then Bert came after me.

Just before we crossed the river we had shot a grouse with a .22, and we had hardly got settled in the cabin before two Indians, Batiste and Michel, who had heard the shot, came along to find out who were around and what they were doing. About the first remark they made on entering the cabin was, "All same bear den," and, of course, it was about correct, for one doesn't build a mansion when you never figure on using it after that winter. When we said that we were going to float down on a raft, Batiste cheerfully told us, "Tahtsa bad river, you likely lose all your stuff."

After a few days of not very successful beaver hunting, we built a raft and I set off down the river to bring back our boat. The trip certainly had its thrills, but I got down safely, only to find that the boat had dried out badly and I, therefore, had to spend a day or two caulking the seams with resin I collected from the spruce trees.

Then came my first effort at poling a boat up a fast stream, and by the time I reached the cabin and Bert, I had had enough experience to make a passable poler, though I would not class myself as either a Volga or Nile boatman.

Despite Batiste's cheerful prophecy, we arrived home with no mishap and then proceeded to get along with our different summer tasks. Bert went down Ootsa Lake, twenty miles on a raft to his own land; Jack spent most of the early summer on the pack-trail to Hazelton getting in supplies, while I stayed at home and busied myself in all different kinds of work, mostly fencing, clearing land, gardening, fishing with nets in Ootsa Lake, tending the stock and milking the cows.

# 10. On Pioneers and Natives

I think it is about time that we met a few of the other people in the district, for there were quite a few who had settled here before we arrived in 1910. I believe that the first man to spend a winter in Ootsa was Jake Henkel, but the next year he moved over to the north shore of Francois Lake, where he spent the rest of his life and established a fine home and farm there. Incidentally, the present government ferry which operates on Francois Lake, right in front of his old home, is named the *Jacob Henkel* in his memory.

The first actual settlers on Ootsa Lake came in during 1904. They came in from Kemano, an Indian village on the coast where, today, the huge hydro-electric generating station is situated. They had to climb the coast range of mountains and then drop down to Tahtsa Lake before following the Tahtsa River and on to halfway along Ootsa Lake, where they staked land. The three men who made that first trip were Harry Morgan, Jim Macdonald, and a fellow by the name of Goodwin. The latter was out of the district before we arrived and Jim Macdonald left soon after we came in. Harry Morgan remained here until his death in 1936. He was one of our most colourful settlers, being engaged in the early years mostly in running a pack-train, bringing in supplies for survey parties, and what-not over the Bella Coola trail.

Other early settlers in our neighbourhood were Mark Brennan, a Newfoundlander who came in 1906, Olaf Anderson, who came in 1907, Bob and Jim Nelson from Northern Ireland, and their partner Kelly, an Irish-Canadian, who came in 1908, George Lawson and

Shorty Matheson, a gay, care-free little Norwegian. These men pretty much made up the population of Wistaria in 1910. Most of them were away part of the year, earning grub-stakes at different jobs along the railway which was being constructed from Prince Rupert.

At Ootsa Lake, near Harry Morgan's, were Billy Ellison, George Lewis, George Wakefield, the three Bennett boys from England, the Mitchell family from Oklahoma, the Irish family of Eakins from the Fraser Valley, Harry Morgan's brother Jim and his young wife and son, Ford Dodds, a Seventh Day Adventist, Johnny Barker, who came here in 1906, Hank Raymond, and the Horr family, who came in about the same time that we did.

It was not a very big population stretching over thirty miles, but in the next year or so, quite a few others came in, several of whom came in as members of survey gangs — Percy Boden, Tommy McKinley, Billy Rist, and Charlie Hinton. There were others who had been working on railway construction — Jacob Lund, Erland Larson, and Jim Stoynoff, a Bulgarian, Pete Lawson, lately arrived from Scotland to join his brother, and a young wife from England for Harold Bennett.

But what we lacked in numbers was certainly made up for by the general friendliness and hospitality of everyone. I am afraid that Jack and I did not in those days enter much into the community life of the district, for we were always busy at home, and, being right on the western edge of the settlement, we would have had long distances to travel. As our nearest neighbours were about eight miles away, we were mostly out of touch with what was going on.

As the population increased, there was certainly no lack of entertainment, especially in the wintertime, for there was a continual succession of parties at the different homes and, in spite of the smallness of most of the homes, there always seemed room enough for a dance, and music was always available.

Though most of the travelling was done by saddle horse, or by sleigh in winter, distance seemed no deterrent. Women have ridden up to twenty-five miles with a baby on the horse with them to attend a dance or party at Southbank. One thing they could be sure of and that was that, wherever they landed, they were always assured of good food and the best accommodation possible. I won't say that it was actually up to Hotel Ritz style but, all the same, it really felt to everyone as if it was. There is no doubt that the farther one gets from the centre of population, the greater the hospitality, and in those days, on entering a house, the first question asked of people was "Have you eaten?" and, whether it was between mealtimes or not, there was put before you always the best that the house had to offer. Furniture, as we know it today, was quite non-existent, for even if we had the money to buy it, it couldn't have been carried into the country on a pack-horse. All things like that had to come in by degrees and, to be quite candid, we never felt the lack of them. People who came into a wilderness like ours and stayed there were quite ready to put up with temporary lack of the amenities of civilization and, as transportation improved, that old game of "keeping up with the Joneses" soon played a hand in improving our living conditions.

When speaking of hospitality in our western part of the settlement it would be wrong not to mention especially the two Nelson boys and Kelly who lived together in a log cabin at what is now Wistaria. Every man and his dog were always welcome there and sometimes in the fall, when a bunch of settlers from Ootsa Lake were coming through with their winter supplies, the cabin floor would be literally covered with sleepers and the wants of men and horses were all well attended to.

I feel I must pay tribute to those first pioneer women who braved the long, hard trails into the country, and then settled in to make the best homes they could for their husbands and children. Mrs. Mitchell of Oklahoma and Mrs. Eakin from the Fraser Valley were both quite middle-aged when they came in together over the Bella Coola trail. For the greater part of the way those two women walked in, one of them packing a stable lantern the whole way. Horses could not be spared for use as saddle-horses, and Bill Eakin even put a pack on one of the cows they were bringing in. I wonder how many women of today would be willing to undertake such a trip, not knowing what life held for them at journey's end. Then there was the young, slight Mrs. Morgan who came in over the same trail with her husband and little son Jimmy and who, not so long after, gave birth to the first white child born in the entire district. The nearest doctor and hospital were one hundred eighty miles away and, as it happened, the only attendant at little Lulu's birth was her father. Lulu was born in 1911, to be followed next year by another arrival under even more unusual circumstances.

In 1912 another pioneer woman of the district, Mrs. Sandy Thompson of Tatalrose on the south shore of Francois Lake, tried to reach Hazelton Hospital by saddle-horse to have her first baby, but the stork arrived early, and little Jacobina had the distinction of being born under a spruce tree in lonely Buck Flats, and again the only attending midwife was Sandy, her father. Anyway, the children seem to have suffered no harm, and they are now not only mothers, but grandmothers themselves.

In 1911, a girl from an English Midlands town arrived at Hazelton to marry the eldest of the Bennett boys and she had to make the journey to Ootsa Lake by saddle-horse. In the years to come, Polly Bennett played a great part in the life and development of the district.

A little later, a Scottish girl from the Orkney Islands made the trip from Hazelton. This was Mrs. George Lawson, and she was a near neighbour and friend of ours for many years. I never forgot her story of when she first arrived in Hazelton. Here it is as she told me.

"When Geordie and I went to breakfast at the Omineca Hotel the first morning I was there, the waitress came and asked me if I wanted mush. I didn't know what she was talking about and I said, 'What's mush, anyway?' And I found out it was porridge.

"Then later, we were around town talking to folks and when one man learned I was going to Ootsa Lake, he said, 'How you going to get there, are you going to mush in?' Well, I was all muddled up again until I found out that he meant was I going to walk in. The same day Geordie and I were walking up the street past the Ingenika Hotel and there was a crowd watching two men fighting and we stopped to take a look. Pretty soon one of the lookers-on shouted, 'Hit him in the mush, Jake!' And right there, I figured Canada must be all mush."

I have often wondered whether, in later years, she still held the same opinion.

None of these women, and all the others in the surrounding district had an easy life, but they took it in their stride and left their mark and also many kindly memories with the folks who knew them.

Many people may wonder what the pioneers found to make life interesting in those early days. First of all, there was their work in carving out their homes and farms in the wilderness and always that looking forward to the future and what it might hold in store for them. Working and planning, working and planning, even though many of the plans never bore fruit.

One day Jack was over at Kelly's and the latter was painting quite a picture of what he was going to do. Jack remonstrated gently and said, "Look here, Kelly, you know you'll never do half those things." "Oh, well," said Kelly, "what's life without plans?" And, of course, Kelly, who was quite a philosopher, was very right, and as to bringing all our plans to fruition, who ever does?

It must be remembered that the pioneers were from many different countries, of many nationalities, and that the majority had travelled a great deal, and worked at all kinds of different jobs. Furthermore, the pioneer is usually not of the run-of-the-mill type of the average stay-at-home person, and often has queer kinks in his make-up. Altogether, the frontiersman is not only interesting, but also quite educational in regard to life as it is lived in the four quarters of the earth. Many of them are not really interested in making a great success of life in the ordinary sense of the term, but are quite content if they just get by comfortably, and there is no place where this is easier to do than on the frontier. No big show to keep up, no keeping up with the Joneses if they don't wish to do so, and, usually, a large amount of the necessities can be rustled from the country and from one's own moderate efforts around the home and farm.

To persons of the right type, life in those early days was never dull. As regards Jack and myself, I don't think that we ever had a dull moment. Even our evenings never seemed to lack interest, though we had very little reading material. Our library consisted of *Dombey and Son, Barnaby Rudge, Martin Chuzzlewit,* and *Little Dorrit,* for I am a great lover of Dickens. Scott's *Quentin Durward, Ivanhoe* and *The Talisman,* with Shakespeare and the Bible finished off the list. Not a very great array but good stuff can stand a lot of re-reading, and these books got plenty of that.

As our receipt of mail was so spasmodic, we did not get any newspapers of any kind — we were, therefore, really cut off from all current news. With such a limited supply of reading, a great part of our evenings was spent in conversation. Jack had quite a wide experience in life, first as apprentice in the building trade in Bedford, then a couple of years in the Imperial Yeomanry in the South African War. Then he went to the United States and worked his way through New York, Buffalo, Chicago, Hays City in Kansas, San Francisco and from there up to Vancouver. After working in Vancouver for several months he went to Alaska via the Yukon and down the Yukon River in a small boat with several companions, a trip with plenty of thrills. He ended up at Fairbanks on the Tanana River, which town he used as a base while he was in Alaska. In the summer, he was engaged chiefly in hunting and fishing for the mining camp market. Winters he spent in trapping, and his trapping experiences on the upper Tanana River and up the Kantishna and Kuskokwim Rivers were enough to fill a good-sized book. As for gold mining, he never had the slightest interest in it, and never spent a single day at it. We re-lived his experiences in all these different walks of life and, in the end, I knew just as much about them as he did himself, and in later years I could tell him of some things that had happened to him which he had himself forgotten.

I think that one of his most interesting stories was concerned with his trapping on the Kuskokwim, where he was in sight of the great Mt. McKinley. This was a very isolated area and it was only during last month of his stay there that he ran into the only people that he was to see all winter. He met an Indian, Chief Cheso-e and his family and relations. He could easily have had trouble with this band, as some of the younger fry went along his lines, setting off his traps with sticks while he and Cheso-e nearly met head-on on the issue of who should shoot certain beaver. But in previous experiences Jack had discovered that the only way to deal with Indians was to adopt a really firm attitude and under no circumstances to use a policy of appeasement. This line worked successfully with Cheso-e and his band, and fortunately so, for Cheso-e had the reputation of having killed a man. Matters could have easily taken an unpleasant turn.

One day in the course of conversation Cheso-e said to Jack, "You savvy de bunk?" "De bunk?" echoed Jack. "What do you mean?" "De bunk," repeated Cheso-e and, holding up his hands as if holding an opened book, he said, "All same talkum." "Ah," said Jack, "you mean a book." "Yes," said Cheso-e delightedly. "You savvy him?" "Sure," said Jack. "Alright, I bringum." And away he went and soon returned with the book, which turned out to be the report of the head engineer of a survey gang which had been operating in the area where Cheso-e and his band had been wandering. Cheso-e said he thought the book talked about him, so Jack rapidly scanned through it and, sure enough, he came to the account of how the survey party and Cheso-e had become acquainted.

One day Cheso-e's band killed a bear and, when dressing it for meat, they must have opened its stomach for in it they found some bacon. They were quite sure that where there was bacon there must be white men and, after hunting around in wide circles, they discovered the cache from which the bacon and other provisions had been stolen. Afterwards they came across the survey party itself. As it turned out the men of the party were most pleased to see the Indians, for with the bears having destroyed their cache and everything in it, they were getting near the starvation point.

Cheso-e provided the party with the necessary food and was then hired to guide them to a settlement on the River Yukon. The head man of the party paid Cheso-e very generously. Part of the payment was a United States twenty dollar gold coin. On parting he also told Cheso-e that he was going to write a book about the work and experience of the party and that he would send him a copy of it. That he was as good as his word was proved by the copy which Cheso-e had. The whole band was terribly thrilled as Jack read out to them the account of the story. After that there was never any fear of bad blood between them.

Cheso-e still had his twenty dollar gold piece, carefully tied up in the corner of a handkerchief, and proudly showed it to Jack. Jack sold quite a bit of his outfit to Cheso-e, as he did not want the trouble of taking it back to Fairbanks. But, though he tried, mostly for devilment I think, to get that twenty dollar gold piece in payment, he might just as well have tried to get the moon.

One other incident in Jack's Alaskan experiences is well worth the telling for it seems so inexplicable. At the end of a winter's trapping on the upper Tanana, as he was proceeding downstream to Fairbanks, he stopped off at what proved to be a small store and post office. Jack had absolutely no previous knowledge of the place which the owner said bore the name of "Chicken Creek." In the course of conversation, he asked Jack his name and, on being told, he exclaimed, "Shelford. Why, I have got a letter here for a J. Shelford." When produced, it proved to be a letter from Mother addressed to J. Shelford, Chicken Creek, Alaska. Jack declared that he had never mentioned such a place to Mother or anyone else and, in fact, he had never heard of the place before.

In whatever manner Mother got the notion to address the letter to Chicken Creek I will have to leave to someone else to decide. Had Jack known of the place, some kind of mental telepathy could have been the explanation, but since he had no chance of sending thought waves on the matter, we will have to leave it to the psychologists.

Right from the beginning of our life in this country we have been thrown into quite close contact with a great many of the native Indians and, I frankly say that we have in no way suffered from this contact. We have always been on friendly terms with these people. We have to remember that the first contacts which most of the Indians had were with white men of the rougher type — mostly with men engaged in railway construction or with traders. These men were away from all refining influences, and so it could be only expected that they would tend to show the tougher sides of their characters. Many of the traders had quite a bad influence on the Indians because they always tried to get the better of the Indians in any dealings they had with them, and so, naturally, the Indians felt that that was the proper thing to do and, so, tried to beat the white man in return.

Our friend Sam did pull a fast one on us in the matter of the old snowshoes, and did try to pull off a real financial coup in the matter of hiring out his horses to us but, after that, he always behaved like the real old gentleman that he was. In later years Sam built quite a nice little house for himself but, when it came time to prepare for his journeying to the "Happy Hunting Ground," he felt that he had to return to the old Indian way of life, and therefore, he spent his last days in a tent outside his house.

Sam's half-brother, Andrew, had his hunting ground at the head of Ootsa Lake and passed our place every spring and fall on his trapping trips. Like many Indians at that time, Andrew sometimes voiced the opinion that it was no good that the white men come and take the Indian land and fur. And so one day I had it out with him and told him that, if the white man was to be in the country at all, he had to have some of these things. "Which you like best, Andrew?" I asked him. "No white man come, then you get no railroad, no roads, no rifles, no good fish-nets, no flour, no sugar, no tea, no rice, no matches, blankets, knives, axes, pots and pans, and such things, but live just as Indians used to do on fish, beaver, deer, bear and berries." Andrew looked thoughtful for a few moments and then said, "I think maybe white man better stop."

We always admired Andrew for the fact that, when passing our place, he invariably had a huge pack on his back, for it was the usual Indian custom for the man to walk ahead, just carrying his rifle, and the woman following him, carrying heavy packs. But not Andrew. He always had his big pack and his big smile.

Like Sam, Andrew had to receive a lesson on good behaviour. When we came into the district, Andrew had no boat on Ootsa Lake, except a very poor dugout canoe, and so he was very glad to get the use of our boat for about a month in his spring and fall trips. One fall, when returning past our place, he said that he would have liked to have given us some meat for the use of the boat but that he only had the head of a deer left — but that we could have that if we wished. Any meat was better than none, even though the meat on a deer's head just about amounted to the tongue, so we took it, but we did not feel very good about it when, a few days later, a trader named Dorsey came over to buy a cow from us and told us that he had just got a lovely hind quarter of deer from Andrew, as he was passing through.

Dorsey, by the way, was at that time engaged in a rather interesting type of illicit trading. The new railway was at this time approaching us from both directions, but there was quite a gap, on each side of Burns Lake, where construction was still in progress. Dorsey brought in liquor by packhorse from the end of steel at Houston to Nadina at the head of Francois Lake, and then took it down by water to the foot of

Francois Lake in a small boat. Having arrived at the foot of the lake, he would peddle the booze among the different camps in that area.

Our cow was butchered at Nadina and transported to the camps in the same manner. Until Dorsey slept in our cabin with us, we had never had a cold in the years we had been in the country, but he had a real bad one and he surely left it with us. But he didn't leave it entirely, though, for he still took it away with him, and after selling the beef he returned to his headquarters at Telkwa. He had quite a bad heart condition and the doctor advised him to keep off the liquor. He had been quite careful for a long time, but, having arrived back in Telkwa, he thought a good shot of rum would kill the cold. Well, it may have done so, but at the same time, it killed him also.

But to return to Andrew. The following spring when I was out to a small store which operated for a short while at Nadina, I once again encountered friend Andrew who, as usual, greeted me with his big smile. After an exchange of greetings and some small talk, Andrew ventured, "How's chances to borrow your boat?" "No chance at all, Andrew." said I, and then told him of his sin of the previous fall. "If you had had no meat, Andrew, that's alright, but you had meat and sold some to Dorsey. You tell us a lie and we don't like that, so you can't have our boat." The result was a very crestfallen Andrew.

But evidently he put his brain to work on the problem. A few days later, while Jack and I were putting the roof on a big new loghouse which we were building, we heard chopping up the creek-bed trail, and conjectured that Andrew was fixing camp there. Pretty soon Jimmy, Andrew's eighteen-year-old son appeared and started to talk to us. After a little while Jimmy said, "You boys maybe like a little trout?" Jack and I exchanged grins and Jack said, "Yes, Jimmy, I guess a little trout alright." So away trots Jimmy and shortly returns with more than a dozen trout of about two pounds apiece. They were a really beautiful sample, and we didn't stint our praise or thanks. Of course, very soon came the inevitable question, "Maybe you boys like to lend me your boat." Naturally, Jimmy got the boat and ever after we never had the slightest trouble with them. Andrew is long since dead, but Jimmy and his family are still our very good friends and, whenever Jimmy eats at our table, you could never wish for anyone with better table manners.

Only once have we had any suspicion of trouble with any Indian. During our first winter here, Jack ran a small trapline on the south side of Ootsa Lake, up the slopes of Mt. Wells, or, as we always call it, "The Dome." The following spring on a trip to Wistaria Jack met an old

Indian named "Skin Tyee" from near the Ootsa Lake settlement. After some talk Skin said, "You trap some last winter up on mountain." Jack said that he had, and Skin went on, "That no good, that my hunt-ground. Sometime maybe (and putting his rifle to his shoulder) — poof! No witness!" But that was as far as it went, and we saw very little of Skin in later years.

I have said previously that we have learned many things from the Indians, but I think of all the knowledge we found they possessed, perhaps the most wonderful was in regard to measures to prevent goitre. In many parts of British Columbia, like all other places in the world where the water in the streams and lakes comes from melted snow, goitre can become very prevalent unless proper steps are taken. Evidently the Indians had suffered from it and had discovered the means of preventing it.

From Nadina at the head of Francois Lake they had a packtrail up the river and over the Coast Mountains to Kemano on Gardner Canal, one of the many inlets on the coast. They used this trail mostly to get in a supply of oolichans, a species of small fish which yields a great quantity of oil. While at the seashore the Indians also laid in a good supply of seaweed which, of course, with its high content of iodine, is a fine natural preventative of goitre. One wonders how they discovered the fact, but it would be like almost all other such discoveries, first more or less a matter of chance, followed later by close observation. For several years after we came here, some stores always carried packages of seaweed in stock as there was quite a demand for it from those Indians who lived farther away from the coast.

I think too that the Indian can teach his white brother a great deal as to the most nutritious and tastiest meat on an animal's carcass. The average white man will always choose the hind quarter as it is most suitable for steaks and roasts, but the Indian, if he gives any meat away, will always give away the hind quarter of any game and keep the neck, front quarter and ribs for his own use. Try the two types in a stew and you will find that the Indian's choice is far tastier and nutritious, with its large supply of gelatine, than the flat-tasting hind quarter.

Before the advent of the white man, the Indians had to use primitive methods of obtaining fish and game. Fish were mostly obtained by use of the wicker basket fish-trap, placed in streams during the spawning season. A wooden fence across the rest of the stream guided the fish into the trap from which they could not escape. But they also had many other cleverly-made instruments of wood. In later years when iron became available, the Indians were very clever in spearing salmon at suitable spots in a river. I remember watching one of them as he stood on a little rocky ledge on the edge of the Bulkley River at the Moricetown Canyon. The metal spear was not attached rigidly enough to the wooden handle, but was inserted in a hole up the handle and was, at the same time, also attached to the handle by a leather thong. When the salmon was speared the spear disengaged itself from its hole in the handle and the fish could be more easily handled on the leather thong.

Snares of all kinds were much used by the Indians and our old friend Sam spoke of earlier years of caribou being snared in the trails they used. At the present time caribou are mostly confined to the mountain plateaux where lichen, on which they mostly live, is quite widespread. In the summer the caribou roam a great deal in the lower timber areas and are at this time doing this to a greater extent, even being seen in the populated areas. Friend Sam told us that in earlier days large bands of caribou roamed in the timber country and that our farms were on a much-used caribou trail on which they were often snared.

It is not at all difficult to believe such stories of the change in the habits of wild animals for, when we came into the district, there was not a single moose in the whole area nor had there been in previous years. They started to arrive in the year 1911 and are now numbered in the thousands. This is true also of the snowshoe rabbit, or Arctic hare. In early years there was a definite seven-year cycle of these animals during which they built up in numbers from almost zero to the millions and then down to almost zero. But in some way this cycle has been upset and not even the biologists know why in the last twenty years we have had no rabbit cycle but just a small amount of them all the time.

Before getting too far away from the subject of snares, I must relate three rather interesting little incidents. One Sunday as my wife and I were on our way to pick berries, I suddenly heard a little cry behind me and went back to find my wife with her foot tightly gripped in a wire coyote snare which had been left set by the Indians. Fortunately, she had not pulled hard on the snare or she would have found herself suddenly hoisted into the air by the attached springpole. On another occasion I was not so fortunate, as I did pull too hard and suddenly found myself spread-eagled in the air. However, a coyote springpole is not heavy enough to hold a man, and I was soon able to release myself. But a similar case might not have ended as happily. Brother Jack was out on another Sunday with his wife and four small boys. They were walking in Indian file along a trail when they suddenly missed Cyril, the youngest, who was bringing up the rear. On going back, they found him with a snare around his neck. Fortunately, he had not struggled and tripped the springpole, or he could easily have been hoisted into the air and strangled, for at the time he was only a small boy of four or five.

I think I have previously mentioned the system of Indian hunting-grounds under which all Indian families had definitely fixed areas which were respected by all other families. With the advent of the white man this whole system went by the board as the white trapper respected no such boundaries. The Indian had treated his hunting-ground as a farm and had not over-trapped it so as to leave plenty of breeding stock, but now the whole balance was upset and the size of the animal fur catch diminished so much that the provincial government had to step in and itself institute a system of registered trap-lines under which the registered owner, whether white or Indian, has the sole right of trapping. Everyone must agree that this is a feather in the cap of the Indian who earlier recognized the need for such recognition.

Another Indian method, adapted by the Canadian Army in the First World War, was the tumpline, a band of soft-tanned leather, broad in the centre to fit over the top of the forehead and used for packing heavy loads, such as boxes of ammunition and the like up to the Front Line. Evidently, the military authorities found this method preferable to the pack-board in general use in outlying areas in British Columbia. The battalion in which I served had a regular Tumpline Section, and I believe there was also a Brigade Tumpline Section.

# 11. Getting Established

The summer of 1912 was very little different from the previous year as regards work; mostly clearing land and fencing, for, as our cattle began to increase, we had to have more hay and also had to have fences to keep the cattle off the hay land. Jack, as usual, spent most of the summer packing supplies, while Bert was down on his own place.

We did have one very unusual happening, and that was when Mt. Katmai, a volcano in the Aleutian Islands, blew its top about midsummer and the whole atmosphere was filled with ashes. As we had no means of communication with the outside, we thought it was a huge forest fire and that it was smoke that was obscuring the sun. In fact, we were so scared that we dammed up the creek flowing through Jack's eighty-acre meadow so as to prevent any fire from crossing it. Later, however, we noticed that any articles made of iron, such as logging chains, axes, saws, etc., that were lying outside, all got a coating of red rust on them, and all the vegetation had a grey coating. After a while, the news filtered through to us that the volcanic eruption had caused all the trouble. The effect on the vegetation was quite bad for the ash covering so interfered with the breathing apparatus of the plants that they stopped growing, with the result that the hay crop was much shorter than usual.

At the end of the packing season the horses from the numerous pack-trains were put out to winter in different parts of the district and, that fall, Kelly and Jim Nelson brought in over a hundred of these horses to winter and for their winter feed, they had put a big lot of slough hay on the swamp meadows at the head of Ootsa Lake. This slough grass is a broad-leafed grass and, evidently, it made a fine resting place for the volcanic ash that fell all over the countryside. Very shortly after the horses were taken to the meadows and fed on the slough hay they began to die off in considerable numbers. It was not because the horses were in poor condition or because they were not given enough feed for I passed through about the end of November and saw really fat horses dying off with lots of feed before them. After losing about half of the horses, Kelly and Jim got so disgusted that they took the remainder down to their own place and let them rustle their living on the side hills. The result was that they suffered no more horses lost, as the grass on the side hills had not made a good resting place for the volcanic ash.

This year we got a mower in from Hazelton which made haying a lot easier but we still had to rake it all by hand. Gallant little Romeo packed the main body of the mower on top of some sacked grub all the way, without any grumbles and, fortunately, Jack had help in loading him up as a German-American, Bill Behnke, came in with him and spent the winter with him. It was rather amusing that, when Romeo reached the field on my place where we were to start mowing, he said, "I believe this is where you boys figure on starting to mow," and, considerately, lay down all on his own as if he knew that that would make unloading easier; and the heavy mower body was just rolled off him.

After haying was finished, Jack, Bert, and Behnke went to Hazelton for supplies and, as work done on the road during the summer had made it more or less passable, a wagon was used for the first time with Behnke's two mules and two of our little cayuses providing the power. But the road was still far from being a highway and, on their return, disaster nearly struck as they were coming up the steep, narrow, side-hill cut from Francois Lake. The wagon slid off the road and rolled down the hill, taking Romeo and Grey with it. However, Behnke's tow mules who were in the lead hung on to things and kept them from rolling further. It was quite a job to get the mess disentangled, but no real damage was done and, in due course, they arrived home.

The first job on arriving home was to have a good boiling of their clothes, for on the trip the travellers had camped in several abandoned railway construction camps and got themselves a good supply of "greybacks" (fleas). When this was completed, Bert and I again set off for the winter's trapping — this time going up the Whitesail River, which joins the Tahtsa at the Forks. As the ice had not yet formed on Ootsa Lake, we got up to the Forks by boat, but then had to pull our supplies and the boat by hand-sleigh up the five miles of Sinclair Lake to where the Whitesail River enters it. We slept the night at Kelly's

*The rigours of early travel. Easing a freight wagon down a steep hill going down to Francois Lake.*

horse camp and, as they also had slept in the construction camps, we again got well loaded up with "greybacks." With the limited supply of pots and pans, it was almost impossible to "boil-up" so, for a few nights, we "read" our shirts, etc., but, though we made quite a killing, it proved quite impossible to rid ourselves of the pests in this way. However, luck was with us, for we discovered a very effective way of dealing with them. A night of 20 below zero arrived and so we decided to try the deep-freeze treatment on them by hanging all our underwear outside. It worked like a charm, and by morning, every last louse and nit was very plain to be seen, for they all looked like boiled lobsters. A similar treatment for our change, and we were free of the pests all winter long.

When we got to the head of Sinclair Lake, we found the Whitesail River still open and so it was a case of taking our outfit up the river in our small boat — this took two or three trips. Poling a boat in the freezing weather was neither easy nor pleasant, especially as the river was very low and often the boat got stuck on a riffle. The pole got wet and icy and the boat took on an ever-increasing covering of ice so that it made me think I was poling an ocean liner. When it got stuck on a riffle I had to get in the water in my bare legs and pull the boat over the riffle by brute strength, which was not exactly pleasant.

It was while poling the outfit up the Whitesail that I committed a crime for which, at the present time, I would be hung, drawn, and quartered, but for which at that time fifty years ago my conscience did not trouble me in the slightest. Stretches of the Tahtsa and Whitesail Rivers remained open right through the winter, and a good-size flock of trumpeter swans stayed there all through the winter, along with a few geese and ducks.

I guess I had unpleasant memories of our last Christmas dinner and so, when I came across a bunch of swans on the river, I promptly dropped my pole, grabbed my rifle and, with one shot, had our Christmas dinner provided for. And I believe that 999 people out of 1,000 would have acted likewise, in view of the fact that the nearest butcher's shop and, perhaps more important, the nearest game warden, were both at least one hundred eighty miles away. Most certainly I did not feel like a criminal for, in those days, in the fall and spring when the water-fowl were migrating from and to their breeding grounds in the far north, Alaska, the Yukon, and the Northwest Territories, the head of Ootsa, and indeed all the numerous small lakes in the district were literally covered with swans, geese, and every species of duck. We have many lakes close to our home and, on some of them, you could hardly have placed another duck, and yet, in all my fifty years here, I have never bothered them much and don't think that I have shot twenty, all told.

But the dead swan evidently had its own ideas on the subject and, himself, meted out some measure of punishment. While I was freighting our outfit in the boat, we had our camp on the big willow flat at the mouth of the Whitesail so as to be close to the river. We had decided to reserve the breast of the swan for Christmas dinner, and to eat the rest of the meat as we might need it. One night we attacked the drum-sticks and I was really wading into it, for it was a young bird and beautifully tender. Remembering how the bear meat had affected him the previous spring, Bert told me to go easy on the meat or I would make myself sick. But I ignored his warning and said that I was doing fine.

That night we had a terrible storm of wind and snow, and the willow swamp afforded little protection. In the middle of the night I felt the tent fall right on top of us, and said to Bert, "Well, Bert, the tent has fallen down and the ridge-pole is right across my chest, but it is such a terrible night I'm going to leave it there till morning." I imagine that I slept the sleep of the just till morning but, when I did wake up, I was amazed to see the tent standing up just as usual. Evidently it was the swan's leg, and not the ridge-pole, that had got across my chest.

Christmas dinner that year was really good, for we now had our own butter, churned at home, and so managed to make a cornmeal cake, and we also had some delicacies which Jack had bought at

Hazelton from a Mr. and Mrs. Perdue who had stocked up well in Vancouver but, when they got to Hazelton, had cold feet and decided to head south again and so disposed of their outfit to Jack. Our Christmas day menu: Soup a l'Oxo, Roast of Swan with apple sauce, with cake and fruit for dessert. Add to this a good appetite, and you had a feast for the gods.

Trapping that year proceeded much as in the previous winter and, when we had built two cabins and put out the lines from them, we each worked on our own and often did not see each other for weeks. However, any time we went to the main cabin for supplies we always left a note to let the other know that we were alright. Besides the cabin, we also had two tent camps, equipped with stoves; we also worked from campfire camps towards spring. These latter are usually quite comfortable but, that spring, I did get up against a rather tough little cold spell at the end of March when the temperature dropped to about thirty below with a vicious east wind. That was before the days of good warm sleeping bags, and my supply of bedding was not sufficient to keep me warm in such weather. Therefore, I spent about my two most uncomfortable days of my whole trapping career. It was even cold sitting before a roaring campfire during the day, for my camp was on the edge of a small river and there was no shelter from the bitter east wind. It was too cold even to go out on my traplines. But it did not last long, and the next thing I knew was that it was too warm, which made for tough travelling getting my camp equipment and traps back to the base camp, as the trails broke down under the weight of myself and my pack. However, despite these apparently tough experiences and living conditions, we never had any kind of sickness, and colds and coughs were unknown to us in that clean, uncontaminated air.

The summer of 1913 was chiefly spent in getting out logs and squaring them on three sides for a two-storied log house thirty-two by twenty-six feet, erecting it, and whip-sawing the necessary lumber — for Jack was considering the plunge into matrimony with a girlfriend of ours in England. The house-building, added to the ever-present job of packing in supplies and a hay-rake, more fencing and more land-clearing, gardening and a thousand and one other jobs kept us plenty busy, especially as Jack was planning a trip to England during the coming winter to make final matrimonial arrangements.

The house logs themselves gave us plenty of trouble, for neither of us had ever used a broad-axe before, and big spruce logs, about sixteen inches at the butt end, take a lot of hewing to square them on three sides. We also had to haul them over a mile and a half and, for our little cayuses to be able to move the heavy green logs, we had to use the wooden wheels which we had made for our little cart, chaining the heavy end on the axle and dragging the other end.

However, by fall we had the log part of the house built and enough lumber whip-sawed for the roof, floors, partitions, etc., and so Jack was able to get away just after Christmas. The railway, however, was not yet completed and he had to walk over one hundred miles before he made contact with the necessary transportation.

I have often wondered how we early settlers got by without having to make long trips to a doctor or hospital, but I suppose it was because most of us were young and, if any of the weaker variety ventured into the wilderness, they got the right notion and got out before the tough life had time to get them. I did once put an axe into my instep and Jack had to put in three or four stitches, using a glover's needle to do the necessary job. Jack also had a nasty little accident just before his trip home when a tree he was cutting kicked up when it hit another small stump as it fell, struck his finger and put it out of joint, with the knuckle bone sticking through the flesh. Fortunately, he had presence of mind enough, to give it a good yank and put it in joint again while it was still numb and not too painful. Other than these two little accidents we never had anything happen to us, and I don't remember that anyone else did either. I suppose the fact of the matter was that we knew that we could not afford to be sick and so just decided not to be.

I remember when the question of getting a doctor into the district was first mooted, our Norwegian neighbour, Jacob Lund, said, "Doctor! What do we want with a doctor here, nobody is ever sick."

When Jack was home he was talking to an old school friend in our little town of Brackley, who asked him just what the life of a new settler was like, what we had to do, and what obstacles we had to surmount. When Jack recounted a list of the activities that filled our days, weeks and months, Charlie Matthews looked at him and then said, "Look here, Jack, you must think I'm pretty much of a fool if you expect me to believe all that. It's just impossible for me to do all that, and make a living besides." And however much Jack declared that it was all quite true, Charlie still remained quite a "doubting Thomas." Jack told me that the only way he could get most people to believe him was to tell some really good "whoppers."

As Jack was to be away for most of the winter, Bert and I could not both go trapping and so, it was arranged that he should look after the stock and I would do the trapping. As more men were coming in to trap and the trapping grounds were getting a little too crowded for our liking, we decided that I should branch out into a different type of trapping. So far, we had trapped mostly marten, mink, weasel and muskrat, but, in the previous winter, Jack and Behnke had been on top of the "Dome," on the south side of Ootsa Lake, and had discovered that a big herd of caribou habitually wintered on the treeless plateau of the mountain, as, in fact, our old friend Sam had previously told us, and also that fox appeared to be fairly numerous up there. Further more, it was much nearer home, as it only entailed a walk of about six miles to the Head of Ootsa and then a climb of 3,000 feet.

Just before he started on his trip home, Jack showed me his trail up the mountain. It could easily have been our last trip anywhere. On our way out we crossed Ootsa Lake on the ice near the head, and the ice was plenty strong enough. We just sat by a campfire all that night and travelled all next day, hoping to get home before night. We had a pair of big snowshoes and a pair of small trail shoes. I wore the big ones, breaking trail all the way in eighteen inches of snow. For whatever reason, we hadn't the sense to change shoes and ease me off. As a result, when about half a mile from the lake, I was completely played out and we had to camp for the night. As it turned out, this was sheer good luck for next morning we found that the ice at this point of crossing, five miles below the other crossing, had only recently been formed and was quite thin. If we had been crossing in the dark we would almost certainly have gone through. What a nice Christmas Day that would have been, for that was the day it was.

Trapping on the "Dome" was a very different experience from trapping in sheltered timber country. First, I had to pack up enough supplies and bedding and whatnot to enable me to build a cabin, which was not a very difficult job, even for just one man. Though it was close to timber-line, plenty of good even-sized logs were available, and a ten foot square cabin does not entail very heavy work. By this time I had got a little sense rammed into me and built the cabin with a pitched roof, the pitch steep enough to run off all the water from rain or melting snow. Previously, we had just put flat dirt roofs on our trapping cabins, and when the snow on the roof started to melt it was one continual drip inside. One was far better off camped outside as the weather was usually warm by this time and the dripping continued for days after the snow had all melted as the dirt of the roof was saturated with water. So this winter I had a nice dry cabin and that meant a lot in the matter of comfort. It was built directly below two huge cavern-like holes in the top of the mountain, which the Indians very appropriately called "The Eyes," and, indeed, they really looked like the eyes of the mountain and were separated by a strip of land running down between them, which made an excellent nose. At the base of each "Eye" was a small lake which, in the summer-time, had the bluest water in them. The snow never completely melted from the cavern sides of the lakes.

After the cabin was completed, my first job was to get meat. There proved to be lots of it on the mountain. The caribou spent most of the summer in the timber country all round the lower parts of the mountain but, in the fall and winter, they all congregate on the absolutely bare mountain-top. A person who is unacquainted with the feeding habits of caribou at first wonders what in the world they find to eat up there, but, on going over places where they have been feeding, one finds the remains of the silvery grey lichen which they have pawed from beneath the snow. The caribou is close kin to the reindeer and lives on the same kind of food and in similar country. It is much easier for them to rustle their food on the mountain plateaux in the winter than in the timber, where the snow is three to four feet deep. On the mountain the fierce winds sweep the snow almost completely from all the more exposed areas. Moreover, where the snow is drifted and therefore deeper, it usually drifts hard enough for them to travel on it quite easily.

The marvel is how they can endure life up there in the terrific winds which so frequently sweep such plateaux. But they don't seem to notice it in the slightest and their thick coats must be a wonderful protection for them. I have been on that mountain sometimes when conditions were past endurance, with the snow whipped up into a fierce driving sheet, which resembled a sand-storm more than a snow-storm from the way the gritty snow cut into one's cheeks, and yet those caribou would paw in it or lie down in it as if it were a nice quiet day. Later, I made a sleeping bag from caribou hides, and then I knew why caribou could stand just about anything, for I could sleep in that bag in forty below zero without the least discomfort.

During the three winters I trapped on the "Dome" there appeared to be about two hundred caribou, but usually they were split up into small bands, though occasionally I saw the whole bunch in one of the alpine valleys. And a wonderful sight it was. Sometimes, I have sat down all day, watching a herd and waiting to get a shot at them but unable to do so on account of the direction of the wind and the contour of the ground. It would have been tiresome waiting so long if it had not been so interesting watching them. It was most amusing to see a little calf go and bunt its mother out of a nice spot where she had been pawing, and taking it over for himself, obviously telling her to go and find another spot for herself. Usually, it was a warm, sunny day when I tried this waiting game, but I don't think that I ever had any luck, for the caribou never moved in my direction or into a position where I could hunt them.

Even under the most favourable conditions, hunting is not easy on those snow-covered, undulating wastes for it is most difficult to judge distances correctly. Somehow the light seems to have an eerie appearance which is often accentuated by light clouds drifting around. I am not a bad shot, but I must confess that I have done some pretty rotten shooting on that mountain.

The Indians who were in the habit of hunting there were well aware of the deceptive light and when an Indian named Peter Pierre, who had never hunted there, accompanied them on one trip and, taking two boxes of shells with him, boasted of what he was going to do to those caribou, Jimmy and Antoine smiled to themselves and said nothing. Came the hunting and Peter's two boxes of shells disappeared, and no caribou. Finally, his friends had to shoot some for him.

Once or twice, when I was in the midst of the light, drifting clouds, I have had the weirdest deceptive visions. One morning I saw a small bunch of caribou at not too great a distance, and I began to crawl towards them. As I crawled a light, misty cloud floated ahead of me and blotted out the caribou. However I kept crawling ahead and then, in the mist, I dimly saw what appeared to be a fox running across thirty or forty yards ahead of me. I crawled one more step and the animal resolved itself into a mouse, just one yard ahead of me. On another occasion I was near the top of the mountain just above the "Eyes," returning home at night, when I saw what seemed to be either the dark back of a caribou or a fair-sized rock sticking out of the snow. I was needing meat, so stood and watched for a while but, when there was no movement, I decided to get a little nearer, for whatever it was, it seemed to be about a hundred yards from me, though it was hard to judge. Once again I only went one step forward and lo, it was just a small knob of caribou dung on a slight rise in front of me and not six feet away.

At times this deceptive light could be quite dangerous, especially in the scrub timber right next to the bare plateau. Here, the snow would often drift into big mounds around a few scrub trees and, even in bright sunlight, as I have been walking along what I thought to be level terrain, I have had the point of my snowshoe stick right into a high mound of snow before I realized that there was any mound there; at other times, however, one could easily drop off such a mound before he knew that such a drop existed.

Other than the possibility of some accident from dangers such as these, there was really very little danger in a winter on the mountain all by oneself, except for the very real danger from the terrible winds which would spring up so suddenly and of which I will have more to say later. Of course, many men could not stand a life of such solitude, and could easily become ill just thinking of the possibility of accidents, but such men seldom venture on such a life and, if they do, they soon quit it. As to loneliness, it is again just a matter of having the right temperament.

One possible danger in a life like this can be when two men go into partnership in such an expedition and, later, find that they cannot get along together. I was told recently of such a case which happened right in this country, up the Whitesail River, many years ago. A friend of mine, Emil, got linked up with a bad partner, Joe, by name. Before long Joe began to show some streaks of bad character and, in the end, Emil told him that they had better divide up the outfit and go their separate ways. So, after some difficulties, this was done. Then they both decided that they would walk down the river to be amongst other people for Christmas.

As they were walking down Sinclair Lake, Emil suddenly fell through the ice but, fortunately, he kept hold of his rifle. By the look on Joe's face, Emil felt quite sure that he would be really content to leave him to drown and so, holding out the rifle, muzzle foremost straight towards Joe, he ordered him to come and pull on the rifle and get him out. After a moment's hesitation, Joe complied and Emil got out, for evidently Joe figured that the rifle might go off if he decided otherwise.

Later, as they continued their journey, a coyote came into view on the lake and Emil took a shot at it or, at least, tried to. When he pulled the trigger there was no result. The shell was either a natural dud or had been spoiled by contact with the water. Both men involuntarily looked at each other without speaking and, ever since, Emil has wondered if Joe would have pulled him out of the water if he had known that the rifle would not fire.

But now to get back to the mountain and the caribou. I am afraid that with the caribou, as with the swan, I often transgressed the game laws. In the first place, I don't believe I knew whether there was any closed season on caribou in our district in those days but, even had I known, when one was in the wilds he interpreted the game laws as the occasion called for. At that time the caribou were only hunted occasionally by a few Indians, for tourists and hunters from the outside were quite unknown, and the only other things which reduced the numbers of the caribou were the wolves in their periodic visits to this district. In those early days of isolation, you could have put anyone on that mountain with a rifle after he had been on a steady diet of pioneer's rations and the reaction would have been the same in every case. As a matter of fact, I personally know of instances where game officials and others in higher brackets have, in similar circumstances, acted in a like manner.

Of the three animals of the deer family whose meat I have eaten, caribou meat is, to me, by far the tastiest, though I have heard several persons complain that any caribou meat which they have got has been bitter and unpleasant to eat. This was probably due to some kind of food which the animals had been eating at the time. But I have eaten a lot of caribou meat in my time and have never experienced any unpleasant flavour. At any rate Bert and I both made up, to a large extent, for previous deficiencies of meat in our diet, even at the risk of more bad nightmares, and we surely laid in a good stock of the valuable protein.

In the last year or so, we had had quite a lot of meat, rabbit that is. When we came here in 1910, the snowshoe rabbit was almost non-existent, but in the ensuing three years they had increased to millions in number. When they were in small, or moderate quantity, the flesh of these rabbits was excellent but, when they got near to their peak in numbers, they developed different diseases, one of which caused them to have numerous water blisters on their bodies and white specks in their entrails, and it was this disease that made the first inroads into their numbers and started them on the downward path. Then the fur-bearing animals — marten, mink, weasel, fox, coyote, and lynx, which had themselves been increasing rapidly in numbers owing to the increased food supply — steadily depleted the rabbit numbers until they were down again near the point of extinction. Then it was the turn of the fur-bearing animals to suffer. With insufficient food, foxes and coyotes would get mangy, many animals would actually die of starvation, there would be war amongst them for the survival of the fittest, and the Indian and white trappers would take their toll. In this way, the balance of nature was preserved, mostly by Nature herself, as the pendulum swung back and forth.

In the summertime these hordes of rabbits seemed to affect the enormous growth of rank wild vegetation very little and were no problem to us farmers, but, in the winter, they invaded any hay-stacks which were not properly fenced against them and I have seen hard-padded trails, a dozen feet wide, leading to a stack from a willow draw or swamp in which they sheltered in the daytime. At nightfall their advance to the stack sounded like any army on the march, and I suppose it really was just that. In many cases, where they ate right under the stack to the height they could reach, the stack would look like a big mushroom and in some cases, has actually fallen over. That winter, they were in their thousands around our cow and horse barns and, one evening, Bert just stood in his tracks near the barns and shot off a whole box of .22 shells, fifty of them, and getting a rabbit every shot. Undoubtedly, the rabbits which come and feed on the dry hay are already weakened by disease or rapidly get subjected to it by the unsuitable food.

As can readily be imagined, persons who have once seen rabbits decimated by disease in this manner never want to eat another, at least of the snowshoe variety, and I myself have never eaten a single rabbit since that first onslaught of the disease.

As it turned out the caribou meat came at a very opportune time, just as we were quitting the rabbit meat. The caribou were even more useful in the matter of bait for my fox trapping. It was killing two very nice birds with one stone, to get the best meat from the carcass for our own use and use the remains for bait. Oh, yes! I believe I was again transgressing the game law in using game meat for bait, but, I ask you, who would pack horse meat 4,000 feet up the mountain, even if you could get it to the base of the mountain by sleigh on the frozen lake, when there was plenty of the best of bait running around just where you needed it. And it was so much better bait than cold horse-meat, for the smell of the kill soon brought it to the attention of the foxes, and they like nothing better than the "innards" of an animal. Moreover, the legs of the animal were an excellent place to which to fasten the chain of the trap and so, altogether, such bait was about the best ever.

I don't want to give the impression that getting meat and bait was a simple matter. On those wide, bare expanses, it was difficult to get near the animals on a clear, quiet day, for it was so easy to betray your presence by sight, sound, or scent, and so it was mostly a case of choosing a dull, windy, drifting day. I have sometimes killed an animal on such a day, when the temperature was way below zero and, believe me, skinning and dressing it was just about sheer agony. You could manage to skin it with mitts on but, when it came to the disemboweling job, it was hard to decide whether to use mitts or not. If you used them, they got all bloody and wet and so easily froze stiff, and you therefore had cold hands all the rest of the day; if you didn't use the mitts, it was a job to keep your bare hands from freezing;

however, once you finished dressing the animal you could put on your warm, dry mitts, which were leather on the outside and a pair of woollen mitts on the inside. The drifting snow covered your hands and got into the inside of the animal, and, oftentimes, I had to plunge my hands and knife into the warm entrails so as to get warm enough to make a fresh start, and then repeat the process as often as it became necessary. I suppose this sounds like a lot of hardship but, like all things of a similar nature, once it is finished, it is over and done with, and, as soon as I struck out for the cabin, the thought of a big, juicy steak drove all thoughts of it away.

The trapping of fox, in itself, is not simple, for the fox — well, he's foxy, and though I give his cousin, the coyote, top marks for cunning in avoiding traps, the fox comes in a close second. Traps for fox always have to be covered and, on the Dome, the only available covering was snow. On the jaws a piece of paper was carefully placed and then light, dry snow carefully sifted on to it in a thin layer from the blade of the axe. But, on the Dome, this was only half the trouble. Wind and drifting snow occurred practically every day, and the trap had to be placed in a position where the snow would not drift deeply on it but would just skim over it and, at the same time, not blow the trap clear. Even then, the wind could easily change its direction, and that meant trouble.

After the baits were out and the traps set, life became just a daily routine of climbing on to the plateau and roaming all over it to inspect the different sets. But there was always the expectation of seeing a beautiful silver fox in one of the traps, for the fox on the Dome ran to quite a good percentage of silvers.

In speaking of the possible dangers on the mountain, I omitted one very real one — that of snow-blindness. In the warm days of spring, the surface snow melts a little and then freezes and the whole mountaintop resembles one huge, bright mirror. It was at a time like this that I began to notice my eyes acting queerly. Sometimes, I would stand and rest in the hot sun and close my eyes. When I opened them it would seem as if numerous dark shadows flitted past in front of me. Then, at night my eyes would smart as if I had got a bunch of sand in them. This sensation of sand never occurred in the daytime, but in the cabin at night it was really painful. The more I closed my eyes, the worse the pain. It suddenly dawned on me that I was getting snow-blind. I stayed in the cabin for a day to rest my eyes and then always used snow-glasses in bright weather and had no more trouble.

Trapping is looked on by many people as a cruel, heartless occupation, and I am not saying that there is not quite a lot of suffering given to the trapped animals, but it is a case where the bad points are very plain to be seen, whereas, in many other ways of life, the bad points are not so glaring, but are, nevertheless, just as objectionable. Even before so-called civilization hits a country, the creatures of the wild can never be said to have an absolutely carefree life, for the original inhabitants always preyed on them for both food and clothing, and practically every species of animal, bird, insect and fish is continually at war with each other, and they are not exactly over-kind in their methods either. With all wildlife, it is a case of the survival of the fittest. And when left more or less on its own, Nature itself can be very cruel, and the balance of nature brings with it a lot of suffering and misery.

The snowshoe rabbit, of which I have spoken earlier, is a typical case in point. Anyone who has seen the misery of those myriads of sick rabbits cannot maintain that, when left to itself, Nature is always kindly and merciful. The ups and downs in numbers of all creatures automatically brings a lot of suffering, and I believe, that in many cases, the activities of humans in helping to keep a better balance is often beneficial.

We had a real good example of the cruelty of one creature to another in this district a few years ago. Two Forestry officials were watching a huge eagle circling way up in the air like the perfect glider that it is when, suddenly, it plummeted to earth, and then, as suddenly, re-appeared with a small bear cub in its talons, while the mother bear and the remaining cub uttered piercing squeals of mixed rage and terror.

The eagle rose several hundred feet in the air with its prey, and then released it, the cub being instantly killed when it hit the ground. The eagle flew to the top of a dry tree to observe whether everything had gone according to plan and then, later, disposed of the dead cub at will. I have been told since, that this is quite a common practice with eagles and that they are a great menace to small animals, such as young mountain sheep and goats on the bare mountain tops.

With the constant changes in the general economy and the general way of life, trapping is becoming a very spasmodic kind of occupation, partly due to the unsatisfactory financial returns compared to those obtained in other walks of life, and also to the fact that, nowadays, so few men are willing to engage in such a rough, lonely and uncertain lifestyle. Even the present-day Indian engages very little in trapping, especially in areas where other work is available. Who knows? Perhaps this trend towards a virtual cessation in the trapping industry may cause such an increase in some phases of wildlife that Man may be driven to do something about it from a sheer matter of self-preservation.

# 12. The War and a Bride Arrive

The summer of 1914 ran to about the same pattern as the previous summers. Jack returned in early June, having successfully fixed up his matrimonial arrangements, which called for his bride-to-be to come over in the summer of 1915. Necessarily, all time, other than that spent in packing in supplies and in haying, was spent in getting the new house ready. That was quite a job, with the lumber all being whip-sawed and therefore usually not of an even thickness, while the edges all needed a lot of planing. Also, all the floor and ceiling joists and partition uprights had to be hewn out with axes, while Jack made all the windows and doors from our own lumber. Being an excellent carpenter, he made a real fine job of them.

After the house was finished, or at least habitable, a visiting lady neighbour was admiring the large windows and enquired as to how we got them in over the rough trails. Jack told her that we didn't bring them in, but just made them here. "You mean you brought the wood and glass in separately and then fixed them in here?" "No," returned Jack, "we made everything here." "You mean to tell me that you cut down a tree, sawed it into boards and planed them, made all those spars and frames and fixed them together?" "Yes, just that," replied Jack. The lady could handle her tongue quite up to average with the rest of the fair sex, perhaps a little above average, but that really took the wind out of her sails, and she relapsed into contemplative silence for at least a short spell.

Then in August the outbreak of World War I came along to complicate

143

matters. As we were busy haying and never left the farm, while our nearest neighbours lived about ten miles away and had never even been to our place, it was actually six weeks before we learned that war had broken out. When we did hear about it, we were faced with the decision as to what to do about it. Finally, in view of the great deal to be done to fix Jack up for his coming venture into matrimony and to enable him to look after our growing herd of cattle, we decided that, for the time at least, we would stay put. Everyone felt at that time that the War would only last for a short while, and the very meagre news that we got, for we still got no newspapers, didn't give us much information on which to act. So we just kept doggedly on, fixing up things as quickly as we could, with a view to getting Jack settled and in shape to take care of things on his own.

As much of the fixing up could not be done in the deep snow of winter, Bert and I both went trapping on the Dome and had a quite successful season, with no untoward happenings except that, in the early part of winter when the ice on Ootsa Lake was not very thick, as we were walking about twenty yards from shore, we suddenly found ourselves dumped into the lake. Seemingly, we had hit a spot where warm springs had kept the ice thin. Fortunately, the water only came up to our waists and so, after clambering out, it was just a matter of building a big fire and then stripping and drying all our clothes. All of which was no great hardship as it was a lovely day.

That spring as the time was nearing when Safie (Jack's girl) was to sail, the sinking of the *Lusitania* brought a lot of uncertainty into her plans. But after an exchange of cables, which in itself was not easy as our nearest telegraph office was over sixty miles away, it was decided that she should take the chance. Jack went to Montreal to meet her and they were duly married there and, in due course, arrived at Burns Lake station on the newly completed railway. From there on, Safie began to get broken into the rougher side of life in our country. First, fifteen miles by wagon to Francois Lake, followed by a night in an empty cabin, and then a trip of forty miles in a little boat powered with a small outboard motor brought them to Nadina, at the head of Francois Lake. From there, they sent Matthew, the youngest son of our old friend Sam, asking me to bring the horses and some food, especially bread, as early as possible the next day.

The request for bread really put me on the spot. I had not expected them for a few more days, and so I was trying to get our bachelor regime properly wound up before they arrived. The sourdough pot was perhaps the most outstanding part of this regime, and I had made the last batch of bread from it. Packing all your supplies for a number of years for a distance of a hundred and fifty miles tends to make a person very frugal and so, hating to waste any of the accumulated dough, which through the years had formed a thick layer on the inside of the pot, I had scraped off a considerable amount of this layer and mixed it in the batch of bread. Where grub is concerned I have never been a very fussy person and have always been able to eat almost anything, but I must confess that that bread was just about the limit. I believe I did try to wade through it myself, but I just did not dare to place it before the new bride, and so I was up till 2 a.m. baking a batch of baking powder biscuits and a lot of small cakes, which was not difficult as we now had lots of eggs and butter. With this, I dared to make my appearance. I learned later that my cooking really was appreciated.

I think that the highlight of that trip home was to watch the look of wonderment of Safie's face as, bringing up the rear on our little horse Pansy, she watched the pack-horses navigate through the narrow trail, especially the last two miles to the farm. Her two great big trunks were carried by Grey, and I believe that, every moment, she expected to see them smashed to pieces against the trees. But a good pack-horse does not do that kind of thing. I must admit that it was really wonderful to see Grey size up the width of the trail between two trees and gently try to ease his load through. If he found it too narrow, he would back out and find a wider place. In later years Safie often referred to that wonderful display of wisdom on the part of Grey, and I believe we all remembered it, for those two huge trunks really looked like an impossible load for that narrow trail.

At the top of the divide between Francois and Ootsa Lakes we looked down on a most wonderful view which really showed off Safie's new home very splendidly. Down the hill about a mile and a half was the farm and then Ootsa Lake, stretching out to east and west with the Dome to the south of it, while, to the south and west, a glorious view of the Coast Mountains surrounding Whitesail and Eutsuk Lakes showed unbrokenly for forty or fifty miles.

At length, we reached home and, if the apparent isolation facing her struck Safie at all, she certainly never showed it. Right through the years she was a splendid pioneer wife to Jack and a sister to me.

Perhaps here might be a good place to say a few words about those wonderful animals, our pack-horses, for, about this time, their reign, as far as the farming part of the country was concerned, was nearing its end. Gradually roads of a kind were built to serve most areas, and the teams and wagons and sleighs displaced the pack-horses. I don't know from what stock these game little cayuses originated, but I suppose they came from animals brought in by different routes from all over the continent. The Indians were quite well supplied with horses and there were many large pack-trains bringing in supplies for survey parties, mining operations, for stores dotted all around the district, and for many other projects.

The pack-horses used by the settlers usually had quite a nice life, but in the large pack-trains they often suffered considerably, especially as winter approached. From the strain of the summer's work, many of them would be getting weary and thin as the feed was gradually getting less and of less value. Often the last trip would be made so late in the season that early snows came before it was finished. Some horses would just quit through weakness and often died. Their loads would then be added to the loads of the remaining horses and the resultant heavier loads then caused the collapse of others. One packer in the district sometimes "boasted" that he had lost more horses than the rest of the people had owned. Not a very creditable boast but, at least, it was fact.

With the packing season ended, the horses would be put with settlers who made a business of wintering them, but for the greater part of the winter the horses just rustled their own living by pawing in the snow in the stretches of open country until the snow got too deep or too hard-crusted for pawing, at which point they would have to be fed. The horse is often referred to as a patient beast, and this is never shown more than by watching a bunch of horses pawing almost unceasingly for their winter feed.

This may seem like rather cruel treatment after the steady hard work all summer, but in those early days there was plenty of grass everywhere as there were few cattle to graze it off in the summer and, except in bad winters, the horses usually came through in quite good shape.

Our own cayuses were, on the whole, quite a colourful bunch and, like most of the humans in this new country, they all had their distinctive characteristics. Of all our horses of those early days, little bay Romeo was certainly our favourite. When he begged for salt or sugar with his soft, limpid eyes and his fetching little whinny, it would have had to be a man with a heart of stone that could have refused him. He would walk along cheerfully all day with three huindred pounds on his back, as long as the pack was riding comfortably, but if the saddle blanket had a ruffle in it and hurt him, he would invariably walk off into the brush and stand there and refuse to go any further until his pack or blanket was fixed. With it once again in order he would resume his march, cheerful as ever.

Only once did I see Romeo cause any trouble on the trail and that was just after he had got his pack on in Buck Flats when he happened to wander on to a strong wasps' nest. He didn't like the experience and ran away, strewing his pack in all directions.

A fine little puller in harness for his size, Romeo only balked once when he took the notion to lie down in the shafts of our home-made wooden-wheeled cart. As he refused to budge, we tried a treatment of which we had been told previously and, when we poured a jug of water down his nostrils, he jumped up in a hurry and decided to be a good horse in the future.

Billy was not as colourful as Romeo and certainly had not the same winning ways, but he did a lot of good service for us and held up the reputation that Round Lake Tommy gave him, that "He awful strong horse, he all-time pack three hundred pounds of iron." After Billy left us he became the faithful friend and companion of an old prospector at Houston and served many more useful years, though I am sure that he had come of age before he left us, and most certainly had reached years of discretion and wisdom.

Pinto, one of our Bella Coola purchases, had absolutely no eye-appeal, for he was a lanky, raw-boned "critter" and his coat was never bright. His missing eye, which he had lost before we acquired him, also detracted from his appearance and, after trying to use him in harness, we didn't wonder a bit that he was lacking an eye for he would have tried the temper of a saint. We tried him hauling hay in the go-devil, but though he did manage to pull it when empty, with the other horse doing most of the work, after a few forkfuls had been put on it, he would turn his head and look at it and plainly say, "If you put any more on it, I shan't pull it" — and he surely kept his word. The only time I ever saw him make a decent pull was when he stood on top of a wasps' nest and they began paying him attention.

But as a pack-horse Pinto had few peers. When Jack brought in the hay-rake, Pinto had the ten feet main frame stuck length-wise on top of the rest of his pack and, for the whole hundred and fifty miles, he had to walk with his head down so that the frame did not knock out any brains he may have possessed. His missing eye caused him a lot of trouble when crossing a bridge where water showed on both sides. His good eye showed him that there was water on that side, and he tried to keep his rear-end as far as possible from it, and so walked across the bridge in a comical cross-wise manner. Later, when we sold him to a man leaving the district, this trait of his landed him in real trouble for, in crossing a fairly high bridge in the Vanderhoof area, he got his rear-end too far to the offside and fell into the creek below. However, his new owner did discover one gift that he had which we had never suspected, for he said that he was a tireless and easy-riding saddle-horse.

Grey, our other Bella Coola purchase, had all the good looks and colour which were so lacking in Pinto and, with his head held high and a smart step, he made me think of Brigadier Gerard at the head of the Hussars of Conflan, as depicted by Conan Doyle. As a work-horse Grey had his own special ways of being a bad actor. Most cayuses, unless they were in harness steady, reverted somewhat to the wild and almost needed re-breaking after spells of idleness. Grey was a model of good behaviour while being harnessed and hitched up alongside Romeo but, at the command of "Get up, Grey," he really and truly got up, for he immediately turned at right angles and jumped sideways right on to Romeo's back, and down they went in a heap. Fortunately, Romeo never struggled at all, and it was just a case of untangling the mess, only for it to be repeated a second time. This called for action, and so Grey was taken out and tied with a long cinch rope to a conveniently placed willow tree, and chased around for a while with a good willow stick behind him. Then we would cease and say "Alright, Grey, come here," and he would march up to us and, when hitched up again, would give us no trouble at all and pull like a lion.

This was regular routine after every period of idleness and, in the end, we never tried to hitch him up without giving him the run around. It was amusing to see the way in which he wanted to come to us after some chasing around, but we would say "No, you old sinner, you run around a bit more." At the first invitation of "Come, Grey," he would come right up to us and seemed to hold no grudge. Our methods would not be said to conform to the accepted rules of horse-breaking, but the main thing was they worked.

Grey, alas, came to a tragic end. Jack sold him to Matthew, son of our friend Sam, and, one winter, he either fell or jumped from a high rock bluff on the shore of Francois Lake, and the crash on the ice put "finis" to poor old Grey.

I am a great lover of horses, and have had many fine ones in the years since, but I really think that those old cayuses still hold top spot in my memories. But the day of this colourful little animal is now about finished, just as that of his brother, the larger-sized farm workhorse, is also at an end, with the advent of tractors, combines and all other kinds of modern farm machinery. Even to outlying mining operations, where formerly all the freighting was done by pack-horses, this is now done by planes, helicopters, and power boats.

And so, once again, "The old order changeth, giving place to the new." However, in one respect, the horse is more than holding his own for, everywhere, in the towns, villages, and right in the rural areas, increasing use of the horse for riding purposes is in evidence and everywhere riding clubs are springing up, and right in our district, many saddle-horses are being raised.

In the years around the beginning of World War I quite a few new settlers came into the district and all added greatly to the broadening of life here. As usual they mostly consisted of people who could take the rough with the smooth, the only kind of people who are really of much use in a country like ours. Indeed, some showed most unexpectedly to be of that type.

Take, for instance, the mother, two sisters, and girl cousin of Charlie Hinton who came right from London. All of them knew absolutely nothing about life outside a city. "Old Lady Hinton," as the mother was always termed, was well into her sixties when she came, and the journey of over fifty miles from Houston, in a wagon over rough roads, must have been quite a trial for her, for she was of a heavy build and somewhat lame. But she took it like a thoroughbred, as she did, too, the life afterwards, a life that was often far from easy, as, with the completion of the transcontinental railway and the outbreak of war, the whole area experienced a very serious slump.

As I have mentioned previously, one of our biggest problems was getting fresh meat for the table, as game was not very plentiful, and the number of cattle had not yet increased to the point where they were much used for our own personal use. This was quite a hardship for the "Old Lady," for she dearly loved her meat, and she got quite disgusted and scornful when some Nimrod of the district would appear at their home and say that he had seen deer tracks. "Tracks. You can't eat tracks. You can't eat tracks," she would say with disgust, when speaking of it later. Her reaction was predictably similar when others would say that they had "got a shot in." But I think her worst moment came when a visiting bachelor said that he would bring them some "lamb's quarters" when next he came. Her hopes soared at the thought of lamb, but picture her disgust when "lamb's quarters" turned out to be a common pig-weed often used as greens in those early days before gardens were well established.

Altogether, especially considering her age, physical condition, and previous background, the "Old Lady" was quite wonderful and lived till over eighty years old, one of the real personalities of the district.

Charlie married the cousin, while the two daughters soon also married, one to a Norwegian to become Mrs. Anderson, and the other, Beatrice, to Billy Rist, an Englishman. Both turned out to be good farm-wives and also a great help in the life of the community, as they were both very musical.

The biggest boost to the population, however, was the arrival of Mr. and Mrs. Harrison with eleven of their twelve children, ranging in age from just over twenty down to babies. This influx of "young men and maidens" naturally gave community life quite a shot in the arm, especially as the "Old Man," as he was always known, was a real wizard with the violin and cello, and one of the sons, Clifford, followed in his father's musical footsteps.

At this period, public utilities began to appear in the district. A Post Office had been established at Ootsa Lake a year or two previously and now, with our rising population, Wistaria also got a Post Office in 1916, with mail coming in once a week from Burns Lake. Incidentally, this is how Wistaria got its name. Our old friend, Bob Nelson, was chosen to be Postmaster, and the Post Office Inspector wrote to get a suggested name for the new office. The settlers in the vicinity had always spoken of being in the "Banana Belt" because that area was less subject to summer frosts than most other parts of the district, and so Bob sent in the name "Banana." The Inspector refused to consider what he termed "such a ridiculous name" and said that the name could be either "Wistaria," a nice flower name, or "Eversly," a good old English village name. And so became Wistaria.

Later another Post Office was established between Wistaria and Ootsa Lake and, as this was in the vicinity where the Hinton family lived, it was named Streatham, in memory of their old home in London.

The arrival of the large Harrison family soon brought another utility, for thought had to be given to educating the young generation. So in 1917 a school was started with the elder of the Hinton girls as school mistress. In this connection it is interesting to note that, although Wistaria was the community farthest from the railway, it was the first to get a school, even before our railway point at Burns Lake.

That first school was not a very pretentious affair, for it was just a little, unused bachelor's cabin, which had to serve as both school and as residence for the teacher. It was certainly rather of the rough and tough type, but in the minds of many people, the thought persists that present-day school buildings have swung to the other extreme, with almost palatial-type buildings. They also further sometimes wonder whether present-day education is really very far ahead of that obtained in the early days in the little country "Red School House," especially when considering the enormous difference in expense.

That first little school house is also noteworthy for another first, for, one evening the school mistress looked out of the little cabin window to see a huge black wolf gazing back at her at close range. I'll bet that Florence Hinton's thoughts flew back to the tale of "Little Red Riding Hood." That was the first wolf ever seen by settlers in the district, but in the years since, we have had lots of them.

Still thinking of colourful newcomers, I think that Max Enter rates mention. Max was a big "skookum" German-American who had worked in many parts of the world, notably in Siam and Malaya and the Yukon, mostly in gold-dredging work. But when Max got to our "neck of the woods," he really did nothing in particular and just got by with as little work as possible, and in a frontier country, a bachelor can do this on very little money or work. Max was notable for one habit; his cabin was on the south shore of the lake and he made a practice of having a morning dip in the lake any time that it was free of ice, however cold the weather.

As events proved, the lake was to play quite a big part in Max's life. Years later, when the outboard motor came into use, Max was on the lake in a small boat and in careless moving to get more gas, he upset and swamped the boat, which, however, still kept afloat with the engine-end deep in the water. Clinging to it, Max let out some real roars for help, and he could surely roar. Ted Lewis, an old British Navy man, heard his cries and went to his help in the only boat he had, a real light canoe. Ted knew the capabilities of that canoe and when he got a little way from Max, he stood off and said to him, "Now look here, Max, if you try to get into this canoe it is bound to capsize and we'll both be in the drink and it will be the finish for both of us. You can hold on to the canoe and I will tow you to shore, but the first move you make to get into the boat, I'll brain you with this paddle." Max knew that this was common sense and promised to be a good boy and, in due course, they safely reached shore. By this time, Max was just about chilled right through and helpless. Fortunately another old-timer, Johnny Barker was now on hand, and he and Ted built a huge fire and finally got Max unchilled and his circulation restored.

But evidently the lake was determined to get Max and get him it did. He had to cross it to get mail and supplies at Ootsa Lake Settlement and in the spring and fall when the ice conditions were very poor, this crossing was often quite hazardous. Max kept some heavy-built dogs which he used to pull a sleigh across the ice and, on his last trip, he evidently ventured before the ice was safe. Later, his sleigh and dogs were frozen in the ice, but the lake had claimed Max for its own, and no trace of him was ever found.

These have been just a few incidents in the lives of some of our neighbours, but I am sure that very similar stories could be written about almost all the people who came to settle in our country, for the general type of persons lent itself to lives of colour. It was during this period that our philosopher friend, Kelly, gave a very trite answer to a man who was travelling through the country with a view to settling here. The man asked Kelly how long he had been here, and when Kelly told him about ten years, the man said, "Ten years! What in heck have you been doing all that time?" "I'll tell you," said Kelly. "We've been building roads for guys like you to come in on." This was very true, not only as to building actual roads but also in building up the country into such a general condition that persons of that type might be willing to make their home here.

# 13. A Terrible Winter and then the Army

As the winter of 1915 - 16 approached, Bert and I decided that if the war was not ended by spring, we would join up, since, by then, Jack and Safie should be in a condition to get along by themselves. The winter started very nicely and was quite unusually mild up to Christmas but, after that, we had the worst spell of cold weather that has ever been known in this country. For six weeks it was 20 below zero during the day and 40 below at night. If the days are sunny and there is no wind, such temperatures are not too awful, but during this spell we seldom saw the sun, while there was a nasty, persistent east wind with light, floury snow in the air all the time.

Jack's new house was not yet fixed up to withstand such weather and I feel sure that Safie must have felt that this was some country to come to; but if she did, she never showed it. Such weather is bad enough where there is plenty of forest protection from the wind, but it is almost past imagining what it is like another 4,000 feet in the air, and on the absolutely bare mountain plateau. Our trapping cabins were, of course, in the timber, but we had to try to get up on that bare mountain plateau every day. I say try for that was about all it amounted to on most days during that spell. We would start out and get some little way on to that bare mountain and then, almost unconsciously, we would look at each other as if to say "What about it." Without further ado, we would turn around and get back to the cabin with all possible speed. I cannot say that we went back to the warmth of the cabin for there was very little warmth even there in that bitter cold, and I well remember that cups of tea placed right under the stove would get ice on them in a short time.

When at length a half-decent day came along it nearly brought tragedy with it. It was still just as cold as ever, but there was not so much wind. As we were nearly out of meat, we both went up to the bare mountain to see if we could get a caribou. After a few miles we separated to hunt in different directions. I was successful in getting a caribou but by the time I had dressed it, it was getting quite dark. It was too late to try and take out any of the meat, so I just took the heart and liver and started for home.

Almost immediately, disaster struck. The snow in many places on the mountain is blown by the fierce winds into rough, hard, uneven surfaces and in the dusk I stepped with the front and back parts of my snowshoe on hard snow, but with nothing under the middle of the shoe. The result was that both frames of the shoe snapped right in two, just in front of the front crossbar. It was almost impossible to use that shoe. Then, to make matters worse, the two cross-bars of the other snowshoe came out of their sockets so that the side-frames just flopped together. As most of the snow on the mountain is packed very hard, I tried to walk afoot, without the shoes, but the route I had to go was along a slight slope and the wind, which had now risen considerably, blew me over every few steps. Finally, I had to wear the shoe with the crossbars out and carry the other one, but it was just a case of hobbling along.

Another danger was that I had to cross a gully which divided parts of the mountain and, if I struck it too far to the west, I would fall over a straight drop of fifty to one hundred feet. Fortunately, the stars were showing and I was able to get my direction from them. Luck favoured me for I struck the gully in the right place. But I was still several miles from where my route hit timberline and so, as there was a little timber a short way down the gully, I decided to sit out the night. In the gully the snow was both soft and deep, so I had to wear both my snowshoes, and it took me over an hour to go a little more than a hundred yards till I found a dry tree. That night was not exactly a picnic but, with the heart and the liver which I toasted, I did not do too badly.

In the morning the wind and cold were still quite bad, and I was only saved, I think, by the fact that I had made myself a new canvas parka and was wearing it for the first time that day. This parka, drawn tight around my face, sheltered it from the wind and cold but, even with it, I could not face the wind directly and had to adopt a tacking process. At last about 2:30 p.m. I reached the cabin but found no Bert there. Off the mountain as there had been no new snow for several days, the snowshoe trail was padded hard and so I could not tell whether Bert had come home to the cabin and gone off again either to our second cabin or to hunt ptarmigan along some alpine meadows inside timberline. However, I had noticed a new trail branching off our main trail as it crossed the meadows, seeming to come from the direction of the mountain.

In the cabin the ashes in the stove were quite cold and the sourdough pot was frozen solid, as if it had not been used that morning, and the supply of kindling seemed to be untouched. By the time I had cooked a meal and eaten, it was getting too late to do anything that night, which made it two full days since we had set out.

Very fortunately Bert had just completed a nice new pair of snowshoes and, when he did not show up that night, I got away before daylight next morning, taking with me some food and a small can in which to make tea, if necessary. I branched off along the new trail which I had noticed and, for quite a while, I couldn't tell whether anything was wrong or not. He had steered nicely between trees and seemed to have no trouble when crossing wind-falls, so that I did not think he was snow-blind.

However, after a while I found that Bert was going in circles, and then was sure that something was wrong. I was travelling just as fast as I could and, of course, I was now able to cut off a lot of distance and I didn't have to follow his circles, but followed where he had crossed his own trail. Meantime, I was hollering at the top of my voice and believe me, I can really holler. Bert's steps were steadily getting shorter and shorter and, finally, he was only moving by about two or three inches at each step. At last at about 10:30 a.m. I got an answer to my "Coo-hoo"; you can imagine my immense relief. At first Bert seemed quite okay and I suggested that we make a fire and have some tea and something to eat. But before we came to a dry tree with which to make a fire he showed that he was becoming a little light-headed, as he saw several things on the trail which were not there. Once he asked, "What's in that trap — a lynx?" and at another place he thought he saw a bush-rat in a trap, and once he asked who lived in a cabin he could see. And so, as we were really not a great distance from our cabin, I decided that, if at all possible, we would try to get there before stopping. He seemed to have plenty of strength and, with me breaking the trail, the going was not too difficult for him.

About noon, we reached the cabin safely and soon had a meal cooked, though I did not encourage him to eat too much for his first meal in his weakened condition, for he had been walking for two and a half days in the bitter cold without food. Bert surely talked in his sleep that night, but the next morning he seemed quite okay, and I believe he could have gone out on his usual round. However, we stayed in the cabin and, in going over his ordeal, we found that it was after he crossed the gully where I spent the night that trouble struck him. It was the same stretch where I found the wind so bad on the second day that I had to tack so as not to meet it right head-on. The bitter wind had whipped the snow up into his face, like sand in a sand-storm, and as he had no parka he got the full force of it and gradually he found his sight going misty. One of his eyes was in poor shape anyway, for when we were boys together in England and were hunting birds with stones, one of us on each side of the hedge, one of my stones had struck him in his right eye and the sight in it was never very good afterwards. He certainly had no symptoms of snow-blindness and so we concluded that the intense cold and driving snow had chilled the filaments of his eyes and thus affected his sight.

On the sloping mountainside the fierce wind had blown him over and he had lost his axe from his haversack in the fall and later he'd lost one of his mitts and had to wrap that hand in a pair of overalls he had with him, as we always carried them to use as emergency pack-sacks. With the loss of his axe, he couldn't light a fire and so had to keep on walking. It was just unfortunate that he got off our regular trail for it was well-beaten and at that point he was but half a mile from the cabin.

Altogether, the only damage Bert suffered from his ordeal were two large blisters on the back of his hands as a result of frostbite, and even these healed very quickly. His eyesight became quite normal again the following day, and on the next day, he made the trip home by himself to get a new axe and mitten. He had packed his heavy 30.40 rifle all those two and a half days and I can never understand how he did not collapse. I feel sure that I would have done so.

All in all that winter was by no means a success, and the cold made it miserable for both trapper and farmer alike. However, in due course, spring came along with its warm weather. The worst thoughts of that 1915 - 16 winter soon faded, though it has always stood out in our memory as the worst ever. Later when we received letters from old school friends living near Red Deer in Alberta and learned that, in the same cold spell there, it had been 40 below in the daytime and 60 below at night, with the wind seeming to blow right through the walls of their home, we felt that we had been almost kindly treated.

In later years we learned that we people in the northern part of the province were not the only ones to suffer in that cold winter, for all the Lower Mainland and Vancouver Island had been equally hard hit. Temperatures had, of course, not been nearly so low as with us, but had at times almost reached zero, which is mighty cold for that area.

What they lacked in cold they made up for in snow, of which they had several feet which stayed with them for most of the six weeks.

As soon as we came off the mountain Bert walked out the seventy-five miles to Telkwa with the intention of joining the Army. I stayed behind since I had still about a month's work to fix Jack up with the necessary fences. Soon Bert returned, a very disappointed man, for the doctor refused to pass him for the Army because of his injured right eye, mentioned previously. The irony of the thing was that a year later the Army conscripted him in spite of his eye, though it had refused him as a volunteer.

We got the younger of the Blackwell boys to help me with the fencing and, when it was completed, he and I walked out the forty-five miles to Houston in one day and, as there was no train that day we walked the thirty miles along the railway track to Telkwa. As there was now no doctor at Telkwa, Alan and I had to go to Hazelton by train the following day. Alan passed his examination without any trouble but when I came before Dr. Wrinch he wanted to turn me down for flat feet. I asked him what flat feet implied as regard as soldier. "Why," said he, "you can't march." "I may not be able to march," said I, "but I walked the forty-five miles to Houston over a rough, muddy road in twenty-five hours." "Yes," said he, "but you couldn't move the next day." "Maybe," said I, "but I walked thirty miles along the track to Telkwa that day and I will take an eighty pound pack on my back and walk up the Bulkley Valley against any man  you like to choose." "Well," said the Doc, "if that is the way you feel about it, I guess I had better pass you." He did give me one good mark when he said that I had the biggest chest expansion of anyone he had examined, a condition which was probably brought on by about six weeks of steady axe work in our fencing effort. As regards my flat feet, I think that they had probably been brought on by several winters of constant snowshoeing wearing moccasins which, of course, have no heels, and I remember that most of the old-time Indians, who wore moccasins most of the time, seemed to be quite flat-footed. In my three years in the Army I never had the slightest trouble with my feet.

After enlistment we went by train to Prince Rupert and then by boat to Victoria, where we were enrolled in the 103rd Battalion and became one of the "P.B.I.'s." We got to Victoria one Sunday and a week later we were on the move, by boat, train, and boat to England, as the battalion was up to full strength and ready for overseas. As a result, we saw very little of Victoria since most of our week was taken up with inoculations and other routine affairs.

Having arrived at Halifax, we embarked on the huge liner *Olympic,* together with several other battalions — altogether about 10,000 of us. We would have made a fine prize for a German submarine. All went well till we got to the north shore of Ireland, when a dense fog settled around us, our speed was reduced, and we were anything but happy when the ship's fog-horn kept letting out loud blasts, as if to advertise our presence to any sub in the vicinity. That was my birthday, July 29th, and I can truthfully say that it was the most worrying birthday I ever spent. Then about 6:00 p.m. when we were said to be in the vicinity of Belfast, the fog suddenly lifted and, just as suddenly the huge ship turned rapidly completely around and we went round the south coast of Ireland and reached Liverpool safely the next day. "Dame Rumour" said that the reason for our sudden about-turn was because the captain got word that a German sub was waiting for us on the northern route. Well, if this was so, our change of direction certainly paid off, and I am sure we were all willing to take the chance of German bullets in the future, rather than a torpedo and probable drowning right then.

It took very little time after we docked for all the 10,000 troops to disembark and to be whisked away in waiting trains. As usual, the Canadian-born soldiers were inclined to ridicule the tiny British railway carriages and, even more so, the engine with its little "peep-peep" of a whistle. And I must confess that, after the large, roomy Canadian carriages with no partitions in them, the British carriages did seem a trifle small and cramped; and the huge Canadian engines with their hoarse, raucous whistles made the British engines seem like little toys. But when we glided out of the Dockside station, with never a jolt or a tremor, opinions began to change rapidly. "Why, we're moving," said the astonished Canadian boys, and I must admit that we British-born men felt that we were getting a little bit of our own back when we said, "Why, sure we are. You don't expect to be jolted out of your seat like you used to be back home, did you?" And as we progressed on our journey, the smoothness and speed of the train further impressed them. Of course, one couldn't expect the newly-built Canadian lines to have the same well-settled roadbeds as the British railways, for such things only come after years of use, work, and improvement. Now, after being back in Canada for over forty years, one finds that the Canadian railway tracks are showing great improvement with age.

We had no idea where our destination was to be, but eventually, we de-trained at Liphook, a little station on the border of Hampshire and Surrey, and marched to a small tent camp at Oxney. Here we stayed about a week and then went to Bramshott into the lines recently vacated by the 4th Canadian Division, which had left for France and was just in time to take part in the First Battle of the Somme, after first doing a stretch in the Ypres salient.

As soon as the Battalion was well-settled in its quarters we all got "landing leave" in relays, and for most of us old-country boys, it meant seeing, once again, our old homes, parents, relatives and friends. And it is a pretty safe bet that a great many of us would never have got home on a trip if we had not joined the Army. For the Canadian-born boys, it mostly meant a trip to London unless they had relatives somewhere in the country.

As I had only been away in Canada for eight years, things had really not changed very much for me, though, of course, Dad and Mother, who were both in their sixties, had aged somewhat. Our little village, with its three or four acres of green with eight big elm trees dotted around on it and surrounded by the houses of the village, was still the same quiet little spot as of old. Incidentally, I may add that when my nephew, Cyril, who was over during World War II, visited it, he thought that Evenley was the prettiest village he saw in England.

Back at camp life was just routine training but in the evenings most of the troops spread themselves into the various towns and villages in the neighbourhood. Most went into Hazelmere, which is one of the prettiest little towns imaginable, while the lovely sunken road with its covering of beautiful overhanging trees, which led from the camp to Hazelmere, was a veritable "Lover's Lane." But, like most pleasant things, our nice home did not last too long. Losses on the Somme called for reinforcements for the four Divisions already serving in France, and soon A and B Companies were sent on draft to another B.C. Battalion, the 29th, while the remaining two companies were sent to Seaford, on the Sussex coast, to form part of the First Reserve, which was to supply reinforcements to B.C. units already in France.

Though many parts of Sussex are beautiful, I can't say that the bare rolling hills of the South Downs impressed me at all favourably, but then we were not tourists but soldiers. Anyway, about half of the remaining two companies soon went to reinforce the 2nd C.M.R.'s, my friend Alan Blackwell being on this draft and after this, I saw very little of him. By this time Christmas was coming along and, with it, Christmas leave. I had been given a stripe and I and another lance-jack were given passes but, unfortunately, some of our sergeants developed measles and all the sergeants were quarantined. Consequently, their duties fell on us corporals, and Rogers, our Orderly Room clerk, said that either Cookson or myself had to stay on as Orderly Sergeant. I said that I would toss Cookson for it, but Rogers said, "Toss be d---," and tore up Cookson's pass. So, once more, I got home and had a real pleasant Christmas among all our old friends around Evenley.

About a month later, on February 7th, our turn to go to France came along, and going by train to Southampton and then by a tiny pleasure-steamer, we arrived at Le Havre after a very rough crossing during which everyone was seasick except myself and one other man. Why I wasn't sick, I can't imagine for I am not naturally a good sailor.

On landing we had our first experience of marching to the sound of the bagpipes and everyone appreciate the nice steady step set by the pipes. The music seemed to almost pull one along and, on that steady, long climb to the hill tent camp at Le Havre, through which hundreds of thousands of troops must have passed, one needed all the help that one could get. February is seldom a very dry month and, from the state of that tent camp, this particular February was not a bit dry, for the mud was terrible and tents and mud do not make a very good mixture — and at this season of the year, tent-dwelling is not exactly cozy.

However, we did not have to suffer long in that mud for the next day we were introduced to our first ride in the French railway box-cars, on all of which was printed "Huit cheveaux, quarante hommes." After a slow journey, we de-trained at a small station several miles back of Vimy Ridge and were marched to a little village of which we were to see a great deal in the future — Gouy Servins, where we were housed in a bunch of farm buildings with a mixed crowd of reinforcements for the 11th Infantry Brigade. Our stay in the back area did not last very long, for a rather disastrous raid on March 1st, in which our gas was supposed to make things easy for our men but did not do so owing to a change in the direction of the wind just before our attack was launched, caused many casualties. Our colonel, Kemball, was killed as he led the attack, together with several other officers and losses were very heavy amongst O.R.'s. Colonel Kemball was not supposed to actually lead the attack but, when the change of wind took place before zero hour, and no orders came to cancel the attack, he felt that he just had to go over with his men on what he knew was almost bound to be a suicidal attack.

As a result, all we reinforcements were rushed in to fill the gaps in the ranks, and so we were in time for the successful attack on and capture of Vimy Ridge on the 9th of April. As it turned out, I did not actually go over the top in the attack for, on the previous day, I was put on a Brigade Hot Ration party, whose duty was to carry big containers of hot soup to the troops during the night after the attack. I did not exactly fall in love with the weather in this part of France on that memorable night, for it snowed bigger, wetter, and faster snowflakes than I have ever seen it do in Canada, and it must have been a very miserable night for any wounded men who could not go out under their own steam.

The next morning we were put into a battlefield clearing party, not a very pleasant job, for I had to help bury many of my old comrades of the 103rd Battalion. I neglected to say previously that in all drafts over from England, all N.C.O.'s were required to throw in their stripes and revert to the rank of Private, a very proper procedure, for it would have been ridiculous for soldiers with only parade and training-ground experience, to go into the line and give orders to men who had had many months of actual honest-to-goodness fighting experience. And so, I was a Private once more. One other thing which I believe I have neglected to mention is that the battalion to which I was sent, and in which I served all my time in the Army, was the 54th Battalion, which was raised originally in the Kootenays.

The summer following the capture of the Ridge was really as pleasant as one could expect under the circumstances. On active service there are always the odd bad spots, but we had quite a few pleasant rest periods interspersed between spells in the line and the frequent working parties at night. When we were in support, I never got to really welcome the cry in the billets by the Orderly-Sergeant, "Everybody for working party tonight," for the work usually consisted of digging new trenches in fairly advanced positions. At one time I held the erroneous idea that the Engineers did most of the trench-digging, but I soon discovered that a goodly portion of that work fell to the P.B.I.'s, especially in the forward areas. True, the Engineers did take part in those parties, for as we passed a certain spot in our journey up to the work area, Engineers were there to present every man with a shovel and every third man with a pick.

However, in the main, those working parties were to be preferred to continuous spells in the front line, and were certainly not as dangerous, though at times we were subjected to some pretty heavy strafing. One such was my very first effort, digging jump-off trenches for the Vimy show. But it is very remarkable how very few casualties are suffered in such a strafing if you are only given enough time to dig a hole deep enough to enable you to crouch below the surface of the ground before the strafing begins. There would be lots of mud flying, but it has almost to be a direct hit to get you.

I am not wishing to give the impression that the Engineers did none of the hard and dangerous work, for that would be grossly unfair, but only that the Infantry did their full share of such work. However, I believe that, from the point of view of general morale, the working parties were really preferable to sitting around and wondering what the next spell in the line would be like. The rest periods back of the line were the really pleasant spells and were mostly spent in small French villages. Ourton, Houdain, Villers-au-bois, Bouvigny, Coupigny, Noeux-les-mines and Camblain l'Abbe are villages that stick in my memory, with Ourton holding first place, for the Battalion had repeat spells there and the men of the "Cinquante Quatre" were warmly welcomed by the people and looked upon as old friends.

Sports were widely indulged in and we had good baseball and soccer teams, and even the "Physical Jerks" periods were livened by games in which we behaved like a bunch of school kids. All-in-all, that summer in front of Lens was a very pleasant one with, of course, the odd tough periods.

One day we had been showing ourselves too much in the streets of battered Cite de Riaumont and, as a consequence, got a real dose of heavy stuff from the German gunners. Three of us got buried under a pile of bricks, mortar, and tiles when the house in which we were billeted got a direct hit — but we were dug out and suffered nothing more than a temporary jolt to the nerves.

In August, I was given a couple of stripes and, soon after, another one as Lance-sergeant. In the fall preparations were being made for the attack on Lens but, suddenly, all these plans were dropped in early October and we were shifted up to the Passchendaele front where we put in three weeks of what was about the dirtiest period during my stay in France and Belgium. The mud was the worst ever and the actual fighting was nothing to write home about. But very little actual fighting was done by our Battalion as we had a fine record for good work on working parties, so that most of our time was spent in packing bathmats and laying them over interminable stretches of shell-holes filled with water. None of us was at all sorry to get back to the Lens front, after a rest spell at Ourton.

About this time, our Company Sergeant-Major left to go to England on an Officers' Training Course and, though I was only a Lance-sergeant, I was made C.S.M. and, right here, I must pay tribute to all the Sergeants and other N.C.O.'s in the Company for the loyal support they gave me when it could easily have been very different, in view of the fact that I had gone up from Private to Sergeant-Major in just over three months.

I had another stroke of luck as we were preparing to move up into the line, for suddenly out of the blue, I received orders to get ready to go on leave to "Blighty," and that meant that I should have another Christmas at home. It was touch and go whether I made it, but my train from London arrived at our railway station at Brackley about 10:00 p.m. on Christmas Eve, and after a two-mile walk, I reached home once more. As soon as I rang the doorbell, Dad's head popped out of the bedroom window and, without a word to me, he turned to mother and said, "It's him."

All this was very nice for the bunch of us who were in this batch but, picture to yourselves the position of the men in the previous batch for they were due to leave Victoria Station on their return to France on Christmas Eve. Was it any wonder that about forty of these over-stayed their leave by two or three days? Put yourself in their place! But their reception back at the Battalion was not exactly warm, and the result was that they were all lined up in a long row in front of the Colonel, who dealt with them in a pretty summary manner. All N.C.O.'s were reduced to the ranks, but there was one fortunate exception. Our oldest, and perhaps our best Sergeant, had over-stayed his leave by two or three days, just like the others, and the date-stamp on his pass showed the fact. By some quirk of fortune, however, his trip back to the Battalion was made in record time, and he got back at the same time as the men who had not over-stayed. When our Second-in-command of the Company said to him how glad he was that he was back on time, our good Sergeant said, "But my pass is stamped three days late at Victoria Station." "Well," came the reply, "I think you had better lose your pass." And that course of action prevented us from losing our best Sergeant. And here I must confess that the newly-appointed C.S.M. very nearly over-stayed his leave by a day and it was only the fact that a letter asking for a date failed to arrive, that saved his bacon.

The early months of 1918 went by in normal fashion on the front line — support reserve, and rest. And then in late February I was sent on a course at the First Army School at Hardelot near Boulogne. However, we had hardly got settled there when the Germans started their big push against the Fifth Army, and all courses were cancelled and we were rushed back to our battalions.

We went in at once on the Oppy front but, as luck would have it, it was one of the quietest spells in the line that we ever had, for though the fighting here had been very heavy, the London Scottish, the Kensingtons and Cheshires, whom we relieved, had so completely knocked the stuffing out of 'Fritz' that there was not a kick left in him. But these three battalions had suffered heavily and looked a weary, played-out bunch. However, by the amount of work done by parties of Germans in recovering their killed and wounded during our spell there, their losses must have been enormous.

After the heavy German push was at last stopped, the Canadian Corps was taken out of the line for an extended period of rest and intensive training, ready for the Allied offensive, which was scheduled for the fall. Before this offensive started, I was again sent down to the First Army School to complete the course from which I had been whisked away in March. What made this course specially nice was the fact that we were mixed in with Warrant Officers and N.C.O.'s from all the different Canadian battalions and also from all the British battalions in the First Army.

When we got back to the line we found matters changed very much for the better, for the Battle of Amiens, which commenced on August 8th, had given us one of the greatest advances of the whole war and was the commencement of the open warfare-type of fighting, while the old type, with only very limited objectives, obtained with very heavy casualties, seemed to get us nowhere. I know that after the Vimy battle, many of us buck Private strategists felt that the gains were too limited and that, while the Germans were on the run they should have been kept that way. The statements of wounded prisoners that we took from the dug-outs at the base of the Ridge strongly confirmed this, for they said their forces were absolutely disorganized and most of their officers put out of action. From the top of the Ridge the country leading to Lens looked really flat and inviting for open warfare, but I suppose that at this time the Allies had not sufficient reserves to warrant such action. I guess that it took the great push of the Germans against the Fifth Army to show us what results such type of warfare could obtain.

Whenever I think of the Fifth Army retreat, I always remember what a young Englishman, whom I met in Canada some years later, said about it. "When we were training in England, the sergeants all told us that a British soldier never ran away," said he, "but when I reached the Fifth Army at the beginning of the German push, we never stopped running for six weeks."

It was no easy matter getting back to our battalion as the Canadians were now on a totally different front and we found ourselves in a conglomeration of men from almost every unit in the Canadian Corps — men who had been on leave, at Army courses like myself, men from hospital, and men who had been away from their units for a dozen or so other reasons. We were a merry bunch, for we had been away from the stress and strain of frontline work for different lengths of time; it was summertime, the weather was lovely, and the camp was in very pleasant surroundings. Needless to say, the "Crown and Anchor" games were running full blast.

However, a few of us from the 54th managed to jump a ride in a truck to the vicinity of our battalion. It was a most exhilarating ride through Amiens and the country beyond it, and perhaps the nicest sight of all was the huge "Park" of captured German artillery, right at Amiens.

Our first contact with the Battalion was when we happened upon a bunch of wounded, lying in the yard of a small country chateau, turned into a dressing station, where we found wounded from our own company and learned of the loss of many of our old friends, and of the treacherous shooting in the back of our Company Commander by a German prisoner who was being passed to the rear. Needless to say, that German did not last long as a prisoner, but I am happy to say that our Captain survived.

The Amiens battle was the first in which tanks were used in quantity, and some of our men, detailed to form part of the crews, did not report too happy a time in them.

Not very long after rejoining the Battalion, it was moved very secretly to another front and, in the later stages, all the moves were made at night, the daylight hours being spent in the cover of thick woods. Finally, we found ourselves on the Arras front and, on September 2nd, we took part in the attack on the Drocourt-Queant line. Here, it was that I got my "Blighty," in the shape of a bullet through my left shoulder. Personally I could never quite understand how anyone survived at all in an attack of this kind, for it was over dead-level country with the enemy in trenches firing all the machine-gun bullets they could at us, not forgetting the numerous shells dropping around us. The ground resembled a hail-storm, as the bullets hit all around us and, I suppose, it really was a hail-storm, only the hail was bullets.

The reason any of us got through was, I think, because the enemy were getting peppered by our fire just as much as we were by theirs. Besides the fire of us actual attackers, they were subjected to a very heavy artillery barrage and also by a steady machine-gun barrage from our Brigade machine-guns. Naturally, we were the better targets but all the same, their heads as they popped up above the parapet to fire at us, made quite excellent targets. It seems strange that, in an attack of this kind, one has no feeling of fear. I suppose it is that you are in it and have a job to do and there is no time to be scared, and it certainly wouldn't help any if you were.

Walking off the field wounded laid me open to be plugged a hundred times, but I suppose the enemy were too occupied with the actual attackers and I reached the trench where a temporary dressing station had been established and was also able to help our Captain, who had got a bullet in his thigh, to reach it also. Then followed a long walk to the Field Dressing Station, along paths marked "Walking wounded." I have said that one felt no fear in the actual attack but, in this walk, I must say that I did not feel particularly happy when walking underneath our Observation Balloons which 'Fritz' was strafing with big "coal boxes," with the shrapnel dropping all around like hail.

Finally, I arrived at the Field Ambulance and, after one night there, I landed up at a General Hospital in Boulogne. On September 6th, I reached the Lord Derby War Hospital in Warrington and thus ended my actual war experience, for the Armistice arrived long before I was fit for service again. I imagine that Mother echoed the feelings of untold thousands of mothers when she wrote to my sister and said, "You will be glad to know that Arthur is safely wounded."

Now that my days of actual fighting were over, perhaps it is a good time to give my general impressions of the Canadian Army in World War I, of the officers and men with whom I was associated, and of Army life in general. As regards the Canadian Army, I don't think there was a finer bunch of soldiers anywhere, and I believe it is an established fact that the Canadian troops after being once properly established never gave up any ground.

The 54th Kootenay Battalion was very much a western battalion, with a large population of its men consisting of either Canadians from the East who had come to the West or men who had come to Canada from Britain and Europe in the big wave of immigration during the early 1900's, together with the younger men who had been born in the West, and also a goodly sprinkling of adventurous Americans. Generally speaking, they were men who had led a more or less tough life, and so could take the rough with the smooth. They were an interesting bunch to be among for they were of the "hail-fellow-well-met" type and easy to get along with.

After a while, we got a lot of reinforcements from Ontario, since British Columbia had raised more battalions than it could keep up to strength and replace casualties. The difference between the two types could be best summed up by saying that they were Easterners and we were Westerners; they were mostly from old-established communities, and we were mostly of the wandering type. I must say that we Westerners were highly amused at a little incident that occurred as we moved up to the Passchendaele front from the Lens front, soon after the first Ontario boys joined us.

Some of the Ontario men grumbled a little when we had to march most of the way and thought we should be moved by bus. Colonel Carey happened to hear of this and, when we arrived at Ypres, he had all the Ontario men lined up and gave them a talking-to. He told them that he had heard of their complaints, that he didn't expect them to come up to the standard of the Western men, but he wished them to remember that they were now in a Western battalion and to try and come as near to that standard as possible. I think that was about the only time when the Colonel was not exactly popular with some of his men. Suffice to say that those men from around Hamilton turned out to be very fine soldiers and also good fellows in every way.

But Colonel Carey was too fine a Colonel for any resentment to last very long. He seemed to have no fear at all and I well remember one night when we were on a working party, digging trenches in the ruins of a French village. Picks and shovels make quite a clatter when used in such material and I think that I can say that we were all a trifle jittery. The Colonel must have sensed it for he came along as we were working, walked right along the top of the parapet we were throwing up, and said, "Now men, you don't need to worry at all tonight, for 'Fritz' is not going to do any dirty work. Don't whisper," he continued in a sibilant whisper, "they can hear you a lot better if you whisper (and then in a loud voice) than if you talk out loud." You just could not feel jittery any longer with your Colonel acting like that. His whole behaviour was like that, and he could overlook a lot of faults in a man if that man was a good soldier.

After one spell in the line we moved back to Camblain l'Abbe for a rest period, and one of our men, MacIvor, just disappeared for two or three days. When brought up before the Colonel, MacIvor was asked what he had to say for himself. "Well, Sir, when we came into the camp I felt awful tired, and I just went into the brush and lay down and went to sleep, and I didn't wake up for all that time." Now MacIvor had been in the Colonel's Company when they were in the 67th Battalion before it was broken up and one Company sent to the 54th, and the Colonel knew that Mac was a mighty good little soldier, and we knew it too. "Well, MacIvor, don't be doing such a thing again, but we will take your word for it this time. Case dismissed." MacIvor did not do it again, and remained the good soldier that he was, whereas harsh treatment, though quite justified in such a case of A.W.O.L., could have easily turned him into a poor soldier.

Taken as a whole, our officers were a real good bunch and were not a bit hard to work under. Naturally, there were a few misfits, but these just usually disappeared. One of our best-liked officers, Captain D.A. McQuarrie, when badly wounded, was given six months sick leave in Canada, but, after three months at home, he told his father that he was going back to the boys, that the bunch left over here were just not worth being with. And so, Tommy, as he was known by his men, came back and, to the grief of everyone, was killed in action in the last few months of the war. The shell that killed him was a very disastrous one for the Battalion for, besides killing him, it killed another officer, Major McDiarmid, wounded our Adjutant, Captain Foster, so badly that he later died, and also wounded the Colonel.

When one thinks that our Canadian Army was made up of men who had mostly lived a free and easy life and never been subjected to any kind of real discipline, it was nothing short of marvellous that those men could be welded in so short a time into such a fine force. The officers, with no previous experience, had to learn to lead, and the men to learn to be led. As to crime of any sort, it was almost non-existent, and the feelings between the troops and the civilians in Britain, France and Belgium were always excellent.

Altogether we had many happy times in France and Belgium, and the esprit-de-corps of the men was such that we never had the slightest thought that we could lose the war. I think the folks at home had much more worry on that score, as indeed they must have had, for we had none, even in the big German push against the Fifth Army in 1918. Of course, we had the ever-recurring sadness of losing many of our best friends. Wet, cold, mud, hardships and the occasional scare, all passed away and were forgotten, but the memory of our gallant comrades who had passed on never left us.

In the years that have passed, some lines from the poem, "The Battle of Blenheim" by Robert Southey, which I learned as a kid, often recur to me. An old grandfather, living on the site of the battle, speaking to his little grandson, who was playing with a whitened skull, said:

It was a glorious victory, there is not any doubt,
But what they killed each other for I never could make out.

Undoubtedly, just about all the people in the world now share this sentiment, but, unfortunately, there is still enough of the devil in enough people to prevent real positive action in the matter.

That winter of 1918 - 19 in hospital was of course, a real holiday and rest; with the actual fighting ending two months after I got my "Blighty," all tension was released and that made life much more serene for both soldier and civilian.

A visit to the "Pictures" (X-rays) soon after I reached the "Lord Derby" showed that I had no bones broken in my shoulder, and so it was just a matter of time the healer. In less than three weeks I was transferred to an auxiliary hospital at Lytham, since room had to be made at the main hospitals for the never-ending convoys of wounded during the last two months of the war.

Since Lytham was within easy tram distance from Blackpool, it was not hard to keep oneself amused though Blackpool in winter, with its holiday season ending at the end of September, is just another town with no special attractions. But the weather was fine and trips to Southport and Fleetwood plus a leave home to see Dad and Mother made the time slip by pretty fast. Towards the end of January I was transferred back to the "Lord Derby" then to the main Canadian convalescent hospital at Epsom and from there back to our "Reserve Depot" at Seaford in Sussex.

Epsom was quite an abrupt change from the other hospitals as all the accommodation was in regular Army huts and there were no nice nurses around to give that very pleasant feminine touch to life.

From Seaford, it was a quick jump to Kimnel Park, in North Wales, the main demobilization centre of the Canadian Army. I arrived just after a bunch of the troops there, badly worked up by what they considered unnecessary delay in being shipped back home, had really gone on the rampage and in a short, fierce riot had done considerable damage to the camp buildings. It was probably unwarranted but I imagine it gave the authorities a sharp jolt and there was certainly no undue delay in getting us on shipboard and heading for home.

As was only to be expected after my years in the backwoods, during which I hardly saw a dozen women, all the nice nurses in the hospitals caused my heart to give a flip and finally I got engaged to a very pleasing V.A.D. at Lytham. This added greatly to the charm of life in hospital and it also made me more anxious to get back home to get things fixed up for her to come out too.

More about this later but for now I will only say with Robbie Burns that "the best laid plans of mice and men after gang aglee." However it was very nice while it lasted.

I can't say that I ever felt any desire to remain in England. It had

**been** very nice to see Dad and Mother, my brother and sister, and the rest of my relatives and many of my old friends, but to remain there? No! In this I am very definitely not meaning anything disparaging to England, for it is a lovely country and hard to beat for prettiness, but after living in the wide-open spaces of the West, the thought of life in England had lost its appeal. Nevertheless, I still subscribe strongly to the sentiment expressed by one of our great poets: "Lives there a man with soul so dead, who never to himself hath said, 'This is my home, my native land.'"

If I had ever had, during my years in Canada, the slightest feeling that I wished I had remained in London (which I definitely never had had), it would have most effectively drowned out by a chance meeting I had with one of my old comrades in the Savings Bank Department during one of my short visits to London. J.P.A. looked as if he was well on the way towards becoming one of those elderly officials, the thought of whom had caused me to "jump my job" and get out.

We sailed from Liverpool on the *Caronia* early in April, and the Atlantic was like a mill pond all the way over. Naturally we were a gay crowd with never a dull moment. At first the decks were absolutely cluttered with Crown and Anchor boards, so much so that very soon an order came out forbidding their use. However there were all kinds of other sports and with men from all over Canada life never lacked interest. After arriving in Halifax we were entrained at once in waiting trains and were whisked out of Halifax so fast that we hardly had time to catch a glimpse of the terrible damage caused by the explosion of a munitions ship after a collision in the harbour.

The train journey was most uneventful, for we were just a bunch of returning soldiers and not valiant heroes going to fight for freedom as we were on our way overseas. On this train journey, we Warrant Officers were put in a parlour-car with the officers and so we really rode in style; but as we neared Vancouver we experienced one of the most humiliating, yet also most amusing experiences of my whole life.

One of the officers came to us and asked if we were willing to subscribe to a fund for the stewards in the car. We at once voiced our willingness to do so. Then he went on to say that the proposed amount for each person was fifty cents. Just fancy — a whole fifty cents for four or five days of splendid service! It just about took our breath away but we Warrant Officers could hardly tell Commissioned Officers that we thought it should be more. I dare bet that the buck privates in the other cars each donated considerably more than that to their stewards, and for much less service.

Came the last day of the journey, and as we neared Vancouver, the chief steward, a splendid figure of a man, stood up at the end of the car and in a short speech thanked us all on behalf of the stewards for the gift of fifty cents from each person in recognition of the fine service we had received from them. In all my life, I have never admired a man more than I did that chief steward when he gave us that fine sarcastic dig for our meanness. I hope all the officers felt even a little bit smaller than we C.S.M.'s did, though I have often wondered since if the sarcasm was wasted on them.

I still often picture that big, fine steward as he addressed us and I am sure he would have made a fine Colonel or some other important personage. Fifty cents each! I still wilt at the thought of it. On arrival at Vancouver, it took very little time for us to get through the process of demobilization, and then we were civvies once more. Vancouver in April is at its best with all the trees in their new spring attire and lovely spring flowers in bloom everywhere. After the melting snows and brown creeks all along the Great Lakes and the bare, treeless prairies just recovering from wintry conditions, Vancouver seemed like heaven.

I only remained there a day or so, as I was anxious to get home, but even in that short time I ran across several old Army friends in the streets. I had to do a little shopping and then once more I was on the boat making that trip to Prince Rupert through the lovely Inside Passage. But the train journey from Prince Rupert to Houston did not strike such a pleasant note, for there was still quite a lot of snow left in some parts of the Skeena and Bulkley Valleys, though at Houston it had all disappeared.

I got a different jolt at Houston, when I found several of my old friends sporting about a week's growth of beard; after three years in the Army, with shaves every day except when up the line, this did not make a good impression on me. It was no better when I reached home, for there I found brother Jack with a similar growth on his chin. I resolved right then that I would never fall back into that rut, and strange to say, I have kept that resolution and have shaved never less than twice a week.

In later years the wife of one of our Anglican ministers at Burns Lake related to us how she went up into the Peace River country to take up a post as nurse. When she arrived at a little village where she had to stay the night, she went to the hotel to get a room and there, in the lobby of the hotel were a bunch of "bearded ruffians", which made her think that she had landed in a nest of brigands. When she went up to her room she did her best to barricade the door and spent the night in a state of fear and trembling. She was from Ontario and so felt that such villainous-looking men could be nothing but bad. I am sure she found soon that, under their rough exterior, most of these men had hearts of gold and would do anything at all to help her.

It was Easter Day when I reached Houston and I was able to attend the Easter service, held in the new Anglican Rectory by Rev. W. Crarey. At that time he also served our district in the summer and had to travel the fifty miles by saddle-horse for our monthly service.

I set out the next day for home, using "Shank's pony" as there was no other transportation available. I could have gone in from Burns Lake from which there was now a weekly mail-stage running, but we had always used Houston as our rail point and it is hard to break a habit.

It was quite a tough trip, for soon after leaving the valley of the Bulkley, I struck snow up to eighteen inches deep in many places and as the road as not much used the walking was not a bit good. By the time I reached the head of Francois Lake, about ten miles from home, I had developed quite a sore knee. I was able to borrow a horse from our old Indian friend, Sam, and though it was not very pleasant riding on the rough snowy trail, I at least got rid of my pack. It was quite a relief when I got home to find that most of the snow had gone from there and I was naturally given a warm welcome by Jack and Safie and two tiny nephews whom I had never seen before.

There was one sad side to my homecoming, and that was that my friend, Alan Blackwell, who went out with me, did not return; he was killed in the vicinity of Mons, six days before the war ended.

I'll be quite candid and admit that my first reactions on reaching home, with the long, hard trip in, the late snow in all sheltered spots, and no growth of new grass, were not of the brightest, for it was such a contrast to the lovely spring conditions around Vancouver. However, I started work next day and in two or three days I was just about where I left off to go and enlist. Work is a great conditioner and I had the future to think of and to work for.

About the first job I tackled was cutting a nice bunch of logs to build a house for our future home, but just about the time I had got them all cut, letters from my fiancee began to get fewer and soon I got a letter calling it all off.

In all my letters to her I had never tried to hide any of the conditions of life prevailing in our district at the time, and I suppose my description of my trip in from Houston and of the late snow conditions here were plenty to give her a bad attack of cold feet. Added to this was the fact that being the only girl in the family, her parents had always been strongly opposed to the affair right from the start.

Well, it was quite hard to take at the time, but as passing days brought sober reflection, I came to realize that I had been very wise to state all the naked facts in all my letters to her and not try to dress them up to give an unrealistic picture. It put her in a position to assess the whole situation, and the decision she arrived at was probably the best for both of us. If a girl came to a frontier country like ours was at that time, and could not fit in, it would be too bad for everyone.

So that was that, and, after a while, we hauled my nice set of house logs and built some really good barns for Jack with them, and that really wrote "Finis" to Romance Number One.

# 14. Progress and Marriage

The period of World War I had not been kind to our district. With the completion of the Grand Trunk Pacific Railway very little work was available, for the provincial government had little money to spare for road work. Also, the market for even the small amount of farm produce had dwindled with the decrease in population and markets had to be found at a greater distance. Nevertheless, there was steady progress in many ways: cattle herds were reaching sizeable proportions, trapping still provided many with an income, and a few mining prospects supplied some work. About 1922 the timber industry began to develop with the supplying of hewed ties to the railway. It has to be remembered that our district started absolutely from scratch: transportation facilities were almost non-existent, lumber had to be whip-sawed, all firewood was cut by hand, there were no grain binders and threshing was at first done either with the flail or by the old biblical method of using horses to tramp out the grain.

But from 1920 most of these primitive methods steadily disappeared. Small threshing machines were brought in — the first, I believe, by Billy Bickle of Grassy Plains. Cutting of firewood was done with a gas engine and buzz-saw. The Harrison family brought in the first sawmill, a terrific boon, and our roads were steadily improved. The population on Ootsa Lake also received a boost with the influx of several large families, notably the Mohrs, Priests and Van Tines, and three small schools were soon running in the area.

With the advent of the sawmill, building was greatly facilitated and in 1923 a small church was built at Wistaria by the Presbyterian

Church. A good-sized community hall was also built, both entirely by volunteer labour. Both of these buildings have contributed greatly to life in our community through the years. Incidentally, though farthest from the railway, Wistaria was the first to build a community hall, a school and a sawmill and almost equal to Burns Lake in getting the first church.

About this time, too, stores were established at Ootsa Lake and at Nadina, at the head of Francois Lake. This was another big step forward, for previously I had had to make three or four trips by sleigh each winter out to Houston, and these trips could be far from pleasant if the weather did not cooperate. There were only about three habitations in the whole fifty miles and with very little traffic, the road was usually poorly broken.

If the weather was cold, it was certainly no joy sitting all day on the sleigh but fortunately I had a good team; if I got cold I could tie the reins up to the sleigh and walk behind. It was sheer good luck that in none of my trips in those early years did I have to buck any big falls of snow while en route. But it was a great blessing when those long, cold, lonesome trips by sleigh in the winter and by wagon in the summer were no longer necessary, for each trip usually took a week.

Meanwhile, the settlers were all searching for the most lucrative way of making a living. When cattle prices slumped badly in the early 1920's, many turned to shipping cream to creameries by railway and then to growing different kinds of grass seed for which our district proved very suitable: several high awards were won for timothy seed at the Chicago and Toronto Winter Fairs.

Another line of effort which was carried on quite strongly from the late 1920's was fur farming, mostly fox and mink, and this industry did quite well until the start of World War II. Then it declined and finally died, chiefly because fresh food, mostly snowshoe rabbits and fish, became too hard to get and too much time had to be spent in hunting and fishing.

The district also moved ahead in other ways. About 1920 we got our first doctor at Southbank, on the south side of Francois Lake and a few years later a small hospital was established there. However, sickness was not very prevalent in those days, mostly because of the sturdy nature of the pioneers and also owing to the slow methods of transportation which did not allow much intermingling of the population. Regular children's diseases were almost unknown here, and it was very noticeable that when our young generation joined up in World War II they all fell victim to all those childhood diseases from which they had so far escaped.

We also progressed in the matter of church services, for both the Anglican and Presbyterian ministers came in from Burns Lake and held monthly services which were mostly well attended. They provided a welcome meeting place for the settlers, who would always manage to attend church in spite of poor transportation. In those days, a trip of ten miles to church or post office, in sleigh, democrat or wagon, was not looked upon as any special hardship, so I suppose we old-timers just must have been tough.

I should mention here that the first minister to come anywhere in this country was an elderly Anglican minister named Mackay, who walked in from Burns Lake in about 1912 with his young son, carrying all their belongings on their backs. Parson Mackay was a real old pioneer and he and his son took up land here and built a small home in which he held services, right on the shore of Ootsa Lake. However, this distant outpost was at that time far from being ready for a resident minister; Parson left us soon after the outbreak of war but memories of him remained very bright among the old-timers for many years.

In the midst of all this general progress, I felt that I had better join the movement. After allowing time the healer to do his good work, I got in touch with another of my old nurse friends, one of the Nursing Sisters of the "Lord Derby". I was very lucky to make connections with her for she had taken a post in a hospital at Kuala Lumpur in Malaya. However, my letter followed her there and, to cut a long story short, this ended with my meeting her at Victoria when she landed from one of the Empress boats.

The trip down to Victoria was by no means an easy one for me, as we had a heavy fall of snow in October of 1922. I really should have gone out to the railway at Burns Lake by the mail stage from Wistaria but instead I took the route I had always taken — to Houston. Once again, I walked the nearly fifty miles, this time on a poorly broken trail and in well over a foot of snow. On the second day it poured rain all day, and I was a pretty bedraggled specimen when I arrived at Tony Reopel's home in Buck Flats, still about seventeen miles from Houston.

The final stages of the journey, first by train to Prince Rupert, and then by boat to Vancouver and across to Victoria, gave me ample time to rest up from my exertions and, as her boat was a day late, I had time to get straightened out before Millie arrived.

A Victoria friend who had taught school at Wistaria the previous year very generously arranged for us to be married from his sister's home. Millie was made to feel really at home there, which gave our

*Wedding photo taken in
Victoria, 1922.*

wedding that homey touch which it would otherwise have lacked. We
have been everlastingly grateful for their great kindness. After our
marriage at St. John's Church, we were taken for a very pleasant drive
around Victoria, and altogether our wedding was celebrated as if we
were one of the family.

The midnight boat started us on our way home and after two days'
shopping in Vancouver we were on the Inside Passage trip to Prince
Rupert. That passage is to us British Columbians a wonderful journey
but I think that Millie compared it unfavourably with another inside
passage that she had taken a few years before — down the Straits of
Malacca. That trip was through beautiful tropical islands, in lovely
warm weather, whereas ours was in cold, foggy weather, with most of
the beauty of the tree-clad mountains hidden by low-hanging clouds.
These conditions didn't give our trip the slightest advantage and I
fancy we lost out in the comparison.

I must confess that I was both a little amused and disturbed when
Millie remarked that the people on the streets of Vancouver seemed a
very drab bunch to her. It was rather natural for in three years she had
become used to seeing the residents of Malaya in their spotless white
garments, with a clean change every day. I couldn't help but wonder what

would be her reaction to the rough garb and general crude conditions of pioneer life. In all walks of life we have our challenges, and I guess this was her challenge. I can say that through the years she has met it in a splendid manner and come out on top, whatever thoughts she may have had on the subject at different times.

Prince Rupert treated us to one of its common downpours, so much so that we had to invest in an umbrella for our short stay there, and have never since had any need for this article.

The train trip up the beautiful valleys of the Skeena and Bulkley was uninteresting because it was all in the hours of darkness, but it was a real joy to find on arrival at Burns Lake that all the snow had disappeared. The mud it had left in its place was not inspiring but there was no snow and it was not cold. We reached Burns Lake on Sunday and in the afternoon we got out to Francois Lake by the mail stage, run by Fay Short in one of the first automobiles to come into the district. As the government ferry made no trips on Sunday, we had to get over the lake in a small gas boat and stay at the Keefe Hotel at Southbank that night.

The next day took us by mail stage — this time in a horse-drawn democrat to Ootsa Lake, where Millie landed in the kindly care of Mrs. Bennett at their little hotel. Millie never forgot that warm welcome and motherly care given her by Polly Bennett on that rather trying journey in from the railway.

Noon the following day found us at the end of the mail route at Wistaria Post Office where we had the usual noisy reception from a goodly number of nearby residents who had gathered to welcome us with jangling cow bells, tin pans and any other contraption that would make a good row. Also there was brother Jack with the democrat to take us to his home until our own was ready. Millie landed in a real bunch of Shelfords, for Jack now had four little sons whose ages ranged from six years to eighteen months. Sister Flora was also there, for she had decided to come out and see how she liked British Columbia. However, Jack's house was a good-sized one and we were not a bit cramped for room.

Our luck had held, for when we got up next morning it was 20 below zero. Wouldn't it have been nice for Millie, fresh from the tropics, if this cold spell had come two or three days earlier, and we had had that drive from Burns Lake in an open democrat in 20 below weather? But we were home and warm and ready to start living happily ever after, which we have been busy doing ever since.

*Our house and outbuildings.*

The summer of 1922 was the driest we had in the district during my many years there. We had no rain at all between April 15th and August 15th, when we had a heavy shower lasting about an hour, and then no more until September 15th. Consequently, most of our crops were very light, especially grain crops and those on land which had been broken up and put down to tame hay.

The growth of wild hay on unbroken land was reasonably good, but we did not have nearly enough feed for our cattle. By this time, we were getting a good-sized herd and so, as soon as we had finished haying on our own place, Jack had to take horses and machinery to some natural slough-hay meadows at the head of Ootsa Lake, about eight miles away, and put up as much as we still needed.

This left me alone to look after the farm and progress as well as I could with my house building, a slow job for one lone man. The house was of logs and was twenty-six feet square inside. It contained seven rooms and a cellar, and logs of that length and mostly more than a foot at the butt end take quite a bit of handling, even when dry.

We now had a sawmill about ten miles away us, but only rough lumber was available, so the lumber for floors, doors, and window casings all had to be planed by hand. This in itself entailed a vast amount of work. Added to this was the fact that none of the lumber was perfectly dry and could not be nailed down permanently; it had to be tacked in position and left to dry before being nailed down, or large spaces between the shrunken boards would have been everywhere.

Even in the winter I had to work alone except for some of the lighter work that Millie herself helped me with, as it took Jack a large part of his time hauling the hay from the head of Ootsa by sleigh on the frozen lake. This was quite a nice trip in good weather and Safie often went with Jack with an extra team and sleigh and brought home a second load, but it all took time, and prevented Jack from helping me.

In a log house all the spaces between the logs have to be caulked like the seams of a boat. Millie did a great part of this while I was busy with the heavier work. I guess it seems pretty crude to get a bride from the Tropics and have her working on the home in this way, but on the frontier, things very seldom go according to schedule. However, by early spring the home was sufficiently fixed up for us to move in, with further work to proceed as opportunity arose.

I sometimes wonder how we pioneers managed to find time and energy enough to build the houses we did. But those houses are still standing and they still contain all the elements for comfortable living.

Those years between the two World Wars were for us years of real happy, pleasant community life, with hospitality, friendliness, and home life at its very best. Practically all transportation was by horse vehicle or by saddle-horse until a few years before World War II, and so people seldom got many miles from home. Visiting was nearly always a full day's job.

Children mostly walked to school with a few of the more distant pupils using horse transportation of one kind or another. The young school-marms of those days were a great asset to the community. Most of them were quite young and entered wholeheartedly into the life of the district. We had often remarked on the fact that in stories written about early days of settlement the young school-marm was usually in the role of heroine, or at least of leading lady. It was not difficult to discover why for very often she was the only eligible young lady among a flock of young bachelors. Some of these young school-marms stayed in the country as settlers' wives, and I don't think they have regretted the step, and they have certainly made good wives.

House parties were frequent. It was almost a miracle how the big crowds managed to dance in the small homes, but dance they did, and everyone had a swell time. Dances and sing-songs were also frequently held in the Community Hall and did not break up until the wee small hours, for everyone brought refreshments and supper was served at midnight. Babysitting was quite unknown in those days and usually the whole family came. Whether in a home or at the Hall, the children were put to sleep in a separate room and seemed to suffer no ill effects.

For many years I took no actual part in the dancing but at length, realizing that Millie would like to dance but would not unless I did, I started to learn when I was 47 years old; being of a musical bent, it did not take me long. I have been a real dance fan ever since.

Even sub-zero weather did not keep people away from the dances; sometimes when it was 20 degrees below, they were there in sleigh loads, with hay in the bottom of the sleigh, and lots of blankets to keep everyone warm. Perhaps the horses had the worst of the deal, but they were well-blanketed, and tied to a bush and fed, and never seemed to take any harm. At most of the dances and meetings, sing-songs were held and much enjoyed by everyone and, even now, one often hears regrets for the passing of those sing-songs.

Church services in those earlier days were well attended, acting as they did as a gathering of all people in the area. In our end of the district we had no regular meeting place for our Anglican services, so these were alternated among the four homes in a small circle, from one to four miles apart. After service, at which fifteen to twenty persons were often present, the whole bunch sat down to a good dinner, often spent the afternoon together and stayed to supper.

Christmas Day was arranged in the same manner among the four families — brother Jack's, our neighbours, the Blackwells, my sister and brother-in-law (by this time Flora had married a Swedish neighbour, Earland Larson), and ourselves. In those early 20's the ministers had quite difficult trips, especially in winter, having to drive fifty or sixty miles in a light cutter, pulled by horses, often in bad weather.

The United Church also held monthly services in the little church at Wistaria, and we usually attended these as well as our own; in fact, Millie often played the organ at their services. The bond that existed between those early ministers and their congregations is very plainly shown by the fact that we still keep up correspondence with all the Anglican ministers and several of the United Church right to this day.

Another type of meeting that was always well attended in the earlier days was the political meeting. All the different political parties held meetings in all the small centres, and our Community Hall was the scene of many very interesting ones, for the audience usually tried to keep things lively by heckling the speakers.

In 1924 I myself got embroiled in the political battle. I had always been a Conservative but, at this time, there was widespread dissatisfaction with both the Liberal and Conservative parties, the former of which was in power in the province at the time. A new party, called the Provincial Party, under the leadership of General A.D. McRae, was formed. I was asked by some friends to stand for the nomination in our riding and at the convention I received the nomination. I was absolutely green at the job and was up against a real tough opponent in the Liberal Attorney-General, Alec Manson, later Judge Manson. He had nursed the constituency very well indeed, and most of his political fences were in good shape, but I gave him a good run for his money and only got beaten by 137 votes.

I have often thought since that if it had not been for my needless modesty, or rather, my sheer political stupidity, I might easily have won. I had had quite a good education in England, was at grammar school till I was nineteen, and got a first class in London Matric. Also, I had financed this education by winning three successive County Council scholarships and some school exhibitions. This, I think, went to show I possessed a reasonable amount of gray matter. But I never advertised these facts; in fact, I didn't even let it be known and ran the election as a reasonably intelligent pioneer farmer; which was quite stupid, for in politics, perhaps more than in any other game, one has to use to the full every card that he possesses.

I ran again for the Legislature in 1928, this time as a Conservative, but again I lost to my old opponent, though the Conservative party did defeat the Liberals and formed the government.

Altogether, I did not run good political campaigns and deserved to lose. Omineca is a strictly rural constituency and most of its inhabitants were folk who had led varied careers, mostly of the working-class. I should have stressed the facts, other than my English education, that I had spent two years in the general labour world at Banff and in the coast logging camps and that as a pioneer farmer, I had a real down-to-earth knowledge of the problems of the constituency.

However, I can say quite truly that these defeats have never caused me any great worry. I have always thought "Whatever is, is well," and I think that was definitely the case here, for the Conservatives came into office just before the Great Depression started in 1929. Under such circumstances it was no wonder that they only lasted one term in office. It had, however, been a wonderful experience, and I got to know the riding and the people of Omineca from one end to the other. This broadened my horizon in a very wide degree and has made my life since much more interesting.

Running a campaign in those days in a widespread constituency like Omineca, which is over 180 miles long and in places spreads out fifty miles from the railway, was no easy task. Money was very scarce at that time and few cars were available; I had to depend mostly on travel on the railway with a lot of walking in areas away from the railway.

One other item I must record is the grit of my little wife, Millie, for she stayed alone at home during those two six-week campaigns and looked after all the work that has to be done on any farm. Not all women could stand such isolation, even though she was only a mile from Jack and his family.

The advent of the telephone line from Houston in the early 1920's was a great step forward. When you are fifty or sixty miles from railway, doctor, hospital and dentist and from bigger stores, the benefit of telephone service can hardly be over-estimated. Next came the radio, and this meant almost as much to us as the telephone for, shut off as we are from all the conventional amusements and entertainment and from ready access to general world news, it put us more on the same level as town folks. Then cars and trucks became more numerous, and these cut out the greater part of the slowness and hardship of travelling; where it had been an arduous week's trip to Burns Lake, it was now only a day for the return trip. Nevertheless, I must say that, happy as we were to get these amenities, in the years when we did not have them life went cheerfully on; we didn't miss what we had never had.

During the twenty years of the inter-war period, the economic life of the district was never stable, nor could it be described as prosperous. We were still very much in the pioneer stage and people were changing and chopping around to find the way of life to which the country was best suited. It was a difficult period, for the population was still quite small. Farming was the chief occupation but local markets for farm products were conspicuous by their absence, and this caused prices for any produce to be very low.

Jack and I changed around like most of the others. When cattle prices slumped, we shipped some cream to make up the deficit, and when that proved not profitable enough we shipped timothy seed for a few years. However, cattle always remained our main effort until we started fox and mink farming in the late 1920's. For a few years this was our most profitable line, but I did very little of the work connected with it. Jack's four boys were by this time husky teenagers; they did most of the fishing and hunting for food for the fur, while Jack spent most of his time looking after the foxes. Bert, who was now in partnership in the mink, was kept pretty busy with them, while my efforts were mostly confined to the general farm work. Our local sale of eggs and butter helped considerably with our overall economy.

*One of the foxes in a pen.*

Like every other part of North America, we had many lean years in what are generally termed the "Dirty Thirties." On the whole, the real farmers came through this period better than most others, but even we were hard hit by the terribly low prices we received for our produce. The price we received for our cattle hurt us the worst. About the mid-Thirties, Bob Nelson, our postmaster, shipped fifteen head of mixed cows and two-year-old steers and heifers, and after driving them out fifty miles to the railway and shipping them to Prince Rupert, he received the princely sum of $189 for the whole bunch — and this happened two years running. One certainly did not amass a big bank account at those prices — if, indeed, we had any bank balance at all. However, by getting odd bits of money from the sale of eggs, butter and vegetables, the bona-fide farmer did manage to squeeze through, and I think the prices we received were far better than those received by prairie farmers for the same products.

In other ways, we were also better off than the prairie farmers, who were wholly dependent on agriculture, for many settlers eked out their living in different ways — some by a little trapping, others by working on some small mining development, still others in a growing tourist industry in this land of forests, lakes and streams and mountains. In the worst of the Depression, however, quite a few were dependent on government relief work on the roads, which served the double purpose of providing a living for those in need and also of improving our roads.

Altogether we came through the Depression very well. The times were indeed tough, but we were tough too, and we had been accustomed in our pioneer life not to expect too many of the luxuries of life, so we did not miss them. Our best asset in these trying times was our spirit of camaraderie, which never faltered; we always found joy in one another's company. With better travelling facilities, our circle of acquaintances widened and in a pioneer country every person has prominent, interesting characteristics. In a thinly scattered population, maybe these characteristics show more than they would do in a more crowded area but, nevertheless, I think that extra ones are present in pioneers. After all, if we hadn't had them, we probably wouldn't ever have wandered into the wilds and been well enough satisfied with the life there to stay.

Among such people it is not easy to pick out the most interesting ones, but I believe that I would choose Mike Tuohy as one of the outstanding characters. Mike was a burly and rather uncouth Irish-American. We saw Mike mostly when he came around with his little threshing machine, and Mike at his best was on his job, with his thick mop of greying hair not only covered but also infiltrated with a goodly quantity of chaff, dust, and every other kind of residue from the threshing operations. Mike once got hold of something else from those same operations. Like most other people of this work, he was in the habit of putting kernels of grain in his mouth and chewing them and, by chance, he got hold of some smutty kernels of barley.

Smut in grain contains the tiny ray fungus, actinomyces, which causes lump-jaw in cattle, and Mike must have got some of this fungus in a decaying tooth, and himself developed lump-jaw. This was not a nice affliction to get, and so Mike decided to go to the famous medical clinic run by the Mayo Brothers at Rochester, Minnesota. On arrival there, he was interviewed by one of the staff doctors who, after a few introductory questions, asked Mike what his usual diet consisted of.

"I eat a pound of steak and some spuds for breakfast, another pound and more spuds for dinner, and the same for supper," said Mike. In an annoyed tone, the doctor said, "Look here, Mr. Tuohy, I want to treat your case correctly, and to do so, it is necessary for me to know just what your usual diet is, and I don't want to be fooled with." "And I'm telling you what my usual diet is, ain't I?" said Mike, and he repeated his regular diet of meat and spuds. Aghast, the doctor said, "You mean to tell me that you eat three pounds of meat a day?" "I do just that, and every day," said Mike.

For some little time the doctor paced back and forth in the room, muttering, "Three pounds of meat a day, three pounds of meat a day." He then went out and collected all staff members he could find to come and see the man who ate "three pounds of meat a day."

Anyway, the doctors cured Mike and his lump-jaw and he never tired of singing the praises of the Mayo Clinic. He even bought a large volume giving the whole history of the Clinic. One day Mike said to me, "You know, Shelford, I'm Irish, and I've got no d.... use for the English, but by G..., you boys can sure be proud that the Mayo Brothers came from England." When he loaned us the book to read we found that they came from Millie's county of birth, Lancashire.

Mike was a great reader and had a nice little library of good books which he greatly treasured. If you loaned Mike a book, it was always promptly returned by mail and insured and he expected you to do the same if he loaned one to you.

After the Second World War had been in progress some time, Mike was again threshing at our place and in almost the same words as before, he again gave grudging praise to the d.... English. "As you know, Shelford, I'm Irish, and I've got no use for the d.... English, but by G..., we've got to hand it to you folks for the way you've stuck up against the Germans and the others, all by yourselves, and made it stick too until at last others stepped in to help." But I hope Mike remembered that he was in Canada, and the Canadians were also in the bunch that stuck.

Mike was an Irish Catholic from one of the wooded States of the eastern U.S.A. Like most of these old eastern loggers, he held to the superstition that Christ's cross was from a poplar tree and you could not get him to use a poplar pole in any of his buildings. Whether he used poplar or other trees for building I don't think Mike's buildings were of very fine architecture. On one of his visits to my place, after he had first been to Jack's, he turned to his companion on the threshing machine, an old neighbour and friend of ours, and said, "Well, Charlie, wouldn't it jar you. Here are these two boys who hardly saw an axe before in their lives, and they put up houses like these, where you and I, who were almost born with axes in our hands, put up shacks like we've got."

Mike was always welcome at any gatherings in the district, for he was a poet of sorts and composed many poems on different aspects of life in the area. His best known effort was "The Hazelton Trail", picturing life in the early days, when our only means of access to this district was by pack-horse from Hazelton. This poem ran to about 250 verses, and remarkably, Mike had all these verses perfectly memorized and could go right through without a hitch.

At an old-timers' Reunion Dinner at Burns Lake in the early 1940's Mike wanted to recite the whole 250 verses as part of the celebration, but the M.C. couldn't quite see it Mike's way, and he limited him to not more than 150 verses. Before he started Mike voiced his bitter disapproval of this but personally I agreed with the M.C., for Mike's delivery was in a sing-song monotone which could get rather tiring. Nevertheless, it was a remarkable feat of memory.

Time at length caught up with Mike, and he retired to a small cabin in Burns Lake. Often he was seen in the streets, always with no hat covering his mop of iron-grey hair, his boots unlaced, and clothes usually not quite up to city standards, but always with a cheery greeting for even a d.... Englishman.

To finish off Mike's story comes a real anti-climax, for the man who had eaten a pound of meat and spuds three times a day for so many years went right off meat; in his retiring days he ate no meat at all but subsisted mostly on package cereals. He didn't die young but I often wonder whether he would have lived longer if he had stayed with his steaks. Mike was rough and he was tough but he was a real likeable character.

Two near neighbours of Mike's were also interesting characters. Mike and Cain Oknianski came from Poland into the district about the same time that we did, and they showed their mettle early by whip-sawing lumber for sale at what is now Burns Lake. Whip-sawing lumber for your own use is trial enough and to spare, but to do it day after day for a living was more than I would have wanted to do. In the ensuing years, they built up a nice herd of thoroughbred Shorthorns and though neither of them ever married, they seem to have come through life quite nicely.

One point about these Polish boys which very much intrigued me is that they took sufficient interest in the affairs of their adopted country to get copies of Hansard regularly from Ottawa for several years — I wonder how many native-born Canadians or Canadians of British origin have that same interest in our national affairs!

One could continue almost indefinitely relating stories about our neighbours and their individual quirks, but I am just going to talk about one other, a little old Norwegian named Shorty Matheson. In the early days one never thought of Shorty without linking him with his two bulls, with which he did considerable work plowing, stump-pulling and working on the government roads.

Shorty always believed in doing things the easiest possible way. When he turned his bulls out to graze at noon he never bothered to take the yoke off them, just let them wander around together to graze their midday meal. In the winter, Shorty would arrange the fence around his haystack so that the bulls could get their heads through and help themselves. At that time we thought it was a shiftless way of doing things but I guess Shorty was just ahead of his time, for now it is the aim of most farmers to do as much self-feeding as possible.

I am afraid that Shorty had a mild scorn for the methods of the "Shelford boys" for he often said, "You Shelfords always seem to want to do things the hard way."

One day not long before he died, Shorty, with a big grin on his cheery little face, came up with his real *piece de resistance* in the matter of making work easier. "Artur," said he, "I've just figured out the best way to harvest spuds. Give the crop a real good harrowing with a spring-tooth harrow and have about six women coming along behind picking up the spuds."

In spite of all his scheming to make work easier, which is a very general practice in present-day farming, Shorty was a great asset to the district in many ways. His cheery grin alone was a great thing to have around, and he was always willing to help anyone who needed help. He never got very far ahead himself but he helped many others in their efforts to do so. Also, he had had a great deal of experience with livestock in the U.S.A. and Canada, and this enabled him to do a lot of useful work. In many cases, some operation was necessary and Shorty was never fearful of using the knife if he thought it was necessary. Crude as his methods often appeared to be, the fact remained they were usually successful. To old-timers, the memories of Shorty will always remain most pleasant.

# 15. Our Wildlife

In any wilderness country — and by this I mean a wild, undeveloped one — it is inevitable that wildlife plays an important part. In this region of dozens of large lakes and perhaps thousands of small ones, big rivers and little creeks, high mountains and little hills, rough rolling country and level meadows, timber and wild grassland, it was naturally part of life in the district.

When we came in the summer of 1910 a few deer were the only game animals in the vicinity, though we learned later that there were large herds of caribou in the mountains south of Ootsa Lake in what is now Tweedsmuir Park, and also a fair quantity of mountain goat. As far as providing a supply of fresh meat for the settlers, the game was just not there. The first moose was seen along the shore of Ootsa Lake in 1912. That same spring I saw moose tracks up the Tahtsa River but did not know what they were. They appear to have drifted in from the Prince George district into which they had come some years earlier.

When we first came, Jack exclaimed at this absence of moose for they had been quite numerous in all parts of Alaska where he had travelled, and he said that the necessary moose feed, mostly willow and other kinds of brush, was more plentiful than it was in Alaska. That is one of nature's secrets, how wildlife migrates from one part of a continent to another, and even dies off in some older habitats, though the necessary food may still be available.

The building up of the moose population was a slow process, and it was not until about 1930 that they became really numerous. Now they are plentiful and a common sight on the roads and farms in winter.

They often become a nuisance feeding at the haystacks, for when the snow gets deep, especially when it gets crusty after a heavy rain or thaw, travelling becomes difficult and painful for them and they then seek out and raid the haystacks. At such times they get very thin and are easy prey to ticks, disease, starvation and predatory animals: losses can be quite severe.

One evening as I was packing a forkful of hay in my farmyard, a moose decided that he wanted some of it — he jumped a high fence and came at a run for that hay, and I had to demonstrate in a very definite manner that I wanted none of him before he stopped his advance.

Regarding the migration of game animals through the years, our old friend, Indian Sam, told us that many years ago caribou were plentiful around where our farm is, and that the Indians used to snare them on their trails. To support this story, several years ago I found a short, cut chunk of petrified caribou horn under a tree on my farm.

Now they are almost entirely confined to the mountains south of Ootsa Lake. Since caribou are not present in many areas, they are a great drawing card for many hunting parties, mostly from the U.S.A.; these are taken in by professional guides with pack-horse outfits, and are a source of considerable revenue to these guides. This area has also the added attraction of a plentiful supply of grizzly bear and some mountain goats, both favourite game with hunters.

Mention of bears brings them up as the next most numerous of the bigger type of animal. Our old friend Sam said that some spring "crazy" come your place. We knew that he was quite correct for as we were looking over the place in our hunt for land, right where my house now stands, we saw a huge grizzly had torn up the dry grass as he walked over it. Several years later in early spring I found one of the cows dead along the shore of a small lake on my farm, and signs showed that a bear had eaten a little of it.

Next afternoon, I went to see if the bear was still around and I found that the whole carcass of the cow had been moved about fifteen yards. It had not been dragged, as the fresh grass and weeds — now nearly a foot high — had not been laid down between the two spots. That grizzly must have been huge and just packed the cow in his mouth. Since then I have learned that this is common practice with grizzlies, also that they like to bury their kill and let it go partly rotten before they eat it. Frankly, I was lucky that I did not find that grizzly, for I had only a 30.30 carbine with me, and that is no weapon with which to meet a big grizzly.

For many years after that we had no trouble with grizzly bear but in 1951 my nephew Cyril, who lives on Jack's old place just a mile from us, lost quite a number of sheep and lambs and some calves, and he suspected a grizzly. One evening, as he was in the sheep pasture looking over things, a big grizzly suddenly jumped over a fence close to him. As Cyril had no rifle he made a valiant attempt to break the record for the hundred-yard dash. Fortunately the grizzly ran into and grabbed an old ram before he reached Cyril.

A few nights later Cyril spotted the grizzly again — this time at a bait of sheep offal which he had put out. He rang me up on the phone and I hurried down, but when we got in the vicinity of the bait no bear was visible. We scouted around and soon we heard a "woof." As we were not quite sure of the direction it came from, we each went in a different direction. Cyril's direction was the right one and he managed to get in a hasty shot, but in the gathering darkness he had no luck. Nothing happened for a few days except that the odd sheep was still disappearing. Then one evening Cyril had three or four officials of the Aluminum Company visiting him. As they were talking outside the house, one of them suddenly exclaimed, "Look at that bear!" There was Mr. Grizzly jumping over the same fence as when he had gone after Cyril. Grabbing up all the artillery they could muster, they sallied forth, but again no bear was in sight. One of the officials said he would take a walk up the trail in the sheep pasture and soon he returned and said, "Well, I sam him alright, but I wasn't tackling that fellow alone with just a 30.30." Evidently the bear had other notions, for he came ambling down the trail right behind him, even as he spoke. The group laid down a barrage and down went the grizzly. The officials wanted to rush toward him but Cyril ordered, "No," as he knew what punishment a grizzly could take. Up struggled the bear and, receiving another blast, he went down again. Once more Cyril restrained the group and once more the bear tried to get away — but one more blast put him down for keeps. When skinned and examined, there were found to be nineteen shots in the bear's carcass.

There has only been one case in the district where a grizzly has attacked and harmed a man. He was a mining engineer named Hughes who was walking on the top of Sweeny Mountain up the Tahtsa River. He only saved his life by feigning dead after he was injured and the bear left him; however, Hughes was badly enough injured that he had to be flown down to Vancouver for treatment.

Black bears are much more numerous than grizzlies, but they are not nearly as dangerous and mostly turn and run when they see anyone. About the only time that a black bear is dangerous is when a person gets between a she-bear and her cubs. Dave Irons, a settler in the Tatalrose district, had the misfortune to get in this position and hastily climbed a tree to get out of danger; however, Mrs. Bear was evidently mad and she climbed after Dave, and when he could climb no higher she perched just below him and gnawed at his feet. By good fortune Dave's cattle were nearby. At his loud calls they came at a run and the loud clanging of their bells made the bear fear for her cubs on the ground and she hastily descended. Dave was then able to get home safely, but his feet had been chewed badly enough that he had to go to hospital for treatment.

On the whole, black bears are not dangerous but they can do a great deal of damage to sheep and calves. I have lost many sheep and lambs, one time five in one night within a hundred yards of home. Bears and coyotes eventually forced me out of the sheep business.

Bears were a real problem for a time. In two summer months we killed twenty-four bears in the four miles between our place and the Blackwell farm. We must have made a good job of them, for we have seen few around since. One of these twenty-four bears I shot up a tree just outside the door of our home. Our dog Laddie put up a persistent barking one morning while we were still in bed. I said to Millie that I thought he had a porcupine treed but when I went outside I found that it was a yearling bear up the tree. Needless to say, he soon dropped out of it and while the meat kept fresh, provided us with some delicious meals, for young, fat bear meat is hard to beat.

Wolves have also been quite numerous at times, giving us some interesting moments and also some bad losses in our cattle and sheep. The first wolf seen in our district was seen peering into the window of her small cabin one evening by our first school teacher, one of the two Hinton sister, who later became Mrs. Olaf Anderson.

In those early years before the moose became numerous, the wolves seemed to come into the area only when the rabbit population became very great, but since the moose population has increased wolves have been more or less steady with us — so much so that the Game Department has had to take stringent measures to control them, for the sake of farm animals and the wild game. At first a local predator hunter was paid a bounty for all the wolves and coyotes he disposed of; at times I have seen big piles of wolves outside Alford Harrison's home and a gruesome sight they looked with their huge heads and powerful jaws. In later years, the Game Department ran its own poisoning program.

We saw the biggest pack of wolves the very first time we saw any. This was in 1923 as we were holding a stockmen's meeting in Jack's house. As the meeting proceeded, we saw six or seven wolves trotting in single file along the far edge of Jack's big meadow. When we got our cattle in that fall we were six yearlings short, and so these wolves had evidently been quite busy.

About this time Jack took his wife and four young boys in the wagon to visit the Blackwells one Sunday. I was milking in the milk pen when they returned and I heard a lot of excited voices. Then I saw Safie running towards the house while Jack and the wagon stayed at the gate. Answering my shouted questions, Safie said there was a wolf following the wagon and Jack wanted the rifle and shotgun, so I ran and got them and hurried to the wagon. Jack said the wolf had left them but that he would turn the wagon round and go back along the road — he was sure the wolf would show up again.

It seems the wolf had joined them a long way back, the drawing card being the collie dog that was with them. Wolves are death on dogs and have killed many in the district, but Paddy was wise enough to keep under the wagon and out of reach of the wolf. But the wolf tried his best and came so close to the wagon that Jack got scared for the safety of the small children and, giving the reins to Safie, he sat at the back of the wagon with the only weapon he had — an open jack-knife.

Well, the wolf did indeed come out and follow us again but he kept about sixty or seventy yards back. I wanted to shoot but Jack said to wait a bit — he would come right close in and I could get him with the shotgun. But Jack was wrong for soon, in the gathering darkness, the wolf faded out of the picture. At a bend in the road I dropped off the wagon and it kept going, but Mr. Wolf never showed up.

We have, very literally, had "the wolf at the door," for before we had a verandah, tracks in the snow showed that the wolf came right up to the door. Evidently, at this time we had no dog or the wolf would probably have killed it. Later, our dog Bingo, a collie, used to sleep on the verandah. One morning I went out to find it looking like a veritable slaughter house, with blood everywhere and a very sick dog lying there. How we never heard the slightest sound of a struggle is a mystery — we must have been sleeping the sleep of the just. The only thing that saved Bingo from bleeding to death was the fact that it was 20 degrees below zero that night, and the intense cold congealed the blood from his wounds.

The Shelford family had one other incident in connection with wolves. This was soon after the boys came home from overseas. Hugh, Jack's second boy, was crossing Ootsa Lake on the ice going to hunt squirrels on the south side of the lake. When he got some distance from land he heard a number of wolves howling on the shore he had just left. Without expecting any results he answered their howls but the wolves decided to call his bluff and soon Hugh found himself surrounded by seven or eight wolves. They acted in a most threatening manner in their efforts to work themselves up to a state that they would have the courage to attack him. Hugh had only a .22 rifle and was further handicapped by the fact that he had lost his left arm in France. However, he lay down on the ice and potted away steadily at them and he felt sure that he hit one of them. At any rate, they seemed to cool off and after a while they left him and he was able to continue on his journey — but all in all, it was not a pleasant experience.

One of our old-time trappers, Tommy McKinley, had a similar experience on Eutsuk Lake and was followed one evening by a pack of wolves but, here again, the wolves seemed to lack sufficient courage to make a definite attack.

The wolf is generally regarded as a cowardly animal as far as humans are concerned, and the Hudson's Bay Company, in all its activities on the frontiers in Canada, has not a single record of a proven case of anyone being attacked and killed by wolves.

It may seem that the members of the Shelford family have had more than their share of contact with bears and wolves, but this is because our farms are the most westerly in this area and to the west of us, the country is all rough virgin forest, the natural habitat of these animals. When any shortage of food causes them to invade our territory, it is our farms they reach first.

Wolves may or may not be a menace to humans, but there is no getting away from the fact that the prolonged, eerie, but nevertheless musical howls of a wolf, or a pack of wolves, can really send shudders and shivers through anyone hearing them and must indeed strike terror into any game animals in the vicinity.

Dogs even seem to realize what the howl of a wolf implies, and I have never known any of our dogs to answer the howl of a wolf. They will always answer the yapping of the smaller coyote, but with a wolf howl they seem to realize that "silence is golden."

Of all the fur-bearing animals in this area the beaver is without question the most interesting, for his industry is boundless, and his engineering skill in building his dams and his houses is amazing. To really understand these two qualities of the beaver, one needs to get a good family of them in a lake or stream close to one's home. As their numbers increase, they need larger feeding areas and so they proceed to put a dam in any place that will flood — land that will produce willows and other bush on which they feed and which will also provide them with water transportation to reach poplar and other trees growing on higher ground, which they cut down and then cut into small chunks. The tree chunks they then drag down to the water and float to their pile of feed in the water close to their house; this pile provides them with food for the winter.

Naturally, they often flood land that a farmer is using and there comes a battle of wills and persistence. The farmer destroys the nuisance dam but, that same night, the beaver restores it. Again, the dam is destroyed, and again it is rebuilt and this process continues almost indefinitely. Often the beaver will quit for a while but then in comes the dam once more and the fight is renewed. It becomes a battle of wills with the odds very much in favour of the beaver until it reaches the point where the number of beaver has to be reduced.

Only a person who has had such an experience can fully appreciate the persistence and cleverness of the beaver. Usually the difficult work is for them to get a start in a fast-flowing stream, but they bring long branches of willow and run the butt ends into the soft bank to hold them temporarily and then weigh them down with mud and stones. For this work they must use their large, flat, strong tails as a kind of trowel or shovel. In the end, the dam is a mass of sticks of all sizes, stones, mud and slough-grass roots. If the beaver feel that one dam is not sufficient to hold back the weight of water, they put in an extra one or two, just as engineers often do. In some creeks, I have seen twenty or thirty dams, one below the other, each one flooding a small section of the stream and producing a good supply of feed and continuous water transportation that is so vital to beaver.

In the body of water in which the beaver house itself is situated the dam has another very important function, and that is to keep the water at a stable level so that the living chamber in the house is not flooded, while at the same time, the water entrance to the house is not exposed.

The air-hole is also a very important part of the house and is constructed right up the centre of the house from the living quarters. It is formed of loosely laid sticks, close enough to keep animals from using it as an entrance but open enough to allow sufficient air to pass through. The rest of the house has quantities of mud and other refuse mixed in with the sticks in order to keep the house warm but no such materials are placed over the air-hole. In winter, an occupied beaver house is easily recognized by the fact that no snow or ice accumulates over the air-hole as it is continually thawed by the warm air from the interior.

Dams are usually not more than twenty yards in length but once in a small river I saw one over fifty yards long. This, of course, had to be commenced in a period of low water, then built up as conditions warranted so as to be able to withstand the greater pressure at high water.

When we came to the district there were beaver in nearly every lake and stream, but after the advent of the white man it became a race between the Indians and the whites as to who should get hold of them. In consequence, the beaver population at one time almost reached vanishing point but fortunately there was just enough seed left so that when both whites and Indians were able to make a better living in other ways, the beaver got a chance to multiply once more. Now we are almost back to our starting position and there are again beaver in almost every lake. Since the price of all wild fur is now quite low, largely due to the competition of materials processed to imitate natural fur and also from the fur raised on fur farms, there is not the incentive to get the fur the tough way by trapping.

However, we are really very glad to see the beaver back again, for by their dams they keep all the lakes at a good level. This in turn keeps the creeks running except in a very dry summer, and removes a lot of the hazard of widespread forest fires. Moreover, a high level of water in the lakes and sloughs creates more food for the fish which in turn provide food for such animals as mink and otter. Added to this, the growth of water vegetation is more luxuriant and makes more food for muskrats, and insect life is greatly increased so that there is much more food for all types of water fowl.

Altogether, the balance is quite heavily weighted on the side of a good beaver population although at times, they can prove a real nuisance. In most countries, the bee is looked upon as the "busy" bee, but in a beaver country one hears much more frequently the term "busy as a beaver."

A beaver's life is not all work. They make a very pleasant sight on a warm summer night as they swim around and, from sheer joy of life, slap the water with their big, flat tails, making a noise almost as loud as a rifle shot. This same loud slap is also used as a danger signal, though how one is distinguished from the other is difficult to understand.

There is another water animal that takes the prize for playfulness and that is the otter. A family of otter can be just as playful as a bunch of kittens and they love to slide, time after time, down a steep bank, preferably on snow, into open water below.

Any talk of wildlife of the district would be quite incomplete without mention of the bird life, especially the water fowl — but this story is a rather sad one.

When we arrived here, and for many years after, any of the smaller lakes containing good food and many parts of the larger lakes were literally covered with all the varieties of duck in the fall during the period of migration to the south; geese and swans were also quite numerous in localities suited to their feeding. In this migration period, huge flocks of geese, swans and cranes were a very common sight in their pretty 'V' formation.

Gradually the numbers of all these water fowl dropped until, at the present time, on bodies of water where there were formerly thousands of them, there are scarcely any at all. What has caused this great drop in numbers we are not sure, but we think that it is the result of the intensive hunting to which they are subjected after they are forced from districts likes ours by the freeze-up, and get into areas where the population is much more dense and where townspeople turn out in their thousands to enjoy a little duck and goose hunting. Another possible reason may be that for some unknown reason the water fowl may have changed their migration route, but this is hardly likely after their wonderful sense of direction in migratory habits has brought them through this area for countless years from their breeding grounds in the Yukon, Alaska, and other northern areas.

Little need be said regarding fish, for where there are countless lakes, creeks and rivers, there are bound to be fish, and this country has lots of them, though in some lakes the coarse type of fish tend to keep down the supply of game fish. Suffice it to say that we are continually getting more and more parties of fishermen, from as far off as the U.S.A., and as the waters adjacent to populated areas get more and more fished out, the number of such fishermen will steadily increase.

Char, or Lake trout, and many species of ordinary trout are found in most of the lakes and streams in the area, but probably the fish most sought after by honest-to-goodness sports fishermen is the steelhead, which is found mostly in the Morice River, which runs into the Bulkley River at Houston, and in the Kispiox River, which enters the Skeena River a little above Hazelton.

And now to finish up with a little fish story. About a mile east of Jack's home was a little lake which we called Eastern Lake on account of its position. In the mile-long creek by which it drained into Ootsa Lake was a waterfall about ten feet in height, and this prevented any of the predatory fish getting into Eastern Lake from the lower lake. The only fish in Eastern Lake were of the smelt type and quite small. How they got there must remain one of nature's secrets.

In the dry part of summer when the creek through their meadow had become a series of pot-holes, Jack's young boys caught some of the small trout there and carried them in lard cans to Eastern Lake and in this way stocked it with trout. Very soon the lake was well-stocked with trout and the native small fish provided the trout with ample food, especially with the natural food in the lake. While the number of fish in the lake remained small, the trout grew to quite a large size, reaching over ten pounds, but now that their numbers have greatly increased, they mostly average somewhat over one pound.

The boys often used to go both swimming and fishing in the lake. One day, Cyril, the youngest boy, attached a baited line to his big toe and proceeded to swim around and, believe it or not, he caught his fish.

# 16. More Progress and Change

Up to the outbreak of World War II the struggle for survival had been pretty tough, but from that time on the whole economic fabric underwent a great and sudden change. Till then, farming and fur farming had been the two mainstays of the district, though during the previous twenty years, a steadily increasing interest in the timber industry had made itself felt. For several years, the tie business had gradually moved ahead. First the ties were hewn with the broad-axe and later on a few sawmills began to saw them. Altogether quite a lot of work was provided and a considerable amount of money brought into the district by this first modest start in timber. But the real expansion of the industry came with the greatly increased demand for all types of lumber after the outbreak of war. Where there had previously been one sawmill, there were now at least twenty.

Up to this time, we had never looked upon the timber in our district as of much commercial value. As a matter of fact, the first settlers were mainly interested in farming and would cheerfully have burnt down most of the timber with the idea that grass would grow in the burnt-over areas and provide good cattle range. What a mistaken idea that was, for, when the forest burnt, most of the good top soil was burnt at the same time. By the time grass and other vegetation started to grow, the dead trees began to fall down and a mess of windfalls effectively prevented any cattle from ranging there. The windfalls took years and years to rot and, by this time, a new growth of timber had grown up. The result was that the district had lost a valuable crop of timber, a lot of good top soil, and had gained not a single thing.

We were fortunate that not much timber was burnt in those days, though a few land clearing fires did get out of hand and did considerable damage. Careless travellers in the woods caused many outbreaks and the odd fire may have sometimes been deliberately set by someone seeking work in fighting the fire; lightning in hot, dry spells was a fairly common cause of forest fires. However, altogether our district was very fortunate.

As a consequence, the lumber industry became the chief source of income, while farming fell to a real low level — that despite a good rise in the price of beef cattle following the outbreak of war. The financial returns from sawmill work were so much higher than those from farming that a large proportion of the younger generation deserted farming, while even those still working their farms spent most of the winter working in the woods. Feed was thrown to the cattle early in the morning and then the part-time farmer rushed off in his car, worked all day in the woods and returned in the evening to throw more feed to his cattle. Needless to say, the cattle, the farm and the whole farming industry suffered from this way of farming.

The loggers certainly made more money than the farmer while they were working, but weather and ground conditions played havoc with the work in the woods. Sub-zero temperatures and deep snow in the winter and the impossible conditions in the spring break-up made transportation of lumber to the railway and hauling of logs to the mill out of the question.

But the industry got the district out of the position of having one way of life — and in so doing gave the farmer a bigger and closer market for his product. The population grew, and Burns Lake, which had been a small railway point, became a thriving lumber town with stores, hotels, mills, two doctors, a dentist, seven churches, a fine new hospital, a movie theatre, and numerous government buildings; the roads, too, all over the district improved above all our expectations.

The money which the lumber industry brought into the district did another important thing — it supplied many farmers with sufficient cash to purchase the new machinery which became so general. One way modern trucking benefitted us farmers was getting our cattle trucked out to the railway. Formerly, we had to drive our cattle from fifty to sixty miles to get them to the railway and it was usually a headache to get them off their home range, for in the timbered stretches it was impossible to use saddle-horses.

My brother-in-law's cattle were usually the most difficult to drive out and one year in desperation we remembered the suggestion of Sam Gledhil, the Bella Coola mailman, that we try tying them snug. The big steers were used in the experiment and when let loose they took off at a wild gallop, which ended very suddenly when each went the different side of a big tree. Both turned a complete somersault and the great wonder was the neither of them suffered a broken neck or any other injury. For us, that ended the "tying snug" method. With the trucks, we just loaded them right in our farmyard and that was all there was to it. Being saved a three-day drive, the cattle arrive at the shipping point in much better condition.

Later, instead of the cattle being trucked to the nearest rail point, large trucks capable of holding as many cattle as a railway car are used and the cattle were taken right down to Vancouver or other points.

The dozen years from 1940 onwards brought a string of upsets into our way of life, which had been so quiet and secluded. First and greatest of these, the outbreak of World War II, found most of our young folks in the armed forces. Three of Jack's boys joined up, leaving one son, Myles, to help Jack and Safie keep the farm running.

It is not hard to imagine the impact that this venture into the outside world had on the boys when one recalls that the four boys had been too far away from school to attend and there were no school buses running in those days. As a consequence, all their schooling had been obtained by correspondence lessons from the Department of Education at Victoria. John, the eldest, saw his first train on his nineteenth birthday in 1935.

One of the most noticeable facts about this great change in the way of life of our youths was that as soon as they mingled with all the other boys in the Forces, they quickly picked up all the ordinary childhood diseases to which they had not been exposed in their former secluded lives — measles, German measles, mumps, scarlet fever and chicken pox assailed them in quick succession.

At the same time, they picked up a broadened outlook and an insight into and interest in world affairs, which they would otherwise probably never have obtained. On the whole, casualties were not very heavy among the boys of the district, and Jack's three boys came home safely, though Hugh, the second boy, lost most of his left arm in his travels, and did so in a most unfortunate manner.

Hugh was taken prisoner in Normandy, the day after D-Day, and while a prisoner being marched between two points near Tours in France, our Air Force unknowingly strafed the column of prisoners. Hugh was wounded in the leg, but not seriously.

Later, the Germans made an effort to get a train-load of prisoners to Germany, and again our Air Force came into the picture, strafing the train and doing quite serious damage to the prisoners. This was where Hugh got his arm so badly injured that it had to be amputated, the job being well done by the German doctor.

Another unfortunate casualty happened in our group to a young Scot, Jock MacIvor, who had lived and worked with us through the Depression of the Thirties. He joined the Army but spent most of his time of service in England; in due course, he married a Scottish lass. Returning home in September 1945, he was on demobilization leave. He spent two days with us and then went to visit other friends and, while on a hunting trip in a boat, accidentally shot himself, three days after his return. This only seemed to back up the very commonly expressed belief in the Army that "If you are going to get it, you are going to get it."

However, our family group suffered worse casualties, for brother-in-law Erland died in 1944 and Jack's wife, Safie, followed in 1945, while her sons John and Hugh were home on leave. This was the first bad break amongst us oldsters, and was further increased in 1951 and 1953 when brother Jack and our good neighbour, Ed Blackwell, passed on. Thus in a few short years our group of families was badly broken up and when my sister moved to the south of the province, it left only Mrs. Blackwell and ourselves.

Another great change in the life of the district came around 1940 with the influx of a large settlement of Mennonites into the Cheslatta area, about thirty miles east of us. The Mennonites are a pacifist Protestant sect, originally founded in the sixteenth century and composed mostly of people from Germany, Russia, and Holland. They still speak mostly German amongst themselves, and the elder people amongst them endeavour to keep all their young folks from intermingling and intermarrying with persons outside the sect. They are an industrious people and are given to raising large families, but as they tend to keep so much to themselves they are really of very little benefit to the community life of the district. In a district such as ours, with its scattered population, close community life is a prime necessity.

However, in spite of the efforts of their elders, the younger generation mixed more readily with the rest of the population and considerable intermarriage took place. They added greatly to general business life in the district, for they became widely distributed and engaged in all the different activities, though they originally came in here to engage entirely in farming.

As a matter of fact, they were very lucky in the time in which they struck our country for, with the commencement of World War II, the

*The last time that we all got together, September 24, 1939.*

price of cattle took a big jump. Even more important was the advent of the lumber industry to the district in a really big way. Small sawmills sprang up everywhere and a great many of them were owned by the Mennonites. Practically all the young men were employed in sawmill work or in the trucking business of hauling the lumber to the railway. But our district is not richly endowed with good quality sawmill lumber and with between fifty and a hundred small mills operating there, the more available timber began to thin out and these small mills could not afford to build the roads necessary to reach less accessible timber. In consequence, the majority of the mills closed down and the men had then to depend on returns from their farms which had been neglected. Furthermore, they had settled much too close together, mostly on farms of only 160 acres, which is not nearly enough acreage, especially as this allows for no outside range for their cattle. Very soon they realized their mistake and began to drift away, mostly to the Fort St. John district in the Peace River.

This drift continued until very few bona-fide Mennonite farmers were left in the whole area. Most of those that remained lived out of the closely settled block; most of the farms were sold to the land-seekers coming in from the U.S.A. These American settlers were not faced with the same handicap of too small farms as they were able to buy several adjoining farms which the Mennonites were only too ready to sell so that they could join the exodus to the Peace River country. Most of the remaining Mennonites were engaged in running stores and garages with a few still running trucks and others working for the provincial Highways Department. And so ended this great adventure into group farming in our district.

But great as were these changes, a far greater one was in the offing — and this was not a change but a real upset.

Before the big upset, Ootsa Lake was situated about midway in a long chain of lakes and rivers which stretched from the eastern slope of the Coast Range of mountains. This water ultimately joined with the water from another string of lakes and rivers to form the Nechako River.

The Ootsa string started in Whitesail and Tahtsa Lakes, both lying close to the Coast Range, and rivers of the same names ran from these lakes and united a couple of miles before entering Ootsa Lake. Ootsa River drained the lake and then passed through two smaller lakes, Natalkuz and Intata, and then was soon joined by the Teta-chuck River to form the Nechako River. The water in the Teta-chuck River originated in what is considered to be the most picturesque lake in the district, Eutsuk Lake, which contains many large islands and several large bays, while on the south shore snow comes down very close to the shoreline all through the summer.

Eutsuk Lake is about fifty miles long, and from its foot a short piece of river, containing the Redfern Rapids, brought one into Teta-chuck Lake. Below Teta-chuck Lake were the beautiful Teta-chuck Falls, and then, after passing through Euchu Lake, this branch joined up with the Ootsa Lake branch to form the Nechako River. The upset changed all this.

In 1949 rumours began to circulate that the level of these two big stretches of water was to be raised to form a huge reservoir to provide water power for a plant to be put in at Kitimat by the Aluminum Company of Canada. The rumours were soon followed by action on the part of the Company. Application for water rights was made and a meeting held at Wistaria to allow for any objections to be voiced against the granting of the water rights.

At this meeting, held in the Wistaria Community Hall, just about everyone from the whole length of Ootsa Lake was present to meet Mr. Neely DuBose, the Vice-President of the Aluminum Company, and other officials of the Company, as well as the Controller of Water Rights in British Columbia.

In this meeting I had the honour of presenting the main brief on behalf of the settlers. In it we frankly admitted that much as we would like to be left untouched in our peaceful community we had no hope, or even desire, to stand in the way of such a step forward in the industrial development of the province. But we wished them to understand what this flooding process would do to our community and all its members.

Our brief portrayed in some detail the building of the community right from the days before the advent of the railway, when all transportation was by pack horse, to its present condition of good homes and farms, church, schools, good stores and good transportation, but most of all, the fine community itself.

We had to impress officials with the great loss that it would bring to everyone in the valley; for the ones who were to be flooded out and would have to find new homes, with all the expense, time, and trouble of re-establishing themselves and for those who would be left, the great loss to be suffered from shrinking of the community, and the consequent loss of our stores and other amenities.

I think we must have made a pretty good case and, during the picnic lunch to which all the residents contributed, Mr. DuBose came to me and said, ''Well, Mr. Shelford, I don't wonder at your folks being just about heartbroken at the thought of the break-up of your community, for I have never seen such a wonderful one, and if I were a member of it, I am sure I should feel just the same.''

A little later, a second meeting for application for water rights was held in Victoria. As the settlers wanted representation at this meeting also, I was delegated to attend, and the Company generously agreed to pay the expense of the trip. However, outside of again stressing the right of the settlers for generous compensation for the disruption of their lives, little else could be done. In due course, the Water Right was granted.

Work started almost immediately on the project, the two main parts of which were the Kenny Dam at a canyon in the Nechako River, and a ten-mile tunnel at the west end of the projected reservoir, at the west end of Tahtsa Lake. Previously, all the water from this area had gone down the Nechako River to Prince George then down the Fraser River to enter the ocean at New Westminster.

But when the project was completed, most of the water went by tunnel from the west end of Tahtsa Lake and running right through the Coast Range of mountains down to Kemano, or Gardner Canal, one of the many fiords on the rugged British Columbia coast.

The tunnel was about ten miles long and gave the water a drop of around 2,800 feet into the power-house at Kemano. From there the power was carried to the aluminum plant at Kitimat by a transmission line some forty miles in length over the difficult terrain of the Kildala Mountain Range, which rises to 7,000 feet. In this way, the water of our drainage basin, which had previously flowed about 800 miles in its journey to the Pacific Ocean, now reached the same goal in a short ten-mile trip.

At the Kenney Dam, the water level was raised about 250 feet but the level of Ootsa Lake was raised only 150 feet. This was, however, sufficient to flood out most of the settlers in our community. Two other small dams had to be built in the Ootsa Lake area, in places where the low contour of the basin would otherwise have allowed escape of water from the reservoir. One of these, Skin's Dam, about three miles east of the Ootsa Lake Settlement, also contained flood gates and a spillway, which were used to control the level of water in the reservoir.

One would naturally think that the large amount of work involved in the project would have brought, at least temporarily, considerable prosperity to our area but in reality the effect on the district was relatively small. The base for the work on the Kenney Dam was at Vanderhoof, from where a good road forty miles in length was constructed to the dam site. The base for the work on the Tahtsa Lake tunnel was at Burns Lake, with all the traffic going along the north shore of Francois Lake and then by a newly constructed road from the head of that lake to the foot of Tahtsa Lake, from where the rest of the journey was accomplished by barge.

The only actual work in our locality was at the Skin's Dam and the other little dam at Bear Lake. Even on these projects, most of the workmen were brought in from the outside, as were also most of the supplies.

During this period, most of the people who had to move out were busy doing so, while the rest of us were busy just staying put, and carrying on with our normal lives. However, the process of moving out involved one very special piece of work. That was the protracted negotiations with the Company for proper compensation for the lands and homes which the settlers were losing, together with their livelihood, the general upset, and the cost of re-establishing themselves in some other place.

The settlers wisely first formed an association to present a solid front in their dealings with the Company. A committee was formed from among their numbers to handle the negotiations and my nephew Cyril was chosen as head of the committee. The latter formulated a more or less stable basis for the compensation demands. This was generally adhered to, though in some cases individual settlers did make their own final deal with the Company.

It must not be thought that the negotiations went through absolutely smoothly for often they took quite a heated and even bitter turn, which was only to be expected; the Company wanted to keep the total cost for compensation to a minimum, while each individual settler wanted his compensation to be at a maximum. In the end, I think the settlers got quite satisfactory compensation, certainly much higher than if no organization had been formed.

The older settlers, especially the early original ones, were in general satisfied with their treatment, for they realized that they were getting far more than they could ever have got on the open market; however, among the younger generation were many who were not content. The feeling among them was that the Aluminum Company had untold millions of dollars and so could well afford to compensate them really handsomely.

The persons who acted carefully and wisely in using their money to re-establish themselves somewhere else far or near, sometimes in an entirely different mode of living, came out very well. Unfortunately, as was only to be expected, a certain percentage felt that such sums of money would last forever and, not using the same care and wisdom, soon found themselves on the financial rocks. As one of those who remained said to me later, "Alcan gave some of us more money than we had ever had before and we just did not know how to handle it."

What of us people who were left? Well, we were not left out in the cold. Through a Trust Fund set up by the company on the insistence of the Minister of Lands, we sixteen landowners who were left did get compensated for our loss of community and all the amenities that go with it, to the extent of about $3,000 each. That was acceptable but when one thinks of all the years of toil and struggle that go into building a community, it was certainly not over-payment. In fact, I have heard some of the displaced persons who are now comfortably re-established remark that we who were left really suffered the most, and are still suffering from the big upset. However, we still have our homes and our roots which have been penetrating further and further into the land.

One of the unfortunate results of the raising of the water level in all our lakes and rivers was the unsightly array of dead trees standing all around the perimeter of the new reservoir. The land area enclosed by the two branches of the reservoir was included in the boundaries of Tweedsmuir Park, named after the former Governor-General of Canada, who opened it in 1936. The whole area of the Park was looked upon as one of the beauty spots of British Columbia, but the flooding left this portion of the Park anything but a beauty spot.

At the time of the inception of the project, very strong and even violent opinions were expressed by many people, including my nephews, to the effect that all the timber and brush should first be cleared from the area to be flooded. When the area to be cleared along hundreds of miles of the shoreline of the new reservoir was considered, the cost would have been enormous, and I doubt whether the Company would have taken on the project at all, if conditions had been imposed calling for such clearance.

A relatively small amount of the easily accessible sawmill timber could have been salvaged if an early start had been made, but most of the timber was not fit for sawmill use, and with no pulp mill within hundreds of miles, there was no possible way of using the timber.

One other rather sad side of the picture for us farmers was that though our district supplied the power for the aluminum plant at Kitimat at such a sacrifice, we didn't benefit by an increased market for our farm produce, situated as we are about three hundred miles from Kitimat by the only travel route.

However, the presence of such a big enterprise in the northern part of the province could not help but supply a big market for farm produce once the farmers got down to arranging a continuity of supply.

In one very important way we benefitted immensely from the work on the Alcan project — the greatly improved roads. The roads along Ootsa Lake were formerly of very indifferent quality, very winding and hilly, especially between Streatham and Ootsa Lake Settlement. Since most of that road was flooded, Alcan had to build a new road and they made a good job of it. We had an almost straight road with an almost level grade.

Good work was also done along the north shore of Francois Lake on which road supplies and equipment were taken to the Tahtsa tunnel project, and with the Highways Department doing work on the gaps, our roads were in quite respectable shape. To us who came in by trail, they seemed like super-highways.

While writing up the profit and loss account of the Alcan project, one other item must be put on the debit side. Before the flooding, in the fall, the Tahtsa River before it entered Ootsa Lake was one of the best hunting grounds for geese and ducks in the northern part of the province. The necessary feed must have been plentiful and, as this stretch of river remained open till late in the fall, it provided a welcome stopping-off place for the waterfowl in their annual migration. I have mentioned previously how the number of waterfowl on our smaller lakes had in recent years almost reached the vanishing point, but this was not so with the Tahtsa River and right up to the flooding it was a favourite spot for hunters from all over this part of the province. However, that was a thing of the past for both the Tahtsa and Whitesail Rivers became part of the huge reservoir, miles wide in spots, and all the feeding grounds were destroyed.

The flooding created a huge body of water which would make a real boating paradise once the unsightly mess of standing and floating dead timber was finally cleaned up. What was once a string of eight lakes became one huge lake. This made the whole perimeter much more accessible, especially as some of the short rivers were not too easily navigable, while the Teta-chuck Falls necessitated a portage. However, this ease of travel did away with a lot of the charm and beauty of a boat trip in the area, especially with the elimination of the beautiful Teta-chuck Falls. The only unspoiled lake was Eutsuk Lake, which was always considered the best of the whole chain. This lake had still to be reached either by a short portage traversed by a tramway between Whitesail and Teta-chuck Lake, or by a short stretch of river to the foot of Eutsuk Lake, which entailed the passage of the Redfern Rapids, not an easy stint for greenhorns.

The people still in the area were in an ironic position. In spite of, and really because of, this flooding of our lakeside, which supplied the aluminum company plant at Kitimat with electricity, we ourselves were still without electric power. This state of affairs was due mainly to the fact that seventy-nine of our settlers were flooded out — and the B.C. Hydro considered that there were not enough settlers left in the district to warrant bringing the power to us. The power line was stalled at Grassy Plains, just thirteen miles from Ootsa Lake.

What does the future hold for the northern part of British Columbia, an area generally known as the Central Interior? That question will by necessity be answered by the younger generation and will be dependent on what the members of it will accomplish on their own, and what aid they will receive from the government in the establishment of new industries.

In the Ootsa Lake district there are left a scant half-dozen of the settlers who came in before the railway and a similar situation exists in the rest of the area. Naturally, we of the older generation are inclined to shake our heads and wonder if the youngsters will measure up to the challenge. And challenge it is indeed, moreso probably than in our own case, for the tempo of life is much faster and the necessity of making so much more money is much greater, in order to meet the expense of the modern way of life.

Most probably, all past generations have indulged in the same sad head-shaking over the succeeding one, though the general pace of life has increased more in the last twenty or thirty years than in many of the preceding centuries, and so is enabling our young folks to go to the parties both near and far in really high gear. However, despite any dire forebodings on the subject, the young folks will probably come through just as well as their forebears.

What are the real results after fifty-one years of pioneering for myself, and thirty-nine years for Millie? Top place must be given to the matter of health. I have almost never had to put myself in the doctor's hands, except for routine check-ups. At one time Millie was not so fortunate. In 1927 she had to undergo an operation for breast cancer. However, the good old doctor at Hazelton Hospital, Dr. H.C. Wrinch, who had come early into the district as a medical missionary, must have made a good job of that work for thirty-three years later, Millie is still going strong and a year or two ago, had her first routine check-up in over twenty years. Sad to relate though, the good doctor himself succumbed to that dread disease several years later.

Otherwise, our lives here have been mostly quiet and more or less uneventful; our only regret is that we have never had any children. But, as one lady-friend remarked, "Well, if you haven't got them to make you laugh, you also haven't got them to make you cry."

Of work we have always had plenty; of money, we have at times not had too much. Now towards the end of the trail, we don't have any worries on that score.

As I mentioned earlier, most of the farmers are now equipped with up-to-date machinery but for us the machine age arrived a little too late, and we have been content to round out our life on the farm with horses and horse-type machinery as of old. We are saved a lot of the worries and expenses of machine farming and for the smaller amount of work that we still have to do the horses are more than competent. I must admit that I am much happier working horses than I would be with complicated machinery.

When I brought Millie into the country, my old friend, Charlie Moore, was one of the those on hand to welcome us at the Wistaria Post Office. Years later he admitted to me that he had shaken his head and said that I had made a poor choice of a farm wife as that little woman would never be able to stand up against the life here. He admitted later that he had been absolutely wrong, as indeed he had. Millie has been as fine a farm wife as anyone could wish for. At the same time, I am not placing her on a pedestal as being superior to all the other farm wives in here, for the pioneer wives of this district have all stood up splendidly — on the whole, better than men.

The life of a wife on a pioneer farm is always a busy one for besides the ordinary routine work around the home, three days a week can be

*The barns on the farm. I built all of them single-handed.*

written off for washing, churning, and bread-making. The chickens take a lot of attention, as does the lone pig kept for home consumption. In addition to all this work, Millie has done most of the work in the garden, helped often with the milking when we milked several cows, and she has always given a lot of help in the hay-field and in the harvesting. She has also helped to harvest potatoes and turnips and in many other tasks.

For a number of years I had to go down to Victoria as a member of the Advisory Board of Farmers' Institutes, usually for just over two weeks. During those times Millie looked after the farm all by herself and preferred to do so rather than have anyone to help her. It is not every woman that could take on such work and responsibility — many would be too scared to be alone at night, with the nearest neighbours three to five miles away.

But it has often not been easy for her, with all the feeding to do, the water-holes to chop and all the hundred and one other chores to attend to. Sometimes the temperature has dropped to below 20 below zero, while at other times considerable snow has fallen to make moving around difficult. I think the toughest break she had was the winter when several of our cows decided to calve while I was away. I returned to a very proud little wife for she had produced six calves from five cows, one cow having twins.

As we get older, of course, life on the farm becomes more difficult. We still have plenty to keep us busy. We have our regular work to do in the daytime, and in the evenings we enjoy writing letters to our many old friends, some of whom we have not seen for over forty years. We have our radio and Millie has her piano and we can always have a chat on the phone. Besides that, I have two secretarial jobs which keep me pretty busy. Most important of all, we are never at a loss for conversation between ourselves and that above everything else makes for congeniality in life.

The problems of retirement are — where to go and what to do? As regards the first of these, we feel that we should like to go further south to a little milder climate, and that, of course, would mean the severance of most of our old ties and friendships. However, we feel that the fullness of our old life should enable us to avoid any emptiness in the new one.

Right here at our own home, the distances are quite a problem for elderly folks. Sixty-five miles to the doctor, hospital and railway, forty miles to our nearest store, and five miles to our Post Office, and neighbours at distances of one, three and four miles are not exactly for old folks.

I am sure that many people would like to ask "If you had your time over again, would you again quit your steady job and again take a chance in a strange country?" If conditions were the same as when I left England fifty-three years ago, undoubtedly I would take the same step. Whether I should chart the same course of life over here is problematical, but I can only say that I could hardly have a happier life than I have had. I might get into some other occupation that was more lucrative but, on that question, I will repeat a quotation which Millie often quotes to me:

Can wealth give happiness?
Look round and see,
What gay distress, what splendid misery,
Whatever fortune lavishly can pour,
The mind annihilates and calls for more.

It is quite possible that if brother Jack had not come and looked me up at Powell River, where I was working on the start of the construction of the big pulp and paper mill, and then persuaded me to come with him into this country, I might easily have stayed there and grown up with the company. Fate determined otherwise, and I am certainly not going to quarrel with Fate on the subject.

Some people might ask whether I would advise a young person to leave his or her old country and take a chance on a new life in Canada. That is a hard question to answer for a person who has been living more or less in the backwoods for the last fifty years.

Times have undoubtedly changed over home since I left, with more and better job opportunities and higher pay. It is, moreover, not as easy to get any old kind of a job here until you could find a better one; it was fifty years ago. Also there is not the same chance of getting free government land as there was then. It is quite important that present-day immigrants be generally well educated with preferably a training in a skilled trade or profession, for the government stresses the fact that the greatest unemployment is centred on persons with no such training.

Fifty years ago, the cry was "Go west, young man, and grow up with the country"; now, the West is just about filled up and the cry has changed to "Go north, young fellow, and grow up with the country."

And it is indeed the North in which new development is taking place and where new opportunities present themselves. Get away from the crowds, the bright lights of the cities and the rat-race and "Go north, young fellow."

One question I have been asked many times, and that is why we went to such an out-of-the-way place so far from the railway. I can only reply that we pioneers must have something in common with the Greatest Man in history and that we were "led by the Spirit into the Wilderness" — but not to be tempted of the Devil, for I think nowhere is that less likely.

At length, in 1965, we came to the conclusion that it was about time that we got off our farm and moved to a place where life would be a little easier for us. Millie had suddenly developed a nasty attack of arthritis, while I, at over 80, was beginning to feel that the work was getting to be a little more than I wanted.

Our farm of over 480 acres needed a lot of fencing and as many of the fences were, like myself, getting rather ancient, a lot of replacement work was becoming necessary. This, plus the routine work of the farm, was just getting too much. Added to this was the fact that we were sixty miles from the railway, doctors, hospital and other necessary services; our Post Office was four miles distant and our nearest store thirty-five miles away.

The farm was therefore listed with a real estate firm at Burns Lake and, very soon, we had numerous prospective buyers to look it over. In that summer of 1965 there were a great many Americans looking for land in our area and most of the persons who came to look over our place were from the states of Washington and Oregon. I was impressed with the quality of all of them, and it was a great pleasure to take them over the place and to talk with them about their own lives and of our own experiences. Most of them were favourably impressed but were faced with that all too frequent trouble — lack of funds to handle the deal. At our age we could not have time payments extending over too many years while in many cases the persons were themselves faced with the problem of selling their own farm in the U.S.A. before they could purchase ours.

However, early in 1966 Mr. Right came along in the person of Mr. Cranston of Portland, Oregon. He was not a farmer but a businessman, who had several times been in our district on hunting trips. Both the district and our place appealed to him and very soon financial arrangements were completed. Mr. Cranston took over not only the farm but all our equipment and livestock and most of the household goods. It was truly a wonderful deal. Just what Mr. Cranston planned to do with our place I did not know, but he had a man working it and many improvements were made. He had other interests in the district and I expected him to prove a real asset to the district in many ways.

And so, after being on the farm for the last fifty-six years, right from the real pioneer days, we left it on July 28, 1966 on our way to Victoria, where we planned to spend our days of retirement.

It might be expected, and certainly most of our friends expected it, that we would feel the break of leaving our old home very much. But I can truthfully say that when I drove the pickup out of our gate with our few very personal belongings in it, I left everything behind and have scarcely given a thought to it since. We had spent all those happy years there but now it was a thing of the past, and our life lay ahead of us, not behind. And although we were leaving the country physically, we were taking a great deal of it with us — we left with all our memories of all those years, and all those good friends. These memories we would cherish always.